Picking Up the Pieces

by John H. Barwick

PICKING UP THE PIECES

A Personal Odyssey – From Academia to Immersion in the Chaos and Drama of Post-War Europe: 1947-1953

John H. Barwick

Railroad Street Press
394 Railroad Street, Suite 2
St. Johnsbury, VT 05819

All rights reserved by the author. No parts of this book may be copied or reproduced without the express written consent of the author.

Published in the United States by Railroad Street Press, St. Johnsbury, Vermont.

ISBN: 9781936711147

1. Memoir

Jacket design by Susanna V. Walden.

First Edition 2011

Railroad Street Press
394 Railroad Street, Suite 2
St. Johnsbury, VT 05819
(802) 748-3551
www.railroadstreetpress.com

Previously by John H. Barwick

My War: A Wartime Memoir 1941-1946

Dedication

This book is dedicated to the memory of my wife, Ilse, who did not live to see this memoir of our early times together.

Ilse
1925-2010

Preface

The "Pieces" in the title of this book are the fragments of humanity left over in Europe after World War II: those who survived the most destructive war in history, now trying to put their lives back together again - either in Europe if possible, or by emigrating to new homes all over the world. Whether large or small, rich or poor, good or bad, everyone was impacted by the war, almost always for the worse. Each one had a story to tell. This book is an attempt to describe a few of these people, the chaos out of which they emerged and the situation in which they then found themselves. It is told through the eyes of an immature, inexperienced young American - myself - as I worked in a variety of public and private programs that helped to make a broken continent whole again.

The book can be read at three levels. First, and most basic, is the historical context - what was transpiring in Europe during the years 1947-1953, the period covered in the book. For most Americans this is an empty page. The US has fought and largely forgotten two more major wars since then. Lately there has been a resurgence of interest in World War II itself, but not in the postwar years despite the fact that enormous events were taking place then. Understanding that history helps to make the settings in which those events took place comprehensible and realistic.

The picture that emerges at level two is of locations and activities to which my disorganized wanderings took me: living with German war prisoners in London, the beach at Biarritz, refugee camps in Germany, and of Cold War political activity in Austria. All of them are interesting, but much less so than the collection of colorful characters that populated these diverse settings: ex-soldiers, resistance leaders, smugglers, war criminals and a few unforgettable ladies. These highly personal encounters at level three are the heart of the book.

This tri-level organization dictates its style - history and setting lending depth and believability to its cast of characters. And this raises the question of how to present these diverse personalities so as to make them as vivid and vibrant as they were in real life. Straightforward reportage would be just that - a reportage.

I decided to the best of my ability to let them speak for themselves in their own words. In practice this meant using conversational dialog to recreate the reality of a situation instead of simply recounting what happened. But this entailed problems. My editor said, "How could you possibly remember accurately a conversation that took place more than fifty years ago? It would inject a whiff of unreality into the book. Readers might think you were making it all up."

No doubt this danger exists. Obviously I could not be expected to remember every word of every conversation. On the other hand, each situation, each encounter, had imprinted itself indelibly on my mind; and each character speaking was so memorable that the words themselves are simply the natural way that feelings would have been expressed. Literal accuracy is not required; the words spoken here reflect the person I remember.

At any rate, I hope this decision works to recreate the events in my European adventure and to bring to life the people behind those events.

Introduction

The spring of 1947 opened onto a future of exciting, endless possibilities for John H. ("Jack") Barwick. Aged twenty-two, I had just completed three years in the Navy. I had commanded my own LCT (Landing Craft Tank) in the European and Pacific theaters, ending up as a lieutenant (j.g.) with one battle star. From there, I went on to complete my senior year at Princeton. Looking ahead, I was now headed for Europe, to London, having been accepted for graduate study at LSE (The London School of Economics), considered the place to be by trendy young liberals, of whom I considered myself one. Better yet, I would be living in relative comfort at home with the family while at the same time enjoying tuition-free studies and a monthly living stipend, courtesy of the newly-enacted GI Bill of Rights. For me, the war had been mostly a world tour, a grand adventure which needed no further rewards. But who in his right mind would refuse such an offer from a grateful nation?

That last year at Princeton was a transformative one. I had been a scholarship student, with the amount of scholarship support more or less in direct proportion to academic performance. Now, with the US Government paying the bills, in addition to my majors – History / Politics – I splurged with electives in art, music, psychology, etc., a rich diet of stimuli that opened up whole new worlds of knowledge, but which also had the effect of shaking up and loosening the discipline that had governed my intellectual progress up to that time.

But such remote considerations were totally lost in the euphoria of the moment. Now that the war was over, especially among young people of college age, there had built up a deep desire to travel, to see the world. This desire had not yet found an outlet, but later would culminate in the student exchange programs of the '50s and '60s, and the tourism to follow. Those lucky few who did manage to break out of the domestic scene became the instant envy of those who remained behind: to get married, have babies, to toil in dreary graduate study programs, or go into the family business. In that spirit, I was helped aboard the Cunard Liner, *Queen Elizabeth*, by a circle of friends, all of whom wished they were going along.

However, this was not a voyage sailing into a new day's sunrise over Europe after the storms of World War II. Far from it. The hot war had turned cold with armed forces on hair-trigger alert, and the unimaginable but all too real specter of atomic weapons in the wrong hands. In many respects this highly charged atmosphere resembled the tensions of 1938-39 when Hitler's speeches were threatening peace on the continent. Now it was the Soviet Union making the threats, backed up with Red Army divisions right up to western Europe's eastern borders.

Where was our defense to come from? Germany was divided, its cities rubble. France, Italy, Poland, and Czechoslovakia were in political turmoil, with the realistic possibility of an elected communist takeover. NATO did not yet exist. American troops three thousand miles away could not match a hundred Soviet divisions already positioned and ready for the order to march. As in 1939, it seemed to be only England as the remaining democracy still on its feet, but this time an England barely able to stand, exhausted and impoverished by five years of war.

To anyone traveling in Europe in the spring of 1947, the thrill of its legendary treasures was tempered by a whiff of danger, a sense of unstable ground underfoot, a feeling that Europe could all too easily fall back into the morass from which it had just emerged. On the ground, there was this curious contrast left behind by allied armies and bombers: beautiful landscapes of neatly tended farms interspersed with quaint old-world villages, and then suddenly miles of rubble where once major cities had stood, panoramas of industrial wreckage: the Ruhr uninhabitable, Hamburg, Berlin, Cologne, Dresden more than 50% destroyed.

Chaos was the only word to describe Europe struggling to recover from the loss of 40 million lives. Many who survived were still in a state of shock, unable psychologically to cope with seemingly insurmountable problems. Among them was a vast swarm of 13 million displaced persons – "DP's," of whom some ten million had been factory workers - "slaves" – forced labor brought into Germany from the east to man the Nazi war machine. To these add twelve million ethnic Germans expelled from their settlements in Eastern Europe, now homeless and unemployed. Finally, there were the remains of the Third Reich's armed forces, millions of men in prison camps all over the world, ready for repatriation to a homeland unable to receive them.

It was into this landscape of ruined splendor that I disembarked at Southampton in July 1947. But before going further into this narrative, an explanation is required as to how the family, and now I, happened to be in England in the first place.

World War II had broken out in September of 1939. Under the leadership of John R. Mott and Tracy Strong, both humanitarians and international statesmen of the first order, the World's YMCA, operating out of Geneva, Switzerland, correctly identified a problem that was sure to emerge and intensify as the war went on: how to deal with captured prisoners of war and enemy nationals, which even at that early stage numbered in the thousands with no upper limit in sight. These captives were housed in camps in Britain and on the Isle of Man where the British army assumed responsibility for providing food, clothing, shelter and security, but no more than that – normal treatment by prevailing standards. Normal perhaps, but leaving a huge gap in terms of the welfare of those incarcerated for years, who could be expected to deteriorate psychologically and emerge unfit to rejoin society as productive individuals.

Working with Sir Frank Willis, head of the British National YMCA, and the British government, John R. Mott and Tracy Strong negotiated an arrangement by which the YMCA would move in to fill these missing needs through a program of education, sports, reading, music, and leadership re-education to counter the virus of Nazism and Fascism that came along with the prisoners themselves. There was even a program to help them reestablish contact with their families at home by mail sent through neutral countries. Religious observation was permitted but deemphasized. Taken as a whole, this was a practical, imaginative program that effectively filled a prisoner's day with a whole variety of free time-options. In retrospect, it was the most successful prisoner-of- war program in the history of modern warfare, setting a standard that has not been equaled, or even attempted, since.

That was the vision. But it had to be implemented, starting with a director to put the wheels in motion. The offer was made to my father, John W., in the spring of 1940, and he sailed for England to assume the title of Director of YMCA War Prisoners Aid. My mother and the family stayed behind.

Fulfillment of the vision meant setting up and administering a YMCA program in the POW camps dotted all over England and Scotland. Starting with just a few in the early days of the so-called "phony war," as hostilities intensified the number of POW camps grew rapidly, until by the time of my arrival there were more than a hundred with a prisoner population of half a million. During the years 1940-1946, John W. spent much of his time on the road visiting camps, and in the process getting to know the British Isles intimately. Given the magnitude of the project, demands for executive direction far exceeded the capabilities of one man, and eventually a staff was organized from American and Scandinavian recruits under John W.'s direction. In recognition of his contribution to the war effort, the British Government conferred on him a status with the equivalent rank of "General." John R. Mott went on to receive the Nobel Peace Prize in 1946.

Meanwhile, with the war now ended my mother and the rest of the family came over to join him. They moved into an enormous Victorian house on the outskirts of London that the YMCA had taken over for a variety of needs. Housing the family was just one of them. We had not been together as a family with all members present for seven years, so my arrival and the reunion were more than special.

For me, it started another seven years, during which I would be away from the US, moving about with no clear-cut objectives or course of direction, but nevertheless living life to the limit - or at least, my limit. Those postwar years – before Europe became a worn out set of tourist clichés and despite the shortages – was the time to be there, and above all, I was young enough for the experience to be fresh, and unencumbered with other cares and responsibilities.

Chapter One

68 Shepherds Hill, London N6

I arrived in England on the *Queen Elizabeth* at Southampton in July 1947. For a new resident, it immediately meant getting used to a few things to which the rest of the family had long since adjusted. For one thing, even though it was July the weather was cool, pleasantly so I thought, in contrast to the sticky, summer humidity back home. And then, daylight seemed to go on forever, courtesy of "double British summer time," which added an hour to regular daylight time, with the result that it never got totally dark, and outdoor activities went on until well past ten o'clock, and even later.

Okay by me. However, the third adjustment was more difficult. Almost forgotten now, those years from 1945 well into the 50's were the "Austerity Period," a time of privation during which the country endured an existence harsher even than in the worst periods of the war itself. Luxuries disappeared completely, fuel for heating and gasoline were almost unattainable, and foodstuffs rationed severely: a few ounces of meat, cheese, butter and fish, powdered eggs, vegetables if you could find them. The one thing available to all in quantity was bread: good, heavy, honest loaves, densely textured and healthful.

As we made our family tour along the coast, these shortages quickly became apparent, in restaurants, and in one or two private homes of friends where we stopped to visit and were offered tea. With a raw wind blowing in off the sea and a steaming mug in my hand, I suddenly understood why England was a nation of tea drinkers. More than tea our hosts couldn't do; a real sit-down dinner would have cleaned out their ration book for a month.

Fortunately, one necessity we didn't have to worry about was petrol (gasoline). Because of John W.'s travel requirements, the YMCA had been allotted an almost unlimited supply. With that assurance, we motored happily along from Southampton before turning north to London. It was all new to me, the small roads, the village architecture, the taverns and ale houses. We had to stop at least once every half hour for refreshments or sightseeing because it was not possible for John W. to keep doing any one thing for longer than that. However, no one minded, the family was together again after seven years of separation, and John W. was obviously enjoying the opportunity to demonstrate his detailed knowledge of the country.

At the end of day three of motoring we entered London from the south and proceeded north to the village of Highgate, which a hundred years earlier lay completely outside the city limits but was now swallowed up by "greater" London. 68 Shepherds Hill was our destination, situated at the corner end of a quiet tree-lined street, on a rise above the sidewalk. Shepherds Hill was a real hill overlooking a small valley with greenery, playing fields, tennis courts and a public swimming pool. Rising above that on the far side stood another "incorporated" village, Muswell Hill, whose church spires were dwarfed by the antennas of an enormous beaux-arts structure. This had been the palace of Alexandra, Queen to King Edward VII, and now serving as operations center for Britain's BBC startup television industry. To the east, Shepherds Hill looked out on the village of Crouch End, another local victim of urban sprawl. Taken as a whole, however, the Shepherds Hill setting was attractive, with long views, many trees, and a sense that the city was somewhere else.

From the street the house loomed up, not particularly inviting or friendly, three stories of dark brick and an iron fence running around two sides of the property. A flight of stone steps ascended from a gate to the entrance. There was no railing. Instead, on either side, two massive ship's hawsers provided support to those who needed it. This quaint touch remained from the original owner, a Scottish sea captain who also gave the property its name -"Blencathara" – lettered on a small iron sign at the gate. Never having lived on such a scale, I was more than a little impressed that this forbidding pile was to be "home" for the next few years.

I don't know – probably never did know – how many rooms were inside, at least twenty-five, maybe more. But they were almost all large, with lofty ceilings, hanging chandeliers, and many fireplaces. Even the kitchen was a domain unto itself. The parlor, or "drawing room," stretched for at least thirty feet or more, and was where most daytime activity took place. This opened onto a large glassed-in sun porch, filled with a veritable jungle of plants, and this in turn gave out onto a lawn, or "garden" as Britons called it, which stretched back about a hundred feet to the end of the property. So the dour, forbidding street-side aspect of Blencathara was more than offset by the interior, and at the rear its openness to nature and the outside.

A reception parlor and two separate dining areas took up more downstairs space. The one dining area was intended for the owner and his family, the other for servants, an anachronism which was ideal for their present use. Upstairs was a warren of hallways, doorways, closets and rooms, some very large, some small, some very cozy with fireplaces. Servants' quarters were on the third floor. But grand as the house was, its imposing size should not be mistaken for luxury. Signs of neglect were everywhere: cracked paint surfaces, stained walls and ceilings, windows that would not open, etc.; the legacy of transient tenant occupation all through the war and thereafter.

Other shortcomings were on a corresponding scale. First, bathrooms: I can recall only two full baths, one on the second and one on the third floor, then half-baths, or "loos" as they were called – three, one on each floor, not nearly sufficient for the needs of those in residence. The full baths were strange affairs: marble and antique fixtures throughout, an enameled bathtub in which you could stretch at full length in water that never seemed to be really hot. The so-called "geyser" – pronounced "geezer"- that, provided it was an "on demand" gas fired system, emitting clouds of steam and only a dribble of hot water. After a time you could no longer see through the vapor, and wondered whether to give up. Against the chill, the fireplaces were more for looks than effect. All burned coal rather than wood. Dirty, hard to handle, harder still to get rid of, coal burning in the grate could also be beautifully cozy and warm. But down in the city centuries of coal use had turned the buildings black, and smoke rising from thousands of chimneys helped make London's famous "pea soup" fogs even more impenetrable. (Coal burning fireplaces were outlawed in the sixties, and a gleaming new city exterior emerged once the grime and soot were gone.)

Now that you have a reasonably complete picture of what the house looked like, I must explain how it was used, by whom, and how life went on there. And to understand that, a word about how it fit into the YMCA War Prisoners Aid Program will be helpful.

By the time of my arrival 68 Shepherds Hill had been a YMCA facility for almost a year. Prior to that it had served as a hostel for workers from the Mennonite Church overseas relief program, a major player in the field of international refugee work, still active today after more than fifty years. By 1946, their work in Britain was winding down. A more pressing requirement existed in Germany: to help rebuild the cities and care for the millions of refugees that flooded the country. In June, the Mennonites moved out, and the YMCA moved in – a good example of coordinated effort characteristic of how the Protestant relief agencies worked together. It was into this scene that my mother, sister, and the boys had made their entry, just in time to help with a massive cleanup of debris left behind, and to be instantly thrown into the midst of the YMCA's program requirements.

Essentially, 68 Shepherds Hill functioned as a hotel, housing the German staff of the War Prisoners Aid London office, its American executive cadre, visiting YMCA officials, clergy from Germany, and other visitors: international observers and persons of note, of whom there was a steady stream. Program administration operated out of an office downtown in the Strand, next to the Charing Cross railroad/ tube station and Trafalgar Square. Four German prisoners helped man the office. Loosened regulations permitted them to travel by tube (subway) to their work from Shepherds Hill, mingling freely with the civilian population, but dressed in a type of coverall clothing that instantly identified them as prisoners. (Can you imagine this happening in the USA, especially since the scars of war were still then visible on every side? At any rate there were no incidents.)

John W. and his executive staff were constantly coming and going on visits to the POW camps, at home scarcely half the time. Their absence, however, was more than made up for by outside visitors. Some were there to help on specific projects such as resettlement planning. Others, particularly German clerics, were there to provide spiritual comfort and a link with home to assure prisoners that they were not forgotten. Also, word of the unique YMCA program had spread far and wide as a model for the treatment of incarcerated captives. This interest resulted in a constant flow of official observers and curious lay personnel, many of whom would arrive without warning.

To all these, the door was always open and the house a hotel in all but name. The operational burden and responsibility fell on my mother, who was more than willing to take it on but who had no experience other than managing a small household. In fact, the task required the skills of a professional hotel-keeper: managing a staff for housekeeping, cleaning, laundry, and cooking; ordering food, fuel and supplies; supervising maintenance and repair, plus detailed bookkeeping and monthly accounting reports to YMCA headquarters. It was almost too much, especially since John W. was not available to help and had no interest in doing so, even if he had had the time. This was typical of his management style: throw an untrained, untried person into the job with little or no supervision. If he survived, and they usually did, fine. If not, get someone else. This extreme style of delegation did much to explain why he was personally so effective as new executives matured and worked out their own salvation under him.

Fortunately, mother was saved from exhaustion and breakdown - although, there were times when she came close – by a household staff of three persons: a general factotum or chief housekeeper, a cook, and a cook's assistant and general handyman. These were all German POW's, who considered themselves fortunate to be in London, away from the camps, with reasonably light work responsibilities. They spoke only a few words of English, and Mother knew no German, but by the time I arrived they had evolved a kind of argot with words from both languages that got the job done and was useful as well for day-to-day chit-chat.

For the next two years I would be living in close proximity with these three Germans as well as those who worked in the YMCA office. Therefore, I'll move in for an individual close-up of some of those with whom I had the most contact, starting with house household staff.

First, Walter, a very weird character about forty years old from the Baltic area of eastern Germany. His manner was oily and obsequious to the last degree, and you always felt there was something calculating and vaguely sinister underneath. He never seemed to sleep, up at all hours moving silently about the house, suddenly appearing when least expected. But he was fanatically neat and a good housecleaner. My father couldn't stand him, however, and vowed repeatedly to get rid of him, needless to say without consulting Mother.

Next, Otto, the cook, about thirty with a wife and child back in Braunschweig. As a civilian he had been a pastry cook, with skills he now used to full effect by turning out an endless flow of cookies, cupcakes, tarts and cakes. Fortunately, our ration allowance was large enough to permit these luxuries. Pastries were his specialty, regular meals were only so-so. But he and mother worked well together in the kitchen.

Heinz was our general handyman, which describes his duties: dishwasher, heavy cleaning, laundry, and just about anything else that needed doing. He was short, good humored and not too bright. He was the German army's "Sad Sack," For those of you who can call up that hilarious wartime cartoon character, a little story here will show you what I mean.

During the war Heinz was drafted off a farm and sent to the Luftwaffe. There, his job was at an aircraft manufacturing plant where he operated a small truck, towing finished planes off the assembly line and parking them in rows outside on the tarmac. One day he made too tight a turn and knocked a wing off the plane he was towing. His supervisors were not pleased. "One more such mistake," they said, "and you will be sent to the front!" Sure enough, a few days later another collision and another ME-110 out of service. And a few days after that, Heinz found himself on the western front with a rifle in his hands.

Those were the household staff. Now, the office group.

Wolfgang (I don't remember his last name.) Of all our prisoners, Wolfgang was most like the image we Americans had of the typical Nazi warrior: young, 25 or so, blond, with chiseled Aryan features. He was well educated, spoke some English, and unlike the other prisoners held strong political opinions that defeat and captivity had not entirely erased. Because he could express himself and was not afraid to do so he was interesting, and someone I greatly enjoyed talking with.

Kurt Miethke: tall, thin, receding hairline, bespectacled, had been a journalist in civilian life. Educated, he spoke good English and used his writing skills for YMCA communications to the camps and elsewhere. He had a typical newsman's cynical detachment when it came to political questions, seeing little to admire anywhere, but usually with good grounds for disillusionment.

I never got to know the remainder of the office staff very well because they were gone much of the time and because they spoke little English. There was Cromy, a big, burly man who had been a butcher back in Kassel; he looked like one's image of a typical German burgher. The others, Axel and Ludwig, were still little more than school boys.

I should mention one other person who was in the house on a regular basis. He was Karl Edward Yden, a Danish volunteer in the program; about thirty years old with an excellent command of English. He was a first class bridge player, useful because bridge formed a means by which some of us could meet on neutral ground in friendly competition.

This was the cast of characters with whom I was to spend the next two years. Of course, Mother was always there, John W. occasionally, and my sister, Betty, from time to time. She also helped out in the YMCA downtown office, mostly with making travel arrangements for visiting dignitaries and YMCA staff traveling to Germany or to world headquarters in Geneva. She had a flat (apartment) in the Albany - a high-rise, modern apartment building next to Regents Park, and was much envied by the rest of us because the building had central heating and a swimming pool, both virtually unknown in the London of that day. The two boys, James and Peter, were also only occasionally in residence, at term breaks two or three times a year from their Quaker school – Bootham – up in York in the midlands.

Chapter Two

German Prisoners Speak Out

I quickly fell into the household routine that was well established and varied little from day to day. Registration at LSE didn't start until October, so I had time to get used to new surroundings and to see a bit of London. During the day everyone was busy. The office contingent walked about fifteen minutes down Shepherd's Hill to the Northern Line tube station at Highgate, and from there it was only another fifteen minutes on the train to Charing Cross. Visiting guests also were also off on their various projects during the day. Some were with us only overnight, others for as long as a week.

Inside the house, a flurry of housekeeping activity continued all day long, and did not end until the dinner dishes were washed and put away. Evenings we just sat around, talked, visited with guests, or played bridge. Once a week was movie night. The YMCA had acquired a 16-millimeter projector and a whole trove of pre-war German films. Showings took place in the dining room with one of the Germans as projectionist. Titles included classics as well as a few commercial releases: "The Blue Angel" with Marlene Dietrich and Emil Jannings – a powerful film; "The Cabinet of Dr. Caligari" – eerie; but by far the most popular among the Germans was a piece of light-hearted musical fluff, "Hallo Janine." We must have seen that one half a dozen times.

For the most part the Germans kept to themselves, which made sense given the language difficulty. There was no formal separation so I had multiple opportunities to chat, to learn about their home lives, families and life in pre-war Germany under Hitler and the Nazis. They also talked about their wartime experiences, but in a more guarded way, and only after I had gotten to know them on a more personal basis. This was made easier by the fact that I also had been in the military and seen active duty in the European theater. It established a common bond that opened up communication as no other could, particularly when it came to politics and the issues that had brought us into conflict.

Our conversations took place over a period of many months. It was not a single encounter or exchange, but fragmentary and episodic, starting with neutral or commonplace topics: family life, civilian work, education, etc., then gradually getting into more sensitive areas: war guilt, war crimes, Hitler and the Nazis, "master race" theories and Jews. Miethke and Wolfgang were well educated and articulate, with a good knowledge of recent history. Sixty years is a long time for a precise memory of those conversations, but my general recollection of how they expressed themselves is true to the spirit.

It wasn't hard for them to open up about their current situation as prisoners. "What has been your experience as a prisoner?" I asked. "How have you been treated?"

Miethke answered for all when he said, "We cannot complain. None of us expected it to be this good. At first we were afraid – that was in France where I was taken. But that was a battleground and much depended on who captured you. You didn't know. There were some bad types out there. We had them, too. But once we got in the POW camps, we felt safe."

"How do you think your treatment as captives compared to the way the German Army treated prisoners?"

Again Miethke answered. "Well, there was a lot of propaganda going on. Nothing the enemy does is ever good, so I think there was much misunderstanding. Also you can't compare the German army to the Americans and the British. By the end of the war we had very little ourselves as far as food and supplies went while the Americans especially had all they needed. So far as I could see, we treated prisoners as well as we could under the conditions that existed. There was a good discipline in the German army; being professional meant observing rules."

Wolfgang chimed in, "Of course, once we could see the war

Picking Up the Pieces

was finished, we all wanted to be captured by the Americans or the British. God help you if you were captured by the Russians. I heard terrible stories from some of our soldiers who were there."

Karl Edward: "Yes, it was on the east front where the code of conduct broke down. There were atrocities on both sides. Right now there are 400-500,000 German prisoners still unaccounted for in the Soviet Union. We'll probably never know what happened to them."

I was curious to learn how they felt specifically about the YMCA program. There was total agreement about this. "Excellent".. "A model for all time"… "What civilized countries should do." And so on.

Going a little further I asked, "What did the program do for you personally?"

"Well, of course, it gave me something constructive to do, working here in the office," Wolfgang replied, "instead of rotting away out there in one of the camps. After years in the army, I think it will be much easier to get back into normal life in Germany."

Miethke said, "I never did entirely believe Goebbels' propaganda about the wicked British and the decadent Americans. Now I know from my own experience how wrong that was. After all, this YMCA program isn't just a few kind-hearted people trying to help us, they are carrying out the policies of their governments."

"Yes," Karl Edward added. "It's laying a foundation for good relations between Germany and England that will last long after we have all gone home. Maybe, we'll see an end to centuries of war in Europe."

That was such a happy thought. Later on, as we got better acquainted, I felt we could talk about more sensitive matters. "You know," I said, "Back in America they think Germany started this war, that Germany is a militaristic state that launched two world wars in a space of only thirty years, and that it needs to be made incapable of doing so again. How would you answer them?"

"It makes me very angry when I hear this," said Wolfgang. "I shall explain. You can't separate World War I and World War II, it was all one war with a false thirty-year peace in between. World

War II was caused by the humiliation of Germany in the Treaty of Versailles where we had to accept total blame for the war, which was ridiculous, and agree to a punishment that was intolerable. The Germans are a proud people. We have a great history. We are not war-making savages."

Karl Edward interrupted. "In the interests of fairness, before everyone complains too much about the Treaty of Versailles, I would like to remind us that when Russia surrendered to Germany in 1917, Germany imposed a treaty on Russia at Brest-Litovsk that was a good deal more severe than Versailles. By its terms, Russia lost huge amounts of territory and was forced to pay an even more unpayable indemnity."

To which Miethke replied, "That is true. Nevertheless, after World War I the allies did make it impossible for a moderate government in Germany to succeed. The reparation payments were beyond the ability of a bankrupt country to pay. The British kept up a naval blockade for years after the war ended that reduced many of us to starvation levels. And you Americans enacted a tariff that killed what little trade did manage to spring up.

He continued. "One more point. In the 1920's we had a catastrophic inflation, the Deutsche mark was worthless. There were riots and disorder all over the country. Communist organizations threatened to take over. The Germans are an orderly people. They will not stand for anarchy or weakness in government, and that is what we had. The allied powers and America were indifferent to the situation, and they helped prepare the way for Hitler to be elected by a democratic majority."

Wolfgang nodded vigorously: "You know," he said, "Germany was never defeated in 1918. Exhausted perhaps, but not defeated. Our cities were untouched by the war; our armaments industry was completely intact, with highly skilled workers; and our people were now filled with hatred for the west and a desire to regain our rightful place in Europe."

"Yes," I said, "but does that mean taking over other countries against their will as Hitler did?"

Wolfgang continued. "If you mean the Rhineland, Versailles took it away from us, and the Saar also, but it soon voted to rejoin the Reich. As far as Czechoslovakia and the Sudetenland are concerned, that was a German speaking part of the mother country, cut off from us at Versailles when the artificial state of Czechoslovakia was created. Just like the South Tyrol, German-speaking and completely Austrian, handed over to Italy as a reward for siding with England and France in 1915. No, I don't agree that you can call these attempts to reunite a dismembered country aggression."

There was a lot that could have been said against their claims, but I didn't want to push the argument. I was more interested in hearing what they had to say, particularly from Wolfgang who reflected unspoken attitudes and wasn't afraid to express them. We were getting to know one another better, so that as time went by it was possible to talk about subjects that even the Germans didn't want to discuss among themselves. For example, the idea of a "Master Race."

"What about that? " I asked, "Do you believe in the Nazi theory of a German master race?"

Miethke laughed. "Just look at Dr. Goebbels himself. Does he look like a pure Aryan type? No, I don't think we Germans ever believed wholly in it. But along with the rest of the vague, ideological nonsense - Rosenberg's Neuheiden movement, for example - it became part of a kind of religion, mostly ignored, even mocked but not openly. I thought it was foolishness."

"Perhaps," said Wolfgang, "but from inside Germany, looking out, there was much reason to consider the idea seriously. Anyone could see the foremost position of Germany in Europe. In the West, France, rotten to the core, was a rat's nest of corrupt politicians and collaborators. Italy, not a serious country, where they are good at singing and chasing women. Poland, a nation of jackals, only too glad to bite off a piece of Czechoslovakia for itself. As for the rest of the Austrian Empire in the Balkans, an ethnic stew of barbarians who all hate each other. That leaves Russia, a great swarm of drunken animals under a cruel despot, more Asiatic than European: Can anyone blame Germany for feeling superior and wanting to save Western civilization from sinking back into the Dark Ages?"

Karl Edward laughed. "I'm glad you left Scandinavia out of that speech. I guess we should now feel superior along with you."

"You misunderstand me," said Wolfgang. "I'm not myself accepting the idea of a German Aryan master race. I'm only saying that when the German people looked around them at the rest of Europe, it was very easy to see that Goebbel's propaganda could be believed."

"Furthermore," he added, "In all of these backward Eastern European countries there were pockets of ethnic Germans, millions of people in all, who were the business leaders, owners, and employers; they made order and prosperity wherever they were, but always thought of themselves as Germans. German blood unites us."

"Well'" I said, "How would the 'master race' believers regard the United States?"

"I don't think you are a race at all, only a mixture of what were at one time pure strains," said Miethke . "Our propaganda called the US a 'mongrel country'."

The one thing they didn't want to talk about was the whole subject of war crimes and particularly the Jews. But it was hard to ignore, since the Nuremberg trials of the top Nazis had recently been front page news in every paper. I asked whether they thought the defendants – Goering, Hess, Streicher, Himmler, et.al - had been given a fair trial. Were they guilty of war crimes?

"Against what laws?" Miethke asked. "There were no laws in Germany against what the Nazis did, and at that time no such international law or jurisdiction existed for 'crimes against humanity.' So Nuremberg was a case where the victors wrote the laws, and executed those men to please public opinion. But who can be surprised? It is always so after every war. The Russians would not even have bothered to stage a trial."

"But the concentration camps and the murder of six million Jews – doesn't that leave a heavy burden of guilt on the German people? Aren't the German people responsible?"

"Yes, undoubtedly it does"." Miethke replied. "But each person excuses himself. It's always someone else who did those terrible things. After all, the concentration camps were a secret, almost always located in isolated spots, many in foreign countries like Poland. But we never really knew about them or what went on inside. The Jews? Well, in my town one day they were there, and the next day they were gone. Nobody asked where."

"How do you feel about it now?" I asked.

"I didn't know then, and I don't want to know now," said Wolfgang. "I want to get on with my life. What's past is past. It doesn't do any good to keep digging into it. We Germans need all our energy to just recover from the war."

Chapter Three

Academic Failure

I registered at the London School of Economics (LSE) in the middle of October 1947. Walking up the Strand to Aldwych, my first impression of the building was that of a big, unfriendly fortress, packed in among equally large impersonal office buildings, pushed right up against the sidewalk with pedestrians and noisy traffic going by – a far cry from Princeton and from my idea of what a great university ought to look like.

Once inside, this impression only got worse: dingy rooms, crowded hallways, grimy windows through which a little light struggled to get in, and a cafeteria which set an all-time low for British cooking standards. This dismal introduction abruptly changed for the better when I met the Dean of Admissions – I forget her name – a most attractive middle aged woman, stylishly made up and dressed, looking like she didn't belong there. She gave me a short welcome speech, had me fill out the usual forms, handed me an information packet, and set up an appointment with my faculty advisor the next day.

I studied the course catalog, trying to map out a tentative program with a course attendance schedule that made sense. The information packet contained a history of the school, much of which I already knew. I knew that its founders included Sidney and Beatrice Webb, leaders of a movement called Fabian Socialism, which aimed at providing an advanced education to members of the working class, or others not likely to be able to afford a degree from Oxford or Cambridge. Although international relations, and political and economic theory were in the curriculum, LSE's offerings were also intensely practical: public administration, planning, taxation, etc., from the national down to the local level. Unlike Oxford with its broad cultural orientation backed up by magnificent libraries in a bucolic, contemplative setting, LSE was an urban factory where working class apprentices could learn the mechanics of making government work.

At that moment, in 1947, LSE was at the zenith of its power and influence. After a dozen years of Tory (Conservative) leadership, the country was ready for a change, and it was to be a thorough one based largely on the "Beveridge Report," a document issued during wartime in 1942. Nothing could be done then to implement its recommendations; that would have to await the end of hostilities. The readiness of the nation to set a new course is shown by the fact that the Tories and their immensely popular leader, Winston Churchill, were defeated in the election of 1946, and replaced by the Labor Party under a mild mannered expert in the intricacies of statecraft, Clement Attlee – a "sheep in sheep's clothing," as Churchill called him.

Once in charge, Labor proceeded to enact the reforms recommended in the Beveridge Report: nationalization of basic industries (coal, steel, railroads, etc.), a vastly expanded welfare program, unemployment compensation, family assistance, and above all a national health program guaranteeing a minimum of health services to everyone, financed out of general revenues.

Nothing on this scale had been seen in the world up to that time, which was why students were flocking to England to witness at first hand the birth of a real "welfare state," and why so many were applying at LSE. LSE was the intellectual hothouse where these radical seeds were sown in the 20's and 30's, to germinate in lectures, books and papers from a faculty made up of the foremost political and economic theoreticians of the day. Foremost among the "socialist intellectuals" was Harold Laski, well known on both sides of the Atlantic. But it would be a mistake to think of LSE as restricted to the propagation of only leftist ideas. Present also was the eminent opponent to welfare statism, F.A. Hayek, who had just published his influential book, *"The Road to Serfdom,"* as well as other famous scholars not identified with political thought. For a student alive to current political ideas, LSE was the place to be. Most of the students there at that time fit this image. The surprising thing to me was how many came from nations and outposts of the British Empire: Africa, India and the Middle East. Many were well past college age, studying to absorb the ideas and skills that they would take back home and use to throw off colonial rule and establish another "emerging nation."

American students seemed less developed by comparison – I certainly was. Inexperienced perhaps, but no less imbued with the heady feeling of being present at a turning point in history. Unlike me, however, these Americans were left wing ideologues and a few fellow traveling communists with a passion for politics that was all consuming. At home they were avid supporters of Henry Wallace and his breakaway "Progressives," opposing Harry Truman, particularly his foreign policy of militant containment of Soviet expansion. I was not comfortable with them, that is, most of my fellow American students. However, there were a few exceptions who had managed to preserve some native common sense and balance, remarkable in that time of deep ideological fractures and intolerance, on both the left and the right.

The best part of my meeting with the dean was learning that my faculty advisor was to be Harold Laski. I couldn't have been more pleased. I had come to LSE to learn the philosophy and dynamics of the welfare state and here I would be talking to its most articulate and best known spokesman.

Our first meeting provided a few surprises. For one thing, he turned out to be quite small and slightly built. He wore a dark suit and tie. His thin black hair, combed carefully in place, looked almost artificial. His view of the world was through a set of perfectly round glasses. But the most surprising thing about Professor Laski was his very slow, deliberate speech delivered in a low but resonant voice.

He started out by asking what I wanted to accomplish at LSE that I couldn't do at home. I explained that at Princeton I had become interested in how pressure groups operated to influence public policy. For graduation credit we had to write a senior thesis. My chosen topic was "The American Catholic Church and The Spanish Civil War." "An excellent subject", Laski commented.

"Thank you, sir. I won a prize with it. I was particularly interested in political pressure exerted by a religious organization in contrast to typical business interests. You know, religious groups are supposed to operate on a higher plane than the Chamber of Commerce."

"So you propose to continue this line of investigation?" he asked. When I nodded he said, "But why aren't you better off doing that in the US? Pressure politics is a more highly developed art there."

"The reason is that I'd like to continue to develop the religious angle, and I'd like to do it while the issue is actually going on. I could have written a much more detailed thesis at Princeton if I could have done it in 1939 instead of 1947. The record was pretty well buried by then. I didn't have many sources."

"All right," he said, "but I still don't understand why you want to do this work here, or how I could be of help."

"Well sir, that is because I've identified another religious group – Zionism, and right now the big issue is Palestine and what is going to happen to it. It's a hot topic in Britain. Your government has been trying to enforce the terms of its mandate in Palestine. There are huge pressures on it to change its position. I thought that could be a very interesting subject to explore - 'Zionism and postwar British foreign policy-' but I would need guidance."

He looked thoughtful for a moment then said, "You've certainly picked a hot topic, maybe too hot. You might want to let it cool off a bit. I say this because I'm not sure we understand the depths of this controversy, and how strongly people feel about it. Also America has no experience in that part of the world. But we'll see. Meanwhile, spend this term doing some basic reading. Make up a reading list for background. We can go over that at our next meeting, and I'll suggest several people you might want to talk to." I exited with high hopes.

During the next months over the winter of '47, I continued to pursue the work plan we had discussed. I also attended lectures that had nothing to do with it. I sat transfixed as Sir Charles Webster recreated the diplomatic duel between Napoleon III and Bismarck, and was bewildered listening to Professor Lionel Robbins explain deficit finance. But the most interesting of these collateral activities were the afternoon seminars that Laski held on an informal basis for anyone who wanted to sit in.

They were held in a medium sized room. Every seat was taken, students standing along the walls or sitting on the floor at the foot of the diminutive figure of Laski, who led the discussion seated in a chair. The sessions I remember best were a series in which he invited his audience of dedicated socialists, fervent believers in central planning, to attack the theories of leading conservative thinkers opposed to any and all forms of big government ownership and control. Like a lawyer for the defense of these conservatives, Laski would pick apart claims from the liberal prosecution and demolish their arguments until I wondered which side he was really on.

He took the hardest cases. In one seminar he defended the beliefs of the 19th century churchman, John Henry Newman, as set forth in his statement for religion based conservatism, "Apologia Pro Vita Sua." Newman had left the Church of England to become a Catholic, eventually a Cardinal. With Laski in the defense, even brilliant members of the class had a hard time arguing against Newman's ancient, morally-based bedrock principles of conservative thought. Nor did they fare any better when it came to F.A. Hayek, who advocated an iron discipline of the market as preferable to welfare state handouts and their ever expanding growth. The lesson Laski was teaching here – an important one - was not to settle back into smug orthodoxy, but work to understand the basis of opposing thought, and be able to support your beliefs with reason and not groupthink or slogans.

However, as applied to me, I felt that Professor Laski did not always follow his own precepts. As I grappled with work on my thesis things were not coming together. There was no problem with bygone events; the history was reasonably clear, even though buried in government white papers and minutes of the various Zionist conferences from 1895 on. But bringing this history into the present had so far eluded me.

The issue had reached a fever pitch of intensity with the UN Partition Plan for Palestine, the Arab-Israeli War of 1948, the UN Partition Plan, and pending international recognition of the state of Israel. In my role as investigative reporter, I had not located even one credible source. Jewish classmates tried to be helpful. They took me to all kinds of Jewish meetings and celebrations, but the

Academic Failure

Zionist organization in London was totally unforthcoming. Its downtown headquarters was like a bunker with a steel door and a slit through which they looked you over and said they would make inquiries. I never got past that door. Foreign Office officials with whom Laski had made contact also were evasive the closer the discussion got to interaction between themselves and Jewish organizations. They were not only under attack from the Zionists but were also being heavily pressured by Washington, which after years of scandalous indifference to the plight of the Jewish refugees now had decided to make support of Israel a key element of foreign policy.

More and more I was losing enthusiasm, energy and also objectivity. My reading, plus the news reports coming daily out of Palestine – by April,48, Israel – led me to believe that the international community was sacrificing the independence of a backward people, the Palestinians, out of a mixture of sympathy and guilt for the manner in which Jews had been treated in Europe - a belated gesture of atonement with Palestinians now paying the price. In the US, the whole question had become corrupted by domestic politics. England's policy under Foreign Minister Ernest Bevin, bending under the country's desperate need for financial aid, could no longer resist American pressure. He decided to opt out and leave the whole problem to the UN, itself struggling to get started.

My mood of conflict and lack of tangible success reflected itself in meetings with Professor Laski. I told him about this lack of progress and about my own problems in maintaining an objective analytical stance.

"About the lack of progress, I'm not surprised," he said. "The people who matter don't want to talk about it with someone they don't know, especially a young graduate student with no credentials. There's too much at stake here. About the objectivity issue, I think you have to pull yourself up out of the daily stream of press reports – shocking, I admit – and try to see this episode in the larger sweep of history. I can assure you that in the long run, the influx of Jews into Palestine will be the best thing that could possibly happen to the Palestinian Arabs and the entire Middle East."

"How could that be?" I asked.

"This is just one more episode in the breakup of the Ottoman Empire," he said, "which has been going on for a hundred and fifty years. In its wake we have these fragments, mostly poor, backward, not really civilized as we understand the term. Yet this area has great potential for development. Left to themselves it will remain exactly as it is now, or worse, whereas Jewish immigration can turn it around and literally make the desert flower, as they say. You can see it happening right now."

"Well, I don't know," I ventured. "It's happening by force against the will of the native population, a people that Britain was supposed to protect under the League of Nations Mandate. It's a little like Mussolini going into Ethiopia to improve life for the Ethiopians."

"Not really, but I can see, Mr. Barwick, you have been talking to our Arabists and are in danger of becoming one yourself. Give the whole thing more thought and see me next week."

After that conversation, I couldn't help reaching the conclusion that Laski's position was not very different from the 19th century colonial imperialists who justified penetration and takeover of native territories by conferring on them the gift of "progress," that they were eradicating disease and superstition, bringing justice and realizing economic possibilities. For professor Laski, his belief in material progress rationalized the conquest and physical occupation of a territory by an invading group, and the imposition of an alien culture upon the land, while reducing the native population to second class status.

Also, having parted ways with organized religion years earlier, I had little patience with the Jewish territorial claim to Palestine - that many thousands of years ago the "land" had been "given" to them by God, and that two thousand years of history since then were irrelevant. To incorporate this as a precedent for territorial and sovereignty transfers in international law, to me, seemed simply lawlessness in a religious disguise. How could anyone accept it as legitimate and still believe in the separation of church and state?

No, I couldn't agree with him. I wonder what he would say were he alive today.

Academic Failure

At our next meeting, he was quiet for a long moment, then said, "Mr. Barwick, I have just come from the hospital with bad news. The doctor tells me I have a bleeding ulcer which for various reasons they can't do much about. It could be, possibly is, life threatening. In any case I am advised to cut back substantially on my work here at school. I'll probably keep on with a few students whose work is near completion, but transfer the others to new advisors. In your case it will be to Professor Manning. Unlike me, he's very old school. I think you will find him good to work with. So under these circumstances, we'll leave it at that. I wish you good luck, but we'll let Manning have the last word."

I tried to find the right words for this shocking bit of news. My impression was that I was the first person he had talked with since receiving it, and that he was still trying to understand what it meant. We said good-bye and I left.

Within a year he was dead.

My new advisor, Professor Manning, was Chairman of the Department of International Relations, in appearance elderly with snow white hair and piercing blue eyes. His manner was friendly as he said, "Professor Laski tells me you have been having a spot of trouble with your independent work. Perhaps I can help. We'll see. Shall we begin with a review of progress? Start from the very beginning, if you please."

So I went over the whole story. Manning nodded as if he understood. When I had finished he said, "I would like you to give me a written report covering essentially the points you just made. My thought is to review it with several colleagues whose opinions I frequently solicit on academic matters. Then we can proceed from there. Don't make it too long, a few pages will suffice.".

Writing the report helped clear my head without necessarily pointing a clear direction. I left it in Manning's office, and about a week later there was a message setting a date and time to meet.

After a few preliminaries he said, "Well, Mr. Barwick, shall we get right to the point? And the point is that my colleagues and I all feel that you are embarked on an impossible task. Point #1: we agree that the issue is an important one. Point #2: the timing is bad. We are in the epicenter of this conflict with much remaining to be resolved – if it ever is. Point #3: England is no longer a key factor, perhaps not even a factor at all in it. Your own country is where the important decisions are being made. There and at the UN. We doubt that even the most talented investigative reporter could successfully write this story. Were he to do so, no one would publish it.

"That is our joint opinion. To it, let me add a personal observation, and please do not feel offended by it. You are quite young, and eager to exploit a controversial issue, but lacking the breadth and depth of experience to recognize its pitfalls or to render the necessary judgments. At this stage you might make a good reporter but not necessarily a good historian. If England is where you want to study, we have resources here at the School for a lifetime of productive work in another direction. I would encourage you to take advantage of the opportunity, and will be happy to assist, should you so decide."

Afterwards, I thought he had only confirmed what I myself had begun to believe: that I was embarked on a fool's errand, tilting at windmills, wasting both time and resources. Also, I felt, it was only tact that had kept Manning from using the word "immature." But I understood what he meant and conceded that he was right.

Chapter Four

Weekends Away From London

After that, my interest in pursuing Zionist politics waned to the vanishing point, although I still attended classes and sat in on lectures. But after awhile, even that connection with LSE disappeared.

The truth is that LSE was not the place for me, neither by temperament, nor inclination. I was simply not enough of a political animal to feel at home with all the other animals in the zoo, particularly the left-wingers, their endless arguments and ideological intolerance. I'd come to England to witness the birth of the welfare state and social justice which for me represented an extension of Roosevelt's New Deal. But after living there for a year, I began to realize that there was much more to life in Britain than that; that these social innovations were simply a thin overlay, covering a culture of tradition and native character still very much alive, in the villages, pubs, music halls, fish markets and churches, and especially in the universities at Oxford and Cambridge.

Other than a few daytime visits to Oxford, I never really got to know it more than as an average tourist. But I had made several friends, Americans, enrolled at Cambridge. My first sight of those magnificent buildings struck a responsive chord that only deepened with repeated weekend visits. Maybe because Cambridge was a total contrast to LSE: a grim, gray, grimy big city anthill of budding bureaucrats, as against a spacious landscape of graceful buildings and a winding river – well, you get the idea.

I liked everything about the place: everyone on bicycles, boating on the Cam, student "digs," really little furnished apartments, complete with an elderly housekeeper who kept things in order and even served tea. Dining "commons" had a church-like atmosphere where one of the students rattled off a prayer in Latin to start the meal. There were weekend parties on and off-campus: or we did a pub crawl around town. University rules at that time mandated return by eleven o'clock. The trouble was that eleven always seemed to come too soon; the party was still going strong and no one wanted to leave. However, failure to be back inside the gate was considered a serious offense and non-observance could get one "sent down" – that is, expelled. Getting back in after eleven was easier said than done: the main gate would be closed and access barred by a high iron fence - about ten feet high – around the perimeter. Sober, we probably couldn't have managed. Those less agile were pushed up and over by their friends, landing with a thud on the inside. A wonder no one was hurt.

Unlike LSE, Cambridge epitomized student life, still youthful and fresh but bound by tradition, leading gracefully into serious work and adult concerns. There was a camaraderie entirely missing at LSE, by design, I'm sure. And I was still at an age and of a disposition to which that was important. Professor Manning was right, LSE did have much to offer, but I don't think I ever could have been happy there.

Opportunities for a young American to get to know England and experience English life were on every hand. This was because memories of the war were still fresh. England felt, quite rightly, that only American intervention had saved the country from defeat, and even though the war was over, she still needed American aid to stay alive. There was this almost universal desire to show individual Americans how much that aid was appreciated.

A major organization devoted to good relations between our two countries was the English Speaking Union, under the immediate direction of a Mrs. Phyllis Biscoe. She maintained an active program, much of it for students: get acquainted meetings, assistance in finding lodgings, room- mates, etc., etc. Also, they arranged "hospitality weekends" in private homes outside of the city. That sounded interesting, so I decided to take up an offer which came from a certain H. Robertson Glasgow.

On a rainy weekend in the fall of 1948, I caught the train and chugged about an hour and a half in a southwesterly direction to a village by a small river. Mr. Glasgow was waiting at the station platform, a rail-thin aristocratic looking gentleman of about sixty, dressed in a dark suit, with a bowler hat and an umbrella. We introduced ourselves and climbed into a Rover car dating from the late 20s or early 30s. When I commented on how good the car looked, he said, "We try to keep her scrubbed up and out for a run now and then, but with petrol so hard to come by, it's not too easy." In this ancient artifact we drove for a time along the river and then along country lanes and eventually into a grand driveway leading to a stone house of Georgian appearance set in an expanse of lawn with outbuildings to the side and rear.

Along the way Mr. Glasgow informed me that he got up to London several times a year to visit his brother, who was a sports writer for the Times, specializing in cricket. Other than these visits, he spent his time here as what he called a "farmer." The estate had come down to him through the family, but as a young man he had gone to Cambridge to study agriculture and estate management. In actuality, he was the prototypical village "squire" owning a large tract of land with tenant farmers working under his general direction in a kind of paternalistic relationship.

In comparison to the "stately homes" of England this one was quite small, three stories, perhaps 6000 – 7000 square feet. Inside, it was deathly cold. Other than fireplaces I didn't see any means of heating the place, but there was one of those in almost every room. We entered into a large reception hall. On the walls hung framed ancestral portraits, several of Jacobean or Elizabethan appearance. My room was enormous with long windows looking out on the dripping landscape.

Back downstairs I met Mrs. Glasgow who appeared much younger than her husband, about forty, and was dressed in heavy tweeds over a sweater. After introductions, she asked if I wouldn't like a glass of sherry, or perhaps a cup of tea to offset the weather. Tea sounded good, so we all had tea in the drawing room, scalding hot, kept that way under a quilted "tea cozy."

Warmed by the tea, we decided to brave the elements. Mr. Glasgow thought I might be interested to visit the stables, the sheep pen, the bird house, tool shed, potting shed, hot-house and barn. Also the vegetable garden and the orchard. We had just started the tour when I was astounded to see two peacocks on the lawn, an exotic touch for a working farm.

"I thought they were a jungle bird, native to the tropics," I said. "Can they survive in this climate?" "Oh, to be sure," Glasgow replied. "Don't be deceived by looks – they're actually quite tough creatures. Even with snow on the ground. They can always come into the bird house, and at night they often roost in the trees. Good idea. Foxes, you know. These may wake you in the morning. Terrible screechers."

With that, we continued on the tour. When the tour was over Mr. Glasgow said that they usually do a "lie down" for an hour or two before dinner. He suggested I might want to do the same. I said that was fine with me. "Very well. Downstairs for a cocktail then, say, seven-thirty, with dinner at eight."

When I got down to the dining room a fire was burning in the fireplace, but the room temperature I estimated to be about sixty. Mr. Glasgow was wearing black tie and a dinner jacket; Mrs. Glasgow had on a long blue evening dress with thin straps, leaving her neck and shoulders exposed to the elements. I thought she looked a little blue too. Not being prepared for such formality, I felt a bit self-conscious in ordinary street clothes. "Not to mind," said Glasgow. "We only do this on weekends. Our way of showing off."

"Whisky all right?" he asked. I gladly accepted, it being the first I'd tasted since arriving in England. Whisky, meaning Scotch whisky, was one of those little luxuries that had completely disappeared from the nation's store of spirits. At that time all they could produce was shipped abroad to earn dollars. When I commented, he said that bottle came from a relative in Scotland who owned a distillery. "We drink it with a splash of seltzer, no ice."

About the only light in the dining room came from six candles set on two silver candelabra on a polished table. Mr. Glasgow and his wife sat at either end, with me in the middle. More polished silver gleamed in the candlelight. An elderly serving man appeared and filled our wine glasses from a decanted bottle.

"Well, mud in your eye," said Mr. Glasgow, holding his glass up. "I picked that up from one of your American chaps during the war. Your Air Force commandeered my neighbor's estate for a group of their officers. We had them over a few times – jolly good too. They reciprocated by always leaving behind a few cartons of cigarettes. Beatrice was desolate when they left." "Yes," said Mrs. Glasgow. "Those boys certainly got me hooked on – what were they? – Lucky Strikes, I believe."

After the cream of leek soup, the elderly retainer brought out a platter on which reposed a leg of lamb. Mr. Glasgow carved. "Yes," he said, in response to my surprise at this almost unknown bounty. "We keep two sheep for ourselves, the rest go to market along with nearly everything else from the farm. There's a quota we're expected to meet. Tightly regulated too, to keep it from winding up in the black market. Not uncommon for a couple of spies to stop in to see what they can get us to part with. Completely illegal, of course."

That led to a discussion about farming. He was especially interested in my description of the Amish farmers in Lancaster County, Pennsylvania. "You mean they actually farm without power-driven equipment of any kind?"

"That's right," I said. "No commercial fertilizer either. They use horses or mules instead of tractors, and a windmill to pump water. No electricity, oil lamps in the house, and horse drawn buggies instead of cars. It's their religion. They want as little as possible to do with the outside world."

"Sounds like we could use a bit of that round here. We've got a petrol allowance for the machinery but work horses have been gone for fifty years."

"What are your biggest problems in keeping the farm up?" I asked.

"Taxes and labor," he instantly replied. "Estates like this are going to go the way of the work horses. We can't really make agriculture pay enough to keep up with the taxable value of the land. In this immediate area several great houses have shut down – taxed out of existence."

"What about labor?" I asked.

"Just as bad. During the war, of course, all our men were gone, and the young ones today see no future in farming. They get a little bit of education and, first thing you know, they want to leave."

"All right, Robbie, that's enough complaining," said Mrs. Glasgow, rising. "Shall we all go for coffee while there's still something left of the fire. I want Mr. Barwick to tell us about this place where he lives with all those German prisoners. It sounds fascinating."

Conversation went on until there was no more fire. The next morning broke clear and windy. He was right: the peacocks made a lot of noise – a loud, hoarse screech, quite unpleasant. A late breakfast took place in a morning room overlooking the garden. Food laid out on a sideboard, again in silver dishes, featured scrambled eggs, bacon, grilled kidneys, stewed plums and cold slices of toast with a kind of bitter orange marmalade.

"As a joke, one of your Yanks once asked me where we kept the beer warmers and the toast coolers," said Mr. Glasgow. "He could not get over the fact that we drink our beer at room temperature, same with toast."

Mrs. Glasgow said I might be interested in attending a small, local horse race with them that morning. In the afternoon, they had planned a tea for the neighborhood, including several people who worked on the estate. "Nothing very grand," she said, "but a good chance to meet a few of the locals. They don't see many Americans down here since your boys went home two years ago." Sounded good to me. I was enjoying myself immensely.

Both the horse race and the tea that followed were perfect examples of English country social life; home-grown entertainment, simple, authentic, in which everyone seemed to have his assigned part, with no special preparation necessary since they did these things all the time.

The horse race was called a "Point to Point." There was no track, only a course, about a mile or so, laid out across fields and pastures, through a stretch of woods, and back to the start. No jumps or hazards. Riders were mostly teenagers and a few young adults, everyone bundled up against the wind, with muddy boots from yesterday's rain. The horses were all family pets who had done this dozens of times and seemed to enjoy it. There were maybe half a dozen separate races with about four horses competing in each one, representing farms for the immediate area, although in some cases horse and rider were from different farms. A tweedy type got the competitors lined up. Holding an upraised red flag, he shouted, "Go," bringing the flag sweeping down, and they were off. A few minutes later they reappeared coming down the home stretch, with onlookers cheering, and back to the starting gate which was an actual pasture gate, the horses breathing heavily and steaming, the riders laughing as they dismounted, with hugs all around.

Many of the riders and onlookers were present later at the tea, held in the Glasgow's reception hall. In addition there were a number of older people who sat around the sides of the room. I was introduced to everybody, answered a lot of questions as best I could, because they all spoke with a peculiar inflection that I heard referred to as "west country." One old gentleman was introduced to me as the oldest man in the village. I congratulated him and commented on how good he looked, particularly his head of snow white hair.

"Aye, sir, an' y'be wantin' t'keep yer own like mine – right?" I nodded. "Well, I'll tell ye what y'do – y'boil up a mess o' bay leaves t'a strong tea – let it sit, then rub that into yer head ever'day – That'll grow hair on a broomstick." I thanked him and made a mental note of the idea.

Afterward, and after the guests had departed, I said my own good-bye's with sincere thanks. Mr. Glasgow said I must come back next summer for a spot of angling in the nearby river where one of his neighbors owned a half-mile stretch.

On the way back to London I wondered what my fellow students at LSE would have made of the whole scene: the race and now the tea, the whole community – neighbors, workers, everybody mingling unselfconsciously with the local squire and his wife in a comfortable, settled relationship. I had heard a lot about the English caste system, and knew it to be real, but here at the local level there was none of that to be seen. In fact, I don't believe a day like this could have happened back in "democratic" America.

My weekend visit with the Robertson Glasgows was a journey back into a pre-war England that, except for a few rapidly disappearing estates, no longer existed. In contrast to those that remained, a farm up in Yorkshire where I had stayed once or twice represented the less attractive side of British agriculture in those immediate postwar years.

The YMCA War Prisoners Aid program had established a showcase POW Camp in the midlands, near the village of Norton. As a magnet for international visitors the camp received a great deal of attention from London. My father was constantly making the trip up there to tend to business, sometimes with Mother or other family members going along. After my two brothers were enrolled at Bootham School in York, which was not far distant, the visits became more frequent. I went along on one of them.

How my father became acquainted with the Cade family I do not know, but it was certainly not to be wondered at since their farm lay very close to the camp in a tiny crossroads village surrounded by the gently rolling Yorkshire landscape. Several houses were grouped around a small stone church with a square tower, and a well-tended cemetery where most of its worshipers seemed to be .We heard the church was marked to be shut down for a lack of attendance. The Cades' large house stood right at the main road intersection, with outbuildings and open fields stretching away to the rear, and a large stately cedar tree, spreading its branches, out in front. A small brook ran along one side of the property.

The head of the household, Mr. Cade, was a sick man in his mid-fifties. A lifetime of smoking had left him with a constant wet cough and no energy. I never saw him without a cigarette in his hand or in his mouth. Mrs. Cade compensated for her husband's debility by being the real driving force behind the farm and the many persons who lived there. Helping her were two daughters. One had recently married, and made her discontent with married life loudly known. Apparently, it was a sexual incompatibility, or lack of performance by the groom, because he always wore a hang-dog, semi-apologetic air. I felt sorry for him. He seemed to get no sympathy. A son, Tom, completed the family. In addition, they had taken in two handicapped persons in exchange for a partial cost-of-care-and-living state subsidy. One was a very old man, the other a mentally incapacitated mongoloid – or as we say now, suffering with Down Syndrome.

Picking Up the Pieces

Inside, the house was damp and chilly, comprising large drafty rooms with massive pieces of furniture handed down from more prosperous days. Mrs. Cade supervised operations, saw that the girls kept at their assigned tasks, and that all were properly fed, including two hired men who worked outside on the farm. What leisure time she had was spent tending a vegetable and flower garden as well as the hen house – source of an abundant supply of fresh eggs. Flowers from the garden helped soften the dour, cheerless atmosphere inside.

With Mr. Cade incapacitated, responsibility for running the farm fell on young Tom. As farms in England went it was a fairly large one, over a hundred acres of land devoted to pasture as well as to crops such as potatoes, cabbages, and hay. A herd of cattle and sties with pigs ensured milk and fresh meat for the household and helped feed the country. However, the pride of the farm, a rarity, consisted of several Clydesdale horses – real workhorses, standing fourteen hands high at the shoulder, and weighing nearly a ton – magnificent, gentle beasts who earned their keep every day hauling loaded wagons from one job to another. In truth, though, they were more like pets, much loved, petted, and groomed with their manes, tails and fetlocks combed out to long perfection by the girls.

The burden of responsibility to keep this operation up and running, and to make it pay, was too much for young Tom. Signs of neglect were everywhere: shabby, unpainted buildings, sagging gates and fences. An old tractor and pieces of farm equipment stood haphazardly about, rusting in the rain.

Tom was about thirty years old, muscular and physically up to the demands of farm work, but that was about as far as it went. Of a crude, boorish, peasant mentality, he had inherited none of the independent, dignified bearing his parents possessed, handed down through generations of English farmers.

The void created by lack of management skill or motivation was filled by a love of sport, especially blood sport. Tom was an expert shot, useful at that time because the English countryside was overrun by rabbits. One of his favorite pastimes was what they called "ferreting." Only the most sadistic nature could have found pleasure in it. To begin with, one had to have on hand a cage of ferrets, a small weasel-like animal, easily tamed and domesticated, now popular as a pet. However, in the wild they are fierce and bloodthirsty. The sport consists of carrying a cage of ferrets to a rabbit hole, probably with one or more rabbits in it, and then releasing a ferret into the hole to do its bloody business. As the terrified rabbits ran from the hole, Tom would let them get a bit of distance before expertly picking them off with his 12-gauge shotgun. He took my brother James along several times but was unsuccessful in making him a convert.

Ferreting could account for a considerable rabbit kill, but a much larger harvest came at mowing time when dozens of frightened rabbits fled before the mowing machines, to where several men with shotguns got a good morning practice at moving targets. No wonder that the Cade dinner table, along with local restaurant menus featured "Rabbit Pie" and "Jugged Hare." Butcher shops in town featured the animals, often still in their fur hanging up in the game section.

This sadistic streak in Tom's personality was on full display with poor Percy, the live-in mongoloid, as its victim. Tom enjoyed baiting and teasing Percy, laughing and mocking his awkward motions and movements, and imitating his speech defects and pathetic efforts to communicate. It was not pleasant to watch.

When not employed in killing things, Tom enjoyed the company of like-minded friends and cronies at the local alehouse. One of these was the head game keeper for the Duke of Welbeck, whose estate bordered the Cade farm. This friendship had its advantages to both sides. The gamekeeper allowed Tom a certain amount of illegal poaching, and Tom could be counted on to raise a company of beaters for the Duke's occasional weekend shooting parties.

For those unfamiliar with this uniquely British entertainment, a word of explanation. Invited guests were instructed to bring their fowling pieces (shotguns), and the morning after a night of hard drinking were lined up to await the over flight of birds – grouse rousted out of the brush by the beaters, advancing in close formation. As the birds took to the air, the shooters did their best to bring down as many as possible, firing, reloading and firing until there were no more birds left. Then it was back to the manor for Bloody Marys. My brothers were enlisted as beaters and reported a not very impressive slaughter.

Under Tom's mismanagement, the Cade farm continued its bit-by-bit, piece-by-piece decline. As a result of our family's visits to the area, Mother and Mrs. Cade became fast friends, exchanging gossip and their respective tales of troubles, of which they both had enough to keep conversation going for hours.

I found my visit depressing, and never went back.

Chapter Five

An American Queen

Back in London, American students were caught up in the excitement of the upcoming presidential election of 1948. This critical election occurred at a time when the postwar world was being transformed, and our international institutions were in a state of flux. In New York the UN had been formed but was still feeling its way, mainly as a forum for east-west conflict. At Bretton Woods the entire international financial structure had been reformed. Security arrangements which would culminate in the formation of NATO were just being finalized. Every day seemed to bring a new crisis. The Berlin Airlift was daily flying tons of supplies into the beleaguered city. In Czechoslovakia the Communists had won an electoral victory and taken over the government. Could we lose all that we had fought for in World War II? It seemed possible.

As long as Roosevelt was alive, people felt secure with an experienced, tested hand at the helm. But now that towering figure was gone and in its place sat Harry Truman, a nondescript, average midwesterner, product of the Kansas City Pendergast political machine, a man with no international background or experience. Could he be entrusted with the powers of the office at this dangerous juncture? All this contributed to mass insecurity on the part of the American people, nervousness compounded by the exposure of the Rosenberg spy ring and the fearful knowledge that the Soviets had succeeded in breaking the US nuclear monopoly. Our enemies now had their own atomic bomb.

The Democratic Party had been in power since 1932 – sixteen years – long enough for fractures to appear in its base. And they did – from the right and from the left. On the right, conservative southerners angry at the administration's liberal stance on racial issues broke away under the leadership of Strom Thurmond, taking with them a big chunk of the hitherto "Solid South." On the left, Roosevelt's Vice-President Henry Wallace led a group of dissidents out of the party. These were mainly urban liberals, unhappy with Truman's aggressive anti-Communist policy opposing and blocking Soviet expansion in Europe and Communist advances in Asia.

Both Thurmond and Wallace ran as independents: Thurmond as a "Dixiecrat." Wallace on the "Progressive" ticket. The Republicans rejoiced in these divisions. For their own candidate, they chose Thomas E. Dewey, governor of New York State, famous as a crime-busting attorney general in New York City during the thirties. Polls taken prior to the election overwhelmingly predicted an easy win for Governor Dewey, with a militant anti-Communist, anti-liberal rightist party behind him.

It was a gloomy group of a dozen or so American students gathered together to listen to the voting returns as they were received. British radio did not offer this coverage, so we met in an office kindly provided by the *Manchester Guardian* newspaper. Since they had come to England to study socialism, it was not surprising that, with one exception, their favorite was Wallace. The exception was me. I still found much to admire in Attlee's government and its program of social reform. But in the US, the alternatives to Truman were unappealing: The Dixiecrats totally so; the Republicans, a reactionary group bent on rolling back twenty years of history; and the Progressives, a mixture of big-city blacks and activist intellectuals with no base in the country as a whole.

Reactions in the room were interesting as the hours rolled by. Early returns gave Truman a slight lead over Dewey. Then, gradually, it seemed like the impossible might happen. This slight lead, despite all predictions, never turned negative. You could see the mood of those in the room shift as a Democratic win began to emerge. Despite a youthful infatuation with radical slogans and left-wing politics, their roots in New Deal philosophy began to show themselves, until at the end all were cheering Truman's

Picking Up the Pieces

victory as if they had been for him all along.

The flow of American students into Britain increased every year, but by 1948 was still small: a few at Oxford and Cambridge, some at Edinburgh, but the largest number were in London, at LSE, London University, and some at the Royal Academy of Dramatic Arts. There were other individuals doing private research, but they tended to keep to themselves.

At some time in 1948 a group of American students, mostly from LSE, decided it would be a good idea to form an association. Its purpose would be to bring us into contact with important British figures to meet for an informal presentation and discussion of topics of current interest. The idea met with approval, and meetings started once a month in the space above the bar at the Nag's Head tavern in the center of the city. What we had not anticipated in our planning was the willingness, even the desire of important Britons to make time for a group of American students to explain themselves, and by inference the country, to young people who would take the message home – an investment in future relations. Getting speakers turned out to be easier than we had imagined.

Our first was J. Arthur Rank, head of Rank Productions, at that time the premier British film company with such stars as Alec Guinness, John Gielgud, Ralph Richardson, Trevor Howard, etc., in such titles as "*Brief Encounter*", "*The Man in the White Suit*", "*Oliver Twist*", and many others. In fact, the British film industry was among the first to regain its feet after the war. Rank himself turned out to be a plain-spoken, homespun type, a Yorkshire flour manufacturer who had somehow gotten into the business of financing feature film productions. One success had led to another until by 1948 he and his company were international industry leaders. The forty or so of us who attended had a wonderful time talking with this basically simple man for over two hours.

Over the next six months we were to host R.A. Butler, head of the Conservative Party; Harold Laski, of course; Lord John Hope, of the "Hope Diamond" family – a rising young Conservative; Dennis Brogan, a Cambridge scholar in Anglo-American studies; and the editor-in-chief of the *Times* newspaper, Britain's must-read morning daily. The only person who turned down our invitation was Bertrand Russell. In response he wrote: "Forgive me for declining the kind invitation to address your group, but I have decided to devote all of my remaining energies to combating the spread of nuclear armaments. Sincerely, B. Russell."

Every one of these was a major coup for a tiny group of unknowns, but perhaps our greatest success – at least from a PR perspective – was with Eleanor Roosevelt. We learned from the news that she was planning to be in Britain in a few months. Emboldened by success, we thought, "Why not try to get her to meet with us?" As secretary, it became my duty to extend the invitation, which I did via mail to her Hyde Park, NY, address. Weeks went by and we had about given up hope of a response when a letter arrived signed by her secretary stating that Mrs. Roosevelt was favorably disposed to our proposal if it could be arranged so as not to conflict with previous commitments. We were advised to make contact with someone – I forget his name – at Boozy and Hawkes.

Boozy and Hawkes turned out to be a firm of music publishers with elegant offices on Regent Street. Three of us were assembled there to meet our contact, a young patrician type, to work out details. We explained who we were, who had been our guests so far, and why we wanted to meet with Mrs. Roosevelt. He was sympathetic. She did have one free afternoon that might work out.

"Where would this take place?" he asked. We explained that we met at the Nag's Head, over the bar. "Oh my goodness, no. That will never do." he said. "We must find you something better than that. Claridges, or the Dorchester, might be possibilities. Now, about expenses, have you got a treasury? This could turn out to be quite expensive." We were forced to admit to a treasury of only a few pounds.

"Let me think about that for a moment," he said. "Meanwhile, I doubt that we can restrict this to your own little group. American students from out-of-town will likely want to be on hand, as well as others. My view is that you must think in terms of at least a hundred people, possibly more. That will be a factor governing our accommodations. Now, what kind of program do you envision?"

We went on to discuss the program, timing, and other details, after which he said, "First, I will arrange for you to meet with the

Picking Up the Pieces

manager of Claridges, to see if they can fit you in, and what that might cost. If and when that is known, I will put you in touch with a Mr. Chester Dale. He has been helpful in the past, and this project is the sort of thing that would have appeal for him."

Claridges was – possibly still is – London's most prestigious hotel; far, far above and beyond anything we had envisioned, but now here we were talking to the manager – just the type you would expect from a traditional, top-drawer London establishment: urbane, with a perfect upper-class accent, but at the same time friendly and not patronizing.

"Yes, of course," he said, after listening to our story. "Claridges would be glad to participate, to help any way we can during Mrs. Roosevelt's visit. What would be required?"

When we told him that the potential audience might number a hundred or more, he said; "Well, I think it would have to be the ballroom. Come along, let's have a look."

This splendid space measured about eighty by fifty feet, with stately columns on one side and crystal chandeliers hanging from a lofty ceiling. "Now, about seating?" he said.

"Well, since we don't know exactly how many to expect, we thought that everyone could sit on the floor - you know, informal," we suggested.

"At Claridges?" he laughed. "No. I'm afraid not. We'll have chairs brought in as usual. Also, since this is to be an afternoon affair we will provide food and drink in the foyer: coffee, tea, cakes, and so forth."

This, we feared, was beginning to get out of hand, but since no one up to that point had been offering any opposition, we allowed ourselves to be swept along by the current, wondering how far it would take us. Everything was working out; the ballroom at Claridges was free on the afternoon Mrs. Roosevelt was available, and our contact at Boozy and Hawkes had been given a cost estimate. Now for the hard part.

Mr. Chester Dale's office was downtown in that part of London known as "The City." that is, the financial district, corresponding to "Wall Street" in New York. His secretary announced our arrival through an intercom. It was hard to believe that the short, fat young man seated behind an enormous desk was, in fact, the "copper king" of the world, with vast mining operations in several continents under his direct control. (This, in confidence, from our B&H contact.) He rose, we shook hands, introduced ourselves, and hsd just launched into our sales pitch.

"No, no," he interrupted with a wave of his hand. "Let me save you the trouble. I'm already on board. So-and-so at B&H has told me all about it. I consider it a great honor for our firm to be able to sponsor an appearance by Mrs. Roosevelt – and for me personally, I might add."

We breathed a sigh of relief – there was no "hard part." All the selling had been done for us, the way paved and all but strewn with flowers – testimony to the memory here of Franklin D. Roosevelt and the high position Mrs. Roosevelt herself occupied in British eyes.

Mr. Dale continued. "It's smashing of you chaps to have organized an affair like this. But let me give you a word of warning: Keep it quiet. No public announcements, nothing in the papers. If the public learn about this, you'll require police assistance to manage the crowds trying to get in."

Time was moving on. We had about six weeks before the actual event. Now the problem of several hundred invitations presented itself: to whom, composition, printing, mailing, answering inquiries, etc. We hadn't planned for all these details. Fortunately, the English Speaking Union came to our rescue. From this point Phyllis Briscoe took over; she had the contacts and the office resources to handle final preparations. But I don't think even she was fully prepared to deal with what happened next.

Chester Dale was right. Despite all preparations and tight security, word of the meeting leaked out. Phones at the ESU rang constantly. People had gotten the impression that this was a public function and wanted in. Some who called were very important individuals and became quite irate when told that attendance was restricted to American students. "Why does she have to come to England to talk to American students?" was the prevailing reaction. But the ruling held firm: No admittance without an invitation.

At last the day arrived: the ballroom lined with hundreds of gilded chairs, a table for dignitaries up front, and refreshments laid out in the foyer. I was stationed outside in front of the hotel to watch for Mrs. Roosevelt's arrival, and to escort her inside and hand her over to the committee. The hotel manager positioned himself with me as we looked closely into every taxicab that slowed down. Our attention was so fixed on the street that we scarcely noticed the sudden presence of a very tall woman in a gray raincoat who had arrived on foot, instantly recognizable as Mrs. Roosevelt. She was not alone, but had with her two young, utterly bewildered Army WAACs.

"I'm Eleanor Roosevelt," she said, "and these are my two new friends, Jean and Betty, whom I just met on the way over here. Since this is a gathering of young Americans I thought it would be nice for them to come along. So here we are, delighted to be with you." We assured her that would be just fine, and proceeded inside, where the committee took over. I resumed watch at the door to the foyer to help check invitations.

Actually, it would not be "just fine." There had been a delicate diplomatic discussion to decide who would occupy the eight chairs at the dignitaries' table. Seats had been reserved for representatives of student groups at Oxford and Cambridge, Mrs. Briscoe, Chester Dale, an officer from the American Embassy, our own Association president, and, of course, Mrs. Roosevelt. All were occupied. Now, suddenly, two more seats had to be added, which were quickly placed at each end.

The audience was seated. When the noise subsided, our president, Sam Davis, made a short speech of welcome. Mrs. Roosevelt had changed into a long dress of lilac color. She wore her hair upswept, and at six feet tall looked every inch a queen as she rose to begin her address.

I came in the ballroom entry to hear her talk and was horrified to find, standing there at the door - timidly as though he was an interloper - Chester Dale, the man who was paying for the whole affair. My God! What a mistake! Someone had flubbed his assignment. I asked Dale to wait a moment, and ran up to the table and whispered in Sam's ear. He immediately came down and escorted Dale up to the table and put him in his own – Sam's – chair. I never did find out who had succeeded in breaking into the charmed circle. In the room every seat was taken, and up front some people were actually sitting on the floor, almost at her feet, when Mrs. Roosevelt came forward to speak.

Her opening remarks were short and delivered in a musical, high-pitched voice with a distinctively upper-class accent, at the end of which she said, "I think it is terribly important that all you young people are here in England, especially now at this time of crisis in European affairs. My husband devoted his life to forging these trans-Atlantic ties. Nothing would be more important to him than to know that those ties are still as strong as they were in the time of war. Policies developed in Washington can only go so far. For success in the long term, they need the person-to-person relationships that you are developing here at this very moment, and I urge you to make the most of this opportunity. But I came here to talk with you, not to make a speech. Tell me what is on your minds, questions you may have about what is happening at home, and I will try to respond."

I will not attempt a blow-by-blow recap of the exchanges that followed. These few examples will give you an idea of the type of questions and comments that came from the audience.

"We were all inspired by your husband's wartime declaration of 'The Four Freedoms.' Now it seems those great goals have been forgotten. The US is backing reactionary regimes all over the world: a reactionary monarchy in Greece, colonialism in Africa and Indochina, and right-wing dictatorships all over Latin America and Cuba. Why?"

"Your opposition to big-city machine politics is well known – Tammany Hall in New York, for example. Therefore, how can you accept the leadership of a man like Harry Truman whose rise to power was sponsored by Tom Pendergast and his Kansas City gang?"

"Mrs. Roosevelt, your courageous act in inviting Marian Anderson to sing at the White House, after she had been turned down by the DAR to sing at Constitution Hall, was a great gesture of racial tolerance and progress. Why aren't we seeing more of that?"

"Will there be war with the Soviet Union?"

None of these questions, and many more over a two-hour period, seemed to faze her in the least. She, obviously, was a consummately skilled public figure, giving her responses in direct, down-to-earth, common sense terms, delivered in a gracious non-combative manner that almost guaranteed acceptance, if not agreement. Those listening, myself included, were brought under her spell, feeling ourselves to be in the presence of a genuinely great person. Nothing in the years that have passed since then has caused me to lose that conviction. As "America's Grandmother" Eleanor Roosevelt created and fulfilled a role unique in America's history.

Chapter Six

Marking Time

Taken as a whole, the British YMCA War Prisoner Aid (WPA) program represented a high water mark in the wartime treatment of incarcerated captives. But its crown jewel was the previously mentioned camp, located up in the Yorkshire midlands not far from Nottingham, and known as the "Norton Camp."

At Norton the WPA had established a "university" for German prisoners, staffed and administered by a faculty drawn from among the prisoners themselves being held in camps all over Britain. By the end of the war, Hitler's war machine, desperate for recruits, had swept up anyone who could carry a gun, including teachers, educators, and professors with the highest qualifications, as well as artists, musicians and others with a background in the arts. They all became cannon fodder. Many wound up as prisoners, the lucky ones in Britain and not the Soviet Union. From this available population, the WPA was able to select enough qualified individuals to establish a respectable curriculum of liberal arts and some technical subjects. There were also performing artists, including a chamber music quartet that traveled around giving concerts in the other camps, and frequently for us at 68 Shepherd's Hill in London.

A critical assist to the program lay in the "Enemy Property Act" by which all assets in Britain belonging to Germany and the other Axis powers had been seized by the government. These assets, among others, included the copyrights for all existing educational text books. With these rights in hand and available for reproduction, John W. set up a printing press in Luton, north of London, to turn out paperback texts in German as a supplement to course presentations.

Naturally, this "Prisoners University" attracted widespread public attention. A steady stream of visitors arrived at 68 Shepherds Hill on their way to visit Norton Camp, many of them from churches in the US and later from Scandinavia, the Netherlands, and Germany where the camp was widely publicized. There, its fame grew to the point where returning veterans were given formal academic credit for courses taken at Norton. As years passed, "alumni" groups would meet; a degree from Norton was considered a prestigious possession.

Looking back with the perspective of sixty years, and the recent experience of watching the US largely mishandle the incarceration of captive Muslim fighters, I believe I failed to take advantage of a once-in-a lifetime opportunity. There I was, living in the very midst of a ground-breaking experiment in dealing with enemy captives, which, for lack of adequate study and exposure, has completely disappeared from the historical record and public awareness. Instead of foolishly embarking on a quixotic pursuit of Zionism and the highly controversial Palestinian problem – impossible to write about, both then and even now – I ought to have taken advantage of my first hand contacts and resources to study and document the British post-World War II experiment in the treatment of war prisoners. Instead of opposition and total non-cooperation, I would have had enthusiastic support. Whether career opportunities lay in that direction, I'm not sure, but they certainly did not in the other. Well, life is often a story of missed opportunities.

Norton Camp and the WPA program of 1947 represented the high point of this effort. By 1948 the number of prisoners had started to decline – according to a planned repatriation policy.

It is difficult today to imagine how bad conditions inside Germany were at the end of the war with its major cities and industries destroyed and the defeated country under a four-power occupation. To have dumped hundreds of thousands of returning veterans into a non-existent economy would have repeated one of the many mistakes of 1918: the creation of an angry, impoverished army of unemployed veterans. So the repatriation of prisoners was held up until Germany was capable of absorbing its returnees. This

Picking Up the Pieces

meant a very few in 1946, then growing to a stream in 1947 and 1948.

Of the Germans living with us at 68 Shepherds Hill, none wanted to go back, even those with families to go back to. The total repatriation process lasted for several years after the end of the war, but each day had its quota of individuals leaving, all with a great deal of apprehension as to what the future might hold for them, based on letters from friends and family describing conditions at home.

One prisoner slated for return and awaiting his orders stayed with us at the house for a few days. He had been a colonel in the regular German army, in action continuously since the war broke out in 1939. Tall, lean, about fifty years of age, with an upper class manner and a military bearing, all he needed was a monocle and a riding crop to fulfill our image of the German military type. Actually, he was quite a gentle person. I forget his name – "Von" something or other.

Between his broken English and my poor German, we managed to communicate. "Von X" had been captured in France in 1944 and had been in POW Camps ever since. I asked him if he was looking forward to his return. "In some ways, yes. Who would want to spend one's life as a prisoner? At the same time, I must admit to being fearful. There is very little for me to go back to. The family's lands in Saxony are all in communist hands. My wife is dead. At least no word since 1945. And then there's the question of what could I do? I don't know. I am a soldier. In Germany maybe there is no more place for one like me. If I could I would like to go to America and start over."

"Yes," I said. "But I'm sure Germany will come back. Too bad you had to waste those years in war and in a POW camp."

"It was not entirely a waste," he said. "I learn a little English and to pass the time I begin to make water color pictures. If you like, I show you some."

He unpacked a small suitcase. "The YMCA give me paints, brushes and the right kind of paper. Here, these I think, are the best ones. It is not possible that I bring them all," he said, handing me one by one almost fifty paintings. Most of them were landscapes on paper about nine by twelve inches. I thought they were very good and told him so.

"You think so? Well, if I cannot find work and make a living, at least I have this to pass the time," he said. I wished him good luck. The next day he was gone.

I was glad to look at Von X's paintings because over the past two years I had developed an almost obsessive interest in things cultural - I now spent hours in The British Museum's rare print room to which as a student I could gain admission. All that was necessary was for me to tell an attendant what works I would like to examine, in this case watercolors, and the attendant would bring to my table a large box with a hinged lid containing about twenty or so matted paintings. It was hard to believe that the original I held in my hands was one of the very few in existence by Thomas Girtin – he died in his early twenties. Or the Turners; they had watercolors by Turner going back to those executed while he was only a boy. Back then it was still a trusting age.

On a less exalted scale, I became a patron of the arts, at least to the extent of purchasing several watercolor paintings at a downtown gallery for much more money than I could easily afford. They were nice but not remarkable. I still have two of them. Not content with that, I went further. There was an antique shop that I often passed. One day a sign in the window announced that it was going out of business and its entire inventory would be sold at auction. I went inside to have a look. In one corner was a cardboard shipping box, filled to the top with a miscellaneous collection of uninteresting papers and documents from the Empire Antiquarian Society. I dug down into the pile and was rewarded with the discovery of a drawing of a battle scene and soldiers in armor. With interest now aroused, I dug further and turned up two more drawings, executed on both sides of a single sheet of paper: the head of what appeared to be a noble gentleman on one side, and on the other a man astride a rearing horse. Both were obviously originals and very, very old. Greatly excited by this time, I buried them far down among the trash with the intention of bidding at the auction, reasonably confident that no one else would do what I did and that there would be no opposing bids. Nor were there. I got the whole thing for two pounds, removed my pictures, and threw away the rest. I then took these to a prestigious auction house - Christies, I believe - to learn more about what I had found. A learned looking gentleman for the appraisal department said, "About the one we are reasonably certain that it is a Vasari, or by one of his school. That is because it is a study, a sketch for a larger battle scene later executed by him. The others, we can say only that they are sixteenth century Italian drawings done by an unknown artist of unknown male figures. If you would like to sell them, we have an auction coming up in ten days, and there is still time to get them into the catalog."

With visions of instant wealth in my head, I readily agreed to the idea. Unfortunately, on the day of the auction I would be traveling on the continent for two weeks and unable to learn the result until I returned, and would have to contain my impatience until that time. This was not easy, and the first thing I did upon returning was to call Christies.

"Yes.... Let me see. Mr. Barwick, yes. Unfortunately, Mr. Barwick, the auction was very poorly attended and did not meet our usual expectations," said my contact.

"Yes, but what did they bring," I asked.

"Only ten pounds, I'm afraid. If you would care to stop by our cashier's office, they will be happy to make out a cheque to that amount for you, less a percentage to Christies for handling the sale."

Well, that was a disappointment. Ten pounds – I should have set a minimum sale price. At that rate I would have preferred to keep them. So ended my career as art entrepreneur.

Interest in art was a relatively new enthusiasm for me whereas music had been a passion for several years – appreciation that is, since I had something less than no talent for any instrument. I think I mentioned that musicians from the Norton prison camp ocasionally visited to put on live concerts: chamber music and some solo works. Among the musicians was one named Sigfried Leistner. He had studied under the famed conductor Bruno Walter and had been himself Direktor of the Leubek Stratsoper, before exchanging his baton for a rifle. Leistner was a most sympathetic character, and, of all the prisoners the one with whom I developed the closest personal relationship, and whom I visited in Leubek after his return. As a professional, he was proficient on several instruments.

Somewhere on his travels, my father had acquired a musical oddity called a dulcitone. This was a small keyboard instrument, perhaps forty inches wide and extending only about five octaves. Instead of strings, it had metal bars, like a marimba, of graduated lengths. When struck they emitted a sweet bell-like sound unlike any other keyboard contrivance. To complete the picture, this little wonder had folding legs, so it could be easily carried on tour and set up anywhere at a moment's notice for an evening of light entertainment. We didn't have a piano, but Leister provided many hours of enjoyment, tinkling out scores from memory: Mozart, Bach and small score works particularly adaptable to this musical cross-breed.

Not content with throwing away my wartime savings on art, I now invested in a huge combination radio/record player console. This was before the advent of modular units, so the whole apparatus was contained in a polished cabinet like a piece of fine furniture. I already had a large collection of classical records (78 rpm's and some LP's). Listening to them with Leistner's commentary was a musical education – my own personal tutor. He taught me a lot about musical architecture: symphonic form, theme and variations, dance forms, and fugue. I began to gain some sense of the structure on which the emotional content of music rested. This was just a beginning and abruptly ended when his repatriation number came up and he went back to Leubek.

Even with Liestner gone, there was opportunity for musical experience on every hand. In some ways this period of austerity and deprivation was also a golden age of the arts in England, partly because of the talent on display but also because of affordability. Since no one had any money, the theater and the concert halls accommodated themselves to the situation by reducing the price of admission to levels not seen before or since. You could attend a concert in the Albert Hall for two and six, and of course we did. The legendary conductors and performers from the continent were making their first postwar appearances in London: soloists Hans Hotter and Kirsten Flagstad at Covent Garden and the Albert Hall; Szigetti, the violinist, and Pierre Fournier, the cellist, at the Wigmore Hall; British master Sir

Thomas Beecham, and Benjamin Britten. We saw these and many more.

Thinking back on this time of disillusionment with academic work but passionate enthusiasm for the arts, I see it as a turning point, away from disciplined study in a structured environment, toward a self-directed pursuit of laudable interests, but in a disorganized fashion and with no real goal in mind, and with no guidance in how to proceed. The experience of the moment was what counted. I was abandoning education, in which I thought I believed, for dilettantism.

These distractions kept serious thought and organized planning from intruding into my latest interests. During this time I dated quite a few girls, most of them English, some quite appealing. One was an aspiring actress studying at the Royal Academy of Dramatic Art – I forget her name. Another was a budding TV producer for the BBC. Her name was Helena Malinowska, and her father was the anthropologist Brontislaw Malinowski, a contemporary of Margaret Mead, famous for his research among the Trobriand islanders of New Guinea. Helena couldn't have cared less about that; she was caught up in the excitement of being in on the ground floor of a new medium.

To keep track of my various social contacts, I made use of a little booklet I was supposed to keep with me at all times. This was the "Alien Registration Book," issued by the government to each resident alien. In addition to a photo and basic information in the front, it contained a number of blank pages, presumably for further official notations. Since I had to have the book on hand at all times the blank pages served double duty as a convenient place on the spur of the moment to enter the names and telephone numbers of friends and organizations.

As ill luck would have it, one day I was stopped for speeding by a traffic constable and issued a summons to appear before the local magistrate. This individual sat behind a high desk on a raised platform and peered at me over eye glasses on his nose. "Yes, Mr. Barwick, I see you are accused of exceeding the speed limit – forty miles an hour in a twenty-five mile an hour zone. Well, Mr. Barwick, you have to realize that we don't rush about as quickly as you people do in America. May I please have your Alien

Registration Book?"

I handed it to him. He turned the pages, examining it closely, then said, "Dear me, Mr. Barwick, what are all these entries that have been made in what is an official document, intended for government use?"

"Well, sir, I guess I shouldn't have put them in there. They're friends of mine, just a way to keep track of them," I said in some confusion.

"Really? I see that many are ladies names. You must be carrying on an active social life." More a comment than a question.

"Nothing out of the ordinary, Your Honor."

"Well, Mr. Barwick, in addition to speeding, I'm afraid you are guilty of defacing an official government document. We will attend to the speeding charge in a moment, but first we will take care of the defacement matter. Here," he said, rummaging around in a desk drawer and producing a rubber typewriter eraser. "Here, Mr. Barwick, I want you to erase every one of these names and restore these pages so we can use them for the purpose for which they were intended. Now let's see you go to work."

Feeling very foolish, I took the eraser and did as he asked. After much rubbing, I handed the book back to him.

"That's a great improvement, but at the expense of your romantic interests, I fear," he said. "Now about the traffic violation, we will let you off with a warning. Please see the clerk on your way out. Case dismissed."

The magistrate was right. There were several girls who probably wondered why they never heard from me again.

Chapter Seven

The Countess

One weekend during my second year in London, I was up in Cambridge visiting friends. It was a quiet evening. We were in one of the "locals" drinking beer when someone remembered that he had been invited to a party being thrown by one of the professors. We decided to check it out.

When we arrived the festivities had been going on for some time. Looking around, I could hardly believe that the surrounding uproar was actually being sponsored by a College Don. Music blasting and blaring, people falling over one another, spilled drinks everywhere. It was almost impossible to talk over the noise, which didn't stop people from trying, in slurred snatches which one could not understand in any case. I wondered if the professor was present to watch his house being torn apart. We were going to have a hard time catching up, but we resolved to try.

At one point a young Britisher accosted me. "You're a Yank, aren't you?"

"Yes," I said.

"I don't care if I never see another Yank again," he said. "The fact is, I'd rather not."

"Well, I can go away, if that will make you feel better."

"No, don't do that," he said. "You're alive. It's the dead ones I don't want to see."

I was beginning to think he was crazy. "Dead ones?" I said. "You mean in the war?"

"They were in the war, I wasn't," he said mysteriously.

"I don't get it,"

"Of course, you wouldn't. I mean, I was digging them up."

Now I was sure he was crazy.

"Yes, hundreds and hundreds of them. Poor sods, thousands of miles from home, and now some bastard comes mucking about with their bones. That was me, and I wish it wasn't."

More mystified then ever, I asked, "where was all this?"

"In France. You should know. You chaps are paying for it – your government, that is."

A light began to dawn. "Oh," I said. "You probably mean the War Graves Commission – the one set up to return the bodies of GI's killed in the war and buried in France – return them to the US."

"Right on," he replied. "I always thought it was a loony order. Our Tommies are still over there, and nobody talks about digging them up and bringing them back. But, three quid a day kept me happy for six months. Now I'd like to forget it. This helps," he said, taking a big swig of his drink.

Let me explain. You probably have never heard of The War Graves Commission. It's one of WWII's dirty little secrets now lost to historical memory, a raid on the US Treasury conceived by the undertaker's lobby and approved by Congress. The sales pitch went something like this: "Why should your beloved boy lie in foreign soil when he could be interred with a proper burial service right in his own home town, at no cost to you or the family?"

Neither the US Congress nor families of the fallen could resist such an offer Never mind that the military cemeteries in France from WWI were beautifully kept and much visited by friends and relatives. With little opposition, the unholy process was approved, and the digging began.

"It makes me ill to think about it," he went on. "Nothing like you'd want it to be. Lots of times we didn't know who was who, only part of a body in one grave, or more than one in another. We'd just stow what we could in the bag and put a name on it. Bloody awful."

"Yeah," I said. "Depressing."

His name was Cedric – we were now on a first name basis – his father was the professor, it was his, Cedric's, party. He soon drifted away and a short time later returned with a pretty blonde.

Picking Up the Pieces

She had rosy cheeks, china blue eyes and a robust build.

"Jack," he said. "I want you to meet Countess von Brach. She's German." We shook hands.

"Virginia," he said, "Jack is an American, but a good sort - for an American."

"American?" she asked. "I hear all Americans are rich, are you rich?"

"Not that I'm aware of," I replied.

"Oh, what a shame," she sighed. "I'm so longing to meet a rich American."

"Why?" I asked. "Are you poor? I thought a countess would have to be rich."

"Well, now you have met a poor one," she said.

"Virginia?" I wondered. "That doesn't sound like a German name. Is it?"

"No, my family gave me an impossible old fashioned name. So, as long as I'm here, I decided to call myself Virginia." All this in perfect English.

This was unusual, but not worth pursuing. "Are you here for long?" I asked.

"For a few more days," she said.

"And then?" I asked.

"I don't know. I've always wanted to visit London."

"Would you be staying with friends there?"

"If I can find a friend to put me up. I make friends easily."

Without any hesitation, I said, "Well consider that you have just made one. Why don't you come and stay with us, that is, my family and me? We have a big house, plenty of rooms. A bit out of the town center but a quick trip in."

She hesitated, then said, "That is very kind of you. Are you quite sure you could stand me for more than an hour?"

"Here," I said, producing a scrap of paper. "This is my phone number. Give me a call when you know your plans."

By this time the party was winding down. We said our good-byes – I never did get to meet the professor – and prepared to go back to the university and climb over the fence.

Back in London, about a week later the phone rang. "Is this Jack?" a female voice asked. "This is Virginia here."

Virginia? Virginia? I had forgotten all about the party. "Oh yes, Virginia. Hi. Great to hear from you."

"Well, here I am, come to see you. Is it still okay?"

"Oh sure." I said, trying to collect my wits. "Definitely. Where are you?"

She was at the Charing Cross tube station with one small suitcase. So I told her how to take the Northern Line and I would pick her up at the Highgate station.

Back at the house she said, "If you don't mind, let's forget the "countess" bit. I'm just "Virginia," and we can leave it at that."

"But you are a real countess, aren't you?" I asked.

"As real as a marriage can make it," she replied.

"Oh, I didn't know you are married." I said.

"Was," she replied. "He was killed in Russia."

"Oh, I'm terribly sorry."

"No, don't be. It doesn't do any good," she said. "If I'm going to be a widow, it will be 'The Merry Widow,' "

And she was as good as her word. "Die Lustige Witwe," smiling, laughing, never serious, always looking for amusement – or better yet, excitement, and if there wasn't any, she did her best to stir things up.

My sober, serious-minded family didn't know what to make of all this. It didn't take long for the "countess" secret to leak out, and when it did, impressed them mightily. They ascribed her constant party-personality as natural to people with titles. Everyone did their best to keep up. Routine dinners became occasions. My sister, who now worked at the American Embassy, had access to the PX and was able to produce wine and whiskey. Calvados, a distilled apple brandy, imported from France, was also available locally, as well as a kind of champagne or sparkling wine made from apples. Virginia turned her nose up at this, but drank it anyway. She found a few albums of dance music and in the evenings the whole place began to sound like a cabaret. Someone had presented my father with a box of cigars, which had been around for some time - he didn't smoke. She insisted that any man present have one after dinner with their coffee. And so on.

Naturally, I was interested in her background, family, education, and so forth, but she didn't want to talk about it and made evasive replies to my questions. About all I could discover was that she had learned her English at school in Switzerland and was not getting along with her family.

In one conversation, suddenly becoming serious, she said, "That is all over – schluss, kaput. I hate Germany. I never want to see it again. Those Nazi pigs – what they have done. I'm so ashamed of my country – it really isn't my country any more. I am reading in the newspapers about a young American – Garry Davis, I believe his name is. He calls himself a "citizen of the world." That's me. I too am a citizen of the world. I don't believe any more in countries. They are all the same. I love people. I believe in people."

That was an uncharacteristic outburst. Otherwise she was resolutely gay and fun-loving, with the result that my own social life escalated into a whirl of activity. In that small suitcase she carried, she found room for a cocktail dress and a formal evening gown. Courtesy of my sister, we went to two functions at the American Embassy, as well as a dance at the English Speaking Union. I was not then, and am not now, a dancer, but Virginia had no problem finding partners and when not at the bar was out on the dance floor while I nursed a drink on the sidelines.

But it was not all superficial amusement. She had a sincere and deep appreciation of the arts that seems inborn to members of a certain class in Europe. Her knowledge of painting and music was at least the equal of my own, so we spent hours in the galleries, she lecturing me on North German Renaissance painting, I lecturing her on Turner and the British water-colorists. It was a standoff.

She loved poetry, from the classics to modern times.. Her current passion was Rilke – a poet of whom I knew absolutely nothing. She had a book of his poems and read them to me in German, translating as she went along – not easy to understand, but undoubtedly great poetry, especially when heard in the original German. Music also. Here, for her, it was Mahler. I had several of his recorded works. Together we listened to "Das Lied von der Erde." A long piece, and when it ended some time passed before we wanted to speak, or pull ourselves up out of the mood it created.

She was a complex personality living her life at the extremes – maybe what Edna St. Vincent Millay meant when she wrote:

> I burn my candle at both ends,
>   It will not last the night.
> But, oh my friends
>   And oh my foes,
> It gives a lovely light.

With this heady mixture and this unsustainable pace my life went on for almost a month. As time passed, my father began to harbor suspicions that Virginia's visit was not as innocent as it appeared, and that she was, in fact, a foreign agent. He had always been intrigued by spy stories, and harbored a kind of paranoia: that things were never as they seemed, and events were being managed and manipulated by unseen powers.

"I don't think it's any accident that she's over here, and especially that she's in this house," he said.

"That's completely ridiculous," I replied. "I just met her by accident at a party up at Cambridge."

"That's what you're supposed to think," he said. "The German government has every interest in knowing who they're getting back among all these returning prisoners. Are there going to be any trouble-makers – unreconstructed Nazis? If I were them, I'd want to know. Look how the Russians have infiltrated their agents into the DP camps in Europe. What better way here than to work through the YMCA with its leads into every camp in the country? Has she ever asked you about this?"

"No, and I doubt she will. I mean, the whole idea is fantastic. You're imagining things," I said.

"Well, I have a few contacts at MI6. Come along with me and let's see what they make of the situation," he said.

"I can't do that. She's a friend – a guest here in our house. We can't go accusing her of espionage, and getting the government all stirred up without a shred of evidence to justify it," I replied with some heat.

"All right for now, but keep an eye on her and let me know if she says anything along the lines I mentioned, or asks too many questions," he said.

Left unspoken, however, was the thought that he was beginning to feel my little affair had gone further than was safe – that I was in danger of becoming infatuated with someone vastly more experienced than I was. And he couldn't see any good coming out of it.

He may have had a point. I had never known a girl even remotely like this – an exuberant, irrepressible personality: cultured, sophisticated, and at the same time primitive and earthy, with no pretense to be anything but what she was.

Hard to resist, and I wasn't trying.

Besides visits to the art galleries, we went to concerts almost once a week, sometimes to the Royal Albert Hall on Sundays when there was usually a program, or performer of special interest. One Sunday evening the program happened to be Verdi, and the conductor, Sir Thomas Beecham. We sat through the warmup selections after which Sir Thomas and the Royal Philharmonic launched into Verdi's "Stabat Mater," a work I didn't know.

But for some reason – no fault of Verdi's – this time the music didn't take. I couldn't get into it. I became restless. Virginia whispered in my ear, "Are you all right?"

"Not really," I said.

"Do you want to leave?" She asked.

"Let's go," I replied.

Out in the lobby, she asked me what was the matter.

"I don't know," I said. "It's not my night for music, especially not religious music. Let's drive around, see what's open."

But it was Sunday evening and everything was shut down. We drove up along the Thames into a semi-industrial area above Putney Bridge to a pub I knew called "The Dove". But it too was closed. So we sat in the parking lot.

"Do you want to go home?" I asked.

"No, let's just sit here for awhile and talk," she said.

"Well, here's something to help the conversation along," I said, reaching for a paper bag in the back seat. In it was a bottle of "Old Grandad" from the PX, courtesy of my sister, which had inadvertently been left in the car.

I broke the seal, unscrewed the cap, and held the bottle out.

"No glass, no ice. This is how they drink it back in Kentucky."

So the "Old Grandad" was passed back and forth a few times. But the mood of the evening just wasn't right. The conversation was going nowhere. My unsettled mind seemed to have communicated itself to her.

On one pass, she didn't take the bottle.

"Here," I said. "Your turn."

No answer.

"Have you had enough?" I asked.

Still no answer. And then I saw that she was crying.

"Oh, Virginia, I'm sorry. You're not well. We'll go home," I said.

"No, not just yet," she said, wiping her eyes and trying to smile. "I want to talk. This is a good time."

"About what? What's wrong?" I asked.

"It's just that I have to go – to leave," she said. "I never really meant to stay with you this long. And now it's time for me to move on."

"Are you sure there's nothing wrong?" I asked.

"Well, when I came to stay, I knew your father worked with German prisoners, but I didn't realize they were living right there in the house with you. You probably thought it would make me feel more at home, and in a way that's true, but it's almost like I never left Germany at all. And my whole reason for coming over here was to get as far away from anything German as I could."

"Well, I hope it's nothing we've done to make you feel unwelcome," I said.

"Not you, certainly, or your mother, I love you both," she said. "But with the German men it's different. They are condemning me for being here. They think my place is back in Germany. I should suffer just like the others. I'm your guest, but I can see it in their eyes. They think I'm some kind of whore."

"Aren't you exaggerating?" I said. "I've never seen anything like that."

"Believe me, Jack, I know my people. It's not possible for me to stay. I don't want to live any longer in the middle of such attitudes, so I have decided to go," she said with such an air of finality that I knew that more talk would not change anything.

Picking Up the Pieces

On the way back in the car, I asked, "You said you were poor – how poor? Will you have enough to get along?"

"Yes, barely," she said. "I'm a soldier's widow, and that brings me a little something. But even if it didn't, I would still leave."

The next morning her bag was standing just inside the front door. "I've said goodbye," she said, "and thanked your mother. Now it's your turn."

"Where are you going?" I asked. "At least, let me drive you."

"No thanks, dearest Jack – I've already rung for a cab. It will be here any minute."

"Well, this is all so sudden," I protested.

"Better that way," she said.

A cab rolled up in front of the house. She kissed my cheek, snatched up the bag and hurried down the stairs. The driver took her bag and stored it in front. She blew me a kiss, got in the cab, and was gone.

Chapter Eight

Seeking the Sun

As the year 1949 made its appearance, a deep malaise settled upon me and, with rare breaks of optimism and good feeling, colored my whole outlook to a dull, dismal gray. In those days, the word depression was not much used, and "clinical depression" not given serious attention as a widespread malady, particularly common among young adults. But, looking back on that episode, it seems pretty clear that that's what I had.

Even today the causes are not known : what brings about an onset, or what causes it to vanish and then reappear. These causes may lie deep within the psyche; but superficially at least there were a number of factors in my life at that moment which could explain it.

First, there was the obvious fact that my post-graduate study had come to nothing. Its original goal had turned out to be ill-planned and unrealistic, and there was left nothing with which to replace it. Academically, at least, I had always been an overachiever, so this setback created a sense of failure – of worthlessness. Also, I had always been project-oriented, needing a project – an immediate goal – to work toward. Now that was missing, and into the vacuum rushed a whole set of distractions – art, music, travel, girls, which served to mask this deficiency. But none could fill the basic void that had been created. Somewhere, deep down, conscience rebelled against the life I was leading, making itself felt in terms of gloom, pessimism, misery and guilt – guilt because my life there with the family was so much easier than that of the other Americans studying in London, living with no advantages on the local economy in cold uncomfortable lodgings. They never said anything to me about it, but the sense of unearned privilege weighed on me.

Massive pessimism became a way of life. Appropriately enough, I tackled the Russian novelists: on a good day, Tolstoy or Turgenev; on a bad day, Dostoievsky – "The Possessed," or better yet, "Letters From The Underworld" in which he finds himself most alive in the darkest depths of despair. Appropriate music would have been Tchaikowsky's sixth symphony.

Even without any internal problems, daily life in England, particularly London at that time, was enough to put anyone into a state of depression. Austerity had reached its depths under the administration of Sir Stafford Crips, a thin, bespectacled, emaciated individual whose person served as an active symbol of the national poverty and his draconian cure. Britons are a stoic, uncomplaining race and with few exceptions accepted penury as the condition of economic survival. For coddled Americans in Britain, once they got over the newness of their surroundings, it became the source of constant gripes and complaints. For me, the outside cold, rain, and fog simply reflected what was going on inside.

I felt an overpowering need to escape, to get away to a place where the sun shone, where people laughed, and music sounded from open windows and doors. Pure escapism, yes, but not entirely. There also had to be a purpose – I could never be a real beachcomber or wanderer. How to resolve this conflict?

The action at that time was in Germany, the great prize of the cold war, with the United States and the Soviet Union locked in an embrace in which neither could find a decisive advantage. Time seemed to favor the US, with aid from the Marshall Plan now beginning to pour in (matched by German counterpart funds), also the west German people, with ant-like energy, were cleaning up their ruined cities and industries. If that was where the future of Europe was to be decided, then that was where I ought to be.

But in my case there was a problem: facility in the language was missing. Despite living among Germans for the past two years, I had developed no real ability – not even for conversational German. The solution I now came up with blended both needs: first, to get away from the fog and discouragement of London's climate, and second, to develop the language skills needed to work in Germany. This was to enroll in The Berlitz School of Languages in London for a crash course of six months in French and German. (My accumulated GI Bill benefits would pay for it.) Then, continue this program for another six months somewhere in the south of France – preferably where there were few or no Americans. Also, at the same time I would be taking lessons in German. At the end of that period, with ability to get along in both languages, I would go to Germany in search of useful employment.

During the next six months at London's Berlitz School on Oxford Street, I pored over maps of France looking for a spot to suit my exacting requirements: the Riviera? too many Americans; Grenoble? a possibility; and then, Biarritz – seaside, lots of sunshine, no Americans, and there was a Berlitz School there with instructors for both languages. What had seemed difficult became an easy choice.

The plan of action specified an hour of German in the morning and an hour of French in the afternoon, each with a private instructor, plus outside study for vocabulary and some reading. My German instructor was excellent; from the start only German, and never, or almost never, lapsing into English. The French instructors – there were several – seemed to be non-professionals, bilingual types temporarily out of work from their real jobs. Little by little, I got the basics of both languages under control, but progress came slowly.

Also, I decided to make the journey to Biarritz in two steps: by channel steamer and train to Paris, then by bicycle under my own power from Paris to Biarritz, about five hundred miles. Departure was set for the middle of March1949. By then, the worst of winter would have given way to sunshine and, hopefully, warmer weather.

One more step remained, to acquire a bicycle. Unlike most Americans, growing up I had never owned a bicycle and had no experience in riding one. Hard to believe, but true. Undeterred, I set out and purchased not one but two Raleigh bikes, reasoning that when finished with them, I would pass them on to my brothers, James and Peter – and this is what happened. Raleigh bikes of that era were the Rolls Royce of their genre: massively built, with beautifully crafted details, but designed for level terrain, preferably with a strong tail wind. Equipped with side panniers and a rear storage unit, fully loaded, a bike would weigh between fifty and sixty pounds – maybe more, I'm guessing.

With spring the day of departure arrived. At the last minute Sam Davis, who headed up our Student Association, decided to come along using the second bike, and then return to London, taking the bike back with him. That was OK. I just didn't want him to decide to stay down there. This was to be an American-free journey, as much as I could make it.

Spring storms whipped the English Channel into mountainous waves and flying spray. The small steamer climbed and fell, pitched and rolled, shuddered and shook. Inside, nearly everyone was seasick, grimly holding on to whatever support they could find to keep from sliding down the wooden benches. The ship landed at Boulogne, and as soon as it did, the sun came out, the gale died down to a gentle breeze. On the train to Paris, outside the window apple trees had started to bloom, and lambs were frisking in the meadows. This is more like it, I thought, as the scenery flashed by.

Easter came early that year, so we decided to stay in Paris for two days over Easter Sunday and depart Monday morning. It was marvelous. We found a small, cheap hotel on the Left Bank, a few steps from the river, on a corner of La Rue St.Julien le Pauvre. Easter Sunday was balmy with occasional sun, the streets almost empty of traffic, but the Cathedral and the churches were busy. We walked about all day, admiring everything.

Monday morning, however, brought the city back to its usual chaos. With me wobbling tentatively on my bike, we threaded our way through the downtown to the outskirts of Paris. At Meudon, a long cobblestoned hill with trolley tracks was nearly my undoing as I whizzed down, too fast to stop or even slow down, huge trucks on my tail. Once outside the city limits, however, the roads emptied out. Gasoline was in short supply – much too expensive – so trucks were scarce and cars almost non-exsistent.

Our route took us to Versailles, then south to Orleans, and along the Loire to Tours, stopping to admire one chateau after another. We averaged about forty miles a day, continuing south through Poitiers and Angouleme. There were a few long hills that slowed us down, but more often it was the wind that always seemed to be right in our faces. With those heavy bikes, fully loaded, wind can make a real difference.

Another impediment to record speed was occasional stops or detours to sample the wines and spirits of whatever region we happened to be in: around Vouvray on the Loire, then a detour along the beautiful Charente river to Cognac, where the Courvoisier people hadn't seen any Americans that year and poured out an enthusiastic welcome.

Emboldened by success, several times along the road we stopped at promising-looking farmhouses with nearby vineyards. When the suspicious farmer or his wife answered the door, we explained that we were American students eager to learn about French wines and viniculture. Suspicious frowns quickly became friendly smiles. My newly acquired French was just barely equal to the occasion, particularly since the farmer always spoke a version of the language unique to his region.

What was easier to understand was down in the cellar: huge, dust covered barrels. The farmer would take a long glass instrument, something like a "turkey baster." with a rubber bulb at one end. This he would insert into the barrel, and from it fill up a couple of old tumblers which we were encouraged to sample. Since there were several barrels, that meant several glasses. "C'est pas mal, hein?" He inquired after each one. We assured him that it was the best wine we had ever tasted, and with many thanks got back on our bikes. Now, well into the south of France, the mid-afternoon sun was beating down and we had not gone far before deciding in favor of a roadside nap.

What had turned into a wine-tasting tour ended in the Bordeaux region, just north of the city. We descended into miles and miles of underground storage caves illuminated only by an occasional low-wattage bulb on electric wires strung haphazardly along the tunnel. At the sides were wooden racks containing what looked like millions of dusty, cobwebbed bottles lying on their sides. In the ghostly half-light workers gave each bottle a quarter turn to prevent the sediment from building up only on one side. Maybe there was more to it, I don't know. Sipping a glass of St.Emilion or Paulliac, I am reminded of those caves and of the poor wretches working in t

Chapter Nine

Biarritz – The Villa St. Hubert

From Bordeaux to Bayonne, we traversed a long, flat stretch with not much in it, and then a quiet ten miles to our goal, Biarritz.

Biarritz was, maybe still is, one of those resorts fashionable during the nineteenth century still living off the glamour of years gone by. Its glory days were during the Reign of Napoleon III, and his wife, the Empress Eugenie, whose palace stood overlooking the sea. It was now operating as the Palace Hotel. During those years, as was the case with so many European resorts, prosperity brought with it massive overbuilding – rows of four and five-story hotels, unattractive to begin with, which then declined as their clientele chased after newer royalty to newer fashion centers. To this neglect, add five years of war from which the town was only just starting to recover.

But even its mildewed, rundown aspect could not hide the natural beauty of the place, tucked into a corner of France just a few miles from the Spanish frontier. Rising inland, the town looks out onto the Bay of Biscay, with two long beaches, and a small rock-bound harbor squeezed in between them with its own private stretch of sand.

This is Basque country, starting with the foothills at the edge of town, climbing into real mountains, the French Pyrenees, that separate France from Spain. Signs of Basque culture were everywhere: distinctive names and spellings on street signs, "*pelote*" courts (the national sport, here called "*jai alai*"), and small, wiry dark-bronzed men. Downtown was not particularly picturesque, the usual assortment of shops and businesses, but away from the town center houses were built mostly in the Basque style, a kind of mountain chalet with wide roofs over white stucco, and flowering vines climbing everywhere.

My immediate destination was the Villa St. Hubert on the Rue Peyroloubilh, located between the town center and the sea, not far from either. Biarritz was not a large place. I knew where I was going, courtesy of an American friend named Bill Cole, who had just left Biarritz, stopping in London on his way back to the States. He told me about this "great little pension" – not at all deluxe, but very affordable. His recommendation was good enough for me.

The house turned out to be exactly as he had described it: on a street corner, set back from the road, moderately large and slightly decrepit from lack of regular maintenance, with vines climbing up and around the window frames. Inside, that same atmosphere of having once seen better days: curtained windows, old-fashioned furniture in the parlor, and a small dining room with about eight or ten tables, some at the windows with a view onto the street. Old-fashioned, but neat and clean.

The proprietress, Mme. Freda, emerged from the kitchen wiping her hands on an apron as I rang the bell on a desk in the foyer. Oh yes, she remembered "Mr. Beel" very well. "Tres gentile, un beau garcon." In no time we made all the necessary arrangements, which included a small room – bed, desk, and incongruously a large easy chair, a bath in the hall and three meals a day. Perfect.

Next stop was the Berlitz School in the town center, run by an elderly lady who, like everything else in Biarritz, seemed to have seen better days. I had written in advance so that all the necessary official approvals had been received and they were ready for me to start at any time, which meant the next morning: German in the morning, French in the afternoon, three days a week for a total of eighteen hours a week of private instruction.

My German tutor, M. Desrosier, was retired from the local lycee where he had taught German for many years, even during the occupation. At the end of the war, Biarritz had had enough of anything German and struck it from their language program, forcing M. Desrosier into involuntary retirement. As a beginner in the language it was hard for me to assess the quality of his mastery, but since he spoke only a few words of English we were forced to keep everything in German - the best way to learn a language.

Lessons were conducted in his home, an attractive villa perched on a slope at the edge of town. Stone steps led up to an entrance at the side amid masses of brilliant red flowering vines. Settled comfortably in the living room, we conducted our lesson while Mme. Desrosier busied herself in the kitchen. He may not have had a perfect accent but Prof. Desrosier was a total master of German grammar which he enforced without compromise. A good thing too, I thought, since with a solid foundation in grammar, adding vocabulary would be easy.

I soon was capable of holding a simple conversation, and at that point we came to a disagreement. The disagreement had to do with music. It developed that both the professor and his wife were ardent lovers of classical music. His instrument was the violin, and hers a piano. which occupied a corner of the parlor and was covered with sheet music.

The issue which put us at opposites was, "Who was the greater composer? Mozart or Beethoven?" An impossible question, but nevertheless one on which each of us had a decided opinion. Since I was still in my "Beethoven period." I held for him. But Desrosier was equally for Mozart. Mozart, he said, was a true genius - "ein echte wunderkind," a genius who had mastered every musical form without apparent effort, his scores without revisions, while Beethoven had to struggle to achieve his epic creations. "Who knows," he said, "to what heights Mozart might have developed had he not died just at the peak of his powers? No, Beethoven was a great master, but of the two, Mozart was his superior."

So the argument went, with the professor highly energized, all thought of a language lesson lost in the heat of debate, obviously enjoying himself mightily as I was myself. These discussions had the effect on both of us of stimulating a good mid-day appetite, particularly since lesson hours were from ten to twelve. As we talked, enticing aromas wafted into the parlor from the kitchen where Mme. Desrosier was preparing the mid-day meal. The result was that, more often than not, I was invited to stay over for lunch which was more like a dinner, always with wine on the table.

French lessons in the afternoon at the Berlitz School didn't amount to much. There was no organized plan for systematic

Biarritz – The Villa St. Hubert

development based on existing skills, but that deficiency was at least partly compensated for by the fact that this was France, and I was speaking French constantly, at home, around town, everywhere. The instructor was just another resort refugee earning a few extra dollars in the easiest way possible. Mine spent a good part of every lesson complaining about the owner - what a skinflint she was, and the starvation wages she paid to deserving people like himself. As far as I could see, based on my experiences in London and in Biarritz, the Berlitz School of Languages was nothing but a rip-off collection of franchises, living on a pre-war reputation for quality instruction. That quality now depended entirely on luck – the individual instructor to whom you were assigned. But at the time it never occurred to me to complain.

Back at the Villa St. Hubert, I was quickly becoming a member of the family. I particularly liked to sit in the kitchen while Mme. Freda worked: prepping vegetables for dinner, baking bread, or washing pots and pans. She was a big woman, not especially beautiful but very emotional and dramatically expressive. She liked to talk as she worked and didn't mind me in the kitchen. With my limited French I made a good audience for her, and for me it was an unpaid language lesson.

"Ah, M. Barweek." she would say, "Vous avez la chance d'etre Americain".(You are lucky to be an American.) "Ici, la vie est dur, vous savez, tres dur." (Here, life is hard, yes, very hard.) "The only good time I can remember was before the war, when I was a girl. Then Biarritz was famous for its clientele – 'le beau monde' - they filled the hotels and gambled every night in the casino. Elegant ladies who knew how to dress, not this riff-raff we get today – no manners, no money to speak of. And gentlemen with their big cars. I was working at La Plage then cleaning rooms. Ah, M. Barweek, the beautiful dresses, the style, the chic."

"What happened ?" I asked.

"The war. The war ruined everything. Just before it broke out, we inherited this pension from my husband's aunt who died. What a good fortune, we thought. Or so we thought. Then everything started to go wrong.

"Marcel and I were married in 1938, still in the good time.. Then, tout-a-coup, boom! The war breaks out. No more tourists, no more holiday visitors, no income to keep things up. The worst of all, Marcel is called for the army, just in time for our defeat by the Germans and the fall of France. He is captured and sent into Germany to work in one of their factories. That left me alone here, trying to keep the pension going even though there were few visitors. I keep thinking he will be returned, but no, for five years they keep him there at hard labor, and when they finally let him go, he is a broken man.."

It was true. Her husband was now a complete contrast to his wife: thin, speaking just above a whisper, tentative in his movements, about forty-five but looking more like sixty. With Marcel just the shadow of a man, it seemed unlikely that little Christian would ever enjoy the company of brothers and sisters.

"At least," said Mme. Freda, "he has given me this child, mon petit chou, Christian. Thanks be to God."

Little Christian was in imminent peril of suffocating from an excess of love from Mme. Freda. When it came to dressing him, every day was a holiday: neatly pressed shirt and short pants, socks and sandals, and a little white cap on top. Thus clad, scrubbed, brushed, and combed, he would wander into the garden and play in the dirt like any normal child and return to cries of mock horror from Mme. Freda.

"Ooh, la-la. Quelle enfant! Mon petit cochon." (Oh my. What a child! My little pig!) "Toujour plus de travail pour ta mamman. Je devrais te gronder. Viens ici, petit cochon, pour un baiser." (Always more work for your mother. I ought to scold you. Come here, little pig, for a kiss.) And so on.

Her romantic temperament, with such restricted opportunities for expression, found an outlet in the love life of her guests. She knew who was sleeping with whom, or was about to, married or single, especially since in many instances it was she who had promoted the affair. It was her firm belief that there was something unnatural about the single life, and about celibacy in particular. As a good Catholic wife and mother, this did not apply to herself; her marriage and child were sacrosanct, the center of her universe, but this still left a lot of room for creative arrangements in the lives of her guests.

In my case, Mme. Freda would inquire closely about girls: did I have a special girlfriend? Was there one back in America waiting for me? What was my opinion of the girls here in France? Did I prefer blondes or brunettes? When I told her I didn't know any French girls, she replied that she would soon correct that deficiency. There were one or two local girls, temporarily unattached, and in about ten days she was expecting "une tres jolie jeune fille, une secretaire dans l'Embassade d'Angleterre" (very pretty girl, a secretary at the British Embassy) who had stayed with her last year, and had been "friends with Mister Beel." This last with a suggestive smile.

Before I could establish contact with the locals, Yvette arrived: A small brunette, very Parisian, about thirty years old, and to my great disappointment speaking excellent English. Mme. Freda lost no time in making arrangements practically guaranteed to lead to something interesting. Yvette's room was next to mine, as were our tables in the dining room. Nothing subtle about Mme. Freda. This, plus a warm introduction, put us on a first name basis in a day's time.

One afternoon not long thereafter I was in my room seated in the large easy chair, memorizing German vocabulary, when there came a knock at the door. "Entrez," I said. Yvette came in, looked around and said, "I was feeling bored and thought I'd look in to see what you were doing."

"I was working on my German ," I said.

She made a face and said "I can think of better things to do. That's a nice big, chair. Do you think it's big enough for two?" And without waiting for an answer she sat in my lap and put one arm around my neck. "Now that's better already."

It wasn't hard to see where this was going, so I wasn't surprised when a moment later she sat up and exclaimed, "Qu'il fait chaud ici." (It's so warm in here)." I'm getting out of these sticky clothes. How about you?"

That's how the affair began and went on for two weeks until she returned to her job in Paris. During that time I made little progress as far as the language went but made up for it in other ways. Yvette had no interest in anything intellectual; art, history, politics, literature were all a matter of total indifference to her. She lived in a world of style, glamour, and sensation fueled daily by the big tabloids: *Paris Match, Star*, and others whose names I have forgotten. She kept up to the moment with "les grandes vedettes (the big movie stars), their comings and goings, affairs, and breakups. Since this was a world of which I knew nothing, there wasn't much for me to contribute to the conversation, which didn't matter because she liked to talk.

One of her great favorites was Edith Piaf, a diminutive nightclub singer with a sad, haunting voice, who sang of failed love affairs and the sad hopeless atmosphere of postwar France. Yvette's eyes filled with tears as we listened to "Les Feuilles Mortes" ("Dead Leaves") and "J'Attendrais" ("I Will Wait For You"), and even I found myself caught into the heartache that poured from the throat of the small chanteuse. Piaf's love affair with the great French middleweight champion Marcel Cerdan gripped the entire country; and none more so than Yvette, who saw a kind of inspired perfection in the coming together of France's two greatest public personalities, only to be dashed by fate. Cerdan was killed when his plane crashed in North Africa en route to a match. Before that, Edith Piaf's themes had been the pain and sorrow of everyday life; now they deepened into tragedy, and the whole country wept with her.

Among the top personalities and performances of that year were a number of pre-war holdovers, Mistinquette, of the fabulous legs, and Maurice Chevalier, under a bit of a cloud for having been too friendly with the Germans during the occupation. But mostly it was an emerging crop of singers that included Yves Montand and Charles Aznevour . Sex kitten Brigitte Bardot was attracting media attention on the beach at Cannes. Everywhere they were playing a swinging tune, "La Seine," which helped lighten the prevailing national gloom and pessimism.

Yvette was my guide into this side of French life, and I shouldn't disparage that since this is what most people watched and listened to. But Yvette didn't care about the sociological aspect, personalities were what monopolized her attention, especially those with style or glamour, of which she was a studious critic: "First, when we say 'style' we mean Paris, only Paris. The rest of France is a barnyard. In Paris, we have the masters, the geniuses of style and fashion. Coco Chanel, Christian

Dior, Givenchy. People come from all over the world to admire and to buy their creations. They are supreme. But style is not the same as glamour. We have no one who can compare to your Rita Hayworth or Lana Turner – the 'sweater girl', ha ha.

"But my favorite" she went on, "is Ginger Rogers. Quelle femme! She's beautiful. She dances like a dream, and she can even act. I could watch her forever. And she has the perfect man to show her off, Fred Astaire. But, of course, he's really not American at all. He was born in Austria. Never mind. They are wonderful. It was Hollywood that made them glamorous, and we don't have a Hollywood."

Yvette and I had a good time during these two weeks, but when she got on the bus for Bayonne to catch the train back to Paris, I can't say I was sorry to see her go. I can take only so much conversation about the entertainment world before I begin to feel like I'd eaten too much cotton candy. Besides, there were lingering shreds of idealism left, the nagging thought that I had come to Europe for serious study intended to lead somewhere. Instead here I was, in actual study only a few hours a week, the rest of the time spent on the beach or under an umbrella at a café table sipping Cinzano, exchanging vacuities with a celebrity worshiper, and not even in French.

As the summer progressed the Villa St. Hubert started to fill up, mostly with regulars who year after year took their modest holiday as Mme. Freda's guests. The majority of this clientele were no longer young. Their cross-table conversation in the dining room endlessly explored the possibilities offered by the weather, and by health and healthcare. Especially popular were "*crise de foie*" (liver crisis) and "*le mauvais aire*" (bad air). Despite this detailed commentary, I never did learn exactly what "crise de foie" was, how to know if you had it, and how to recover from it if you did. I don't think "*crise* de foie" has any exact corresponding illness outside of France. It is an ailment unique to the Gallic temperament. Almost the same can be said about "le mauvais aire". It may be similar to what used to be called the "discomfort index," a high temperature/humidity combination, although I noticed that complaints came and went for no discernible reason, leading me to believe that it had more to do with one's inner state of mind.

Among these regulars at the pension was one M. Pierrot who was there for several weeks, bringing with him his godson, Toto. M. Pierrot was an aging homosexual, dressed usually in a green suit and wearing a reddish toupee which he must have acquired long ago because the rest of his hair had turned quite gray. His manner was always reserved and formal. Upon entering the dining room, he would bow to all present and say, "Bonjour, Medames et Messieurs." Seated at the table he invariably began his meal with a St. Raphael aperitif and a glass of juice for Toto.

Toto was a hyperactive petit garcon of about seven, a little older than Christian and his mentor in misbehavior. M. Pierrot's air of settled authority was severely tested trying to keep Toto in his chair and under control during the evening meal. The child was either under the table or running around the room. "Toto, viens ici " (Come here). " Toto, sois sage" (Behave yourself). Nothing seemed to work.

Disorder escalated when Christian put in an appearance, as he had been expressly forbidden to do. Against one wall of the dining room was a full-length mirror. The two miscreants would stand there and make faces at the glass, attempting to outdo each other in general repulsiveness. Toto had an in-built advantage in that his natural facial features had a distinctive monkey-like appearance needing little in the way of contortion to achieve the desired effect.

Eventually the noise penetrated into the kitchen and Mme. Freda came rushing out. "Toto, Christian…C'est assez, alors. Laisse les clients tranquilles" (That's enough. Leave the customers in peace.)."

Eventually, Toto, Christian, and I became friends. We took "promenades" (walks) up to the lighthouse, and I bought them ice cream cones.

Chapter Ten

An American Casualty

There were a few good examples around town of what could happen when you let yourself get too far from home. One of these was Frank, an Irish-American who had come to France as an Army private during the war. At the end of hostilities he was sent to one of the holding stations to await shipment back home. There were two of these holding stations: one was in Cannes, the other in Biarritz. Frank was sent to Biarritz. While there, he was lucky. Unlike the great majority of soldiers waiting there with nothing to do but kill time, and nobody to kill it with, Frank met Nicole, a cute, petite French girl - or rather, woman. She was about forty, close to his age, and owned a small patisserie.

That was the summer of 1945 when American soldiers were unblemished heroes to the French people who needed heroes given the miserable performance of their politicians and government during the war years. To this appeal were added Frank's easygoing, friendly nature and devastating good looks. Nicole's husband had been killed in the war in 1940, and Frank was single. Both were lonely. They fell in love and were married.

Since there was nothing of importance in the States for Frank to return to, they decided to stay in Biarritz. She had her little business going and Frank would find a job around town, although it was not clear exactly what he was fitted to do.

As the only Americans in town, Frank and I struck up a casual friendship. Walking downtown one morning, I came upon him seated on a sidewalk bench in front of the patisserie. "Hi, Frank," I said. "How's it going?"

"Oh, comme-ci, comme-ca" (so-so) he replied. "Je cherche

partout pour travail, mais pas de chance. (I'm looking for work, but no luck.) Pas de chance - what's that in English?"

"No luck," I said. "I'm sorry to hear that."

"Yeah, pas de chance, that's me. C'est ce qu'il me faut - a little luck for a change."

Frank spoke a queer mixture of French and English in which French was gradually taking over. He could no longer remember many English words, with the result that he couldn't speak either language properly, just this primitive mish-mash.

He looked terrible: graying hair, a bloated red face, eyes bleary and bloodshot. It was about nine a.m. and he was obviously drunk.

After a few more words I went inside for a croissant and a morning coffee.

Nicole was behind a counter featuring a dazzling display of baked goods: napoleons, tartes, gateaux, mille-feuilles, etc, etc.

"Bon jour, M. Jack,' she said. Unlike Frank her one and only language was still French.

"Bon jour, Nicole. Comment ca va? (How goes it?)"

"Pas tres bien, malhereusement." (Not well, unfortunately.) I am so worried about Frank. I don't know what to do with him. And it only gets worse. A glass of wine, yes. It's good for the health, but wine has now become his whole life. When he's not drinking, he's sleeping. Day, night, it's all the same. I can't believe this is the man I married."

"Is there anyone who can help - the doctor? Your priest?" I asked.

"Maybe they could, but he won't talk to them. He says he's OK and that I shouldn't worry."

"I'm sorry, Nicole. I don't know if it will do any good, but I'll try to talk to him."

"Oh, please, M. Jack. He might listen to you. Please do."

Outside, I sat down with Frank. "Frank, buddy, listen, I'm worried - about you, your health. You don't look healthy to me and I think it has something to do with the bottle. Listen, Frank, you've got a good life here, a great wife, a good little business. You don't want to blow it, do you? Why don't you talk to a doctor. See what he says."

"Yeah, Jack, mon ami. You've been talking to Nicole. Il n'ya rien du mal with me (There is nothing wrong) Un p'tit goutte de temps en temps (a little drop now and then) That's all. Rien (nothing) to see a doctor about. Hell, man. This is France. Tout le monde (everyone) drinks wine. Even les enfants (the children).

"Best thing pour toi (for you) Jack, is we have a p'tit verre. You and me. Whaddaya say? We saved la belle France back in forty-four, n'est pas? (Didn't we?) Let's drink to that."

When I left town two months later Frank was still there on the bench. I sat with him from time to time, but could hardly bear to talk to Nicole. For her, a devout Catholic, divorce was out of the question. Hopeless.

Frank never gave up trying to make a drinking buddy out of me. I was his last link to the States, and after awhile I gave up trying to reform him. But we still met now and then, usually on his bench.

One day while we were seated there a friend of his stopped by to say hello. They had scarcely started to talk when the friend stopped mid-sentence and stared fixedly at something or someone on the other side of the street. Then, without a word, he ran over, shouting and cursing, and hurled himself on a middle aged individual. "Salaud ... sale chien ...je vais t'ecraser." They fell to the ground. He had his victim by the throat and was pounding his head on the sidewalk, clearly in the grip of a murderous frenzy.

Frank and I had hold of his arms and were trying to pull him off. A couple of other bystanders joined in and with great difficulty we succeeded. When we did, the intended corpse got shakily to his feet, then ran down the street and disappeared around a corner. "Va t'en, salaud," shouted his nemesis. "La prochaine fois je casse ta gueule." (Get out, you son-of-a-bitch. Next time I break your neck.)

After he had gone, I asked Frank what that was all about. "Deux avocats - what's that? - two lawyers. Yeah, well during the occupation, that guy on the trottoir - the sidewalk - denounced l'autre, mon ami Paul, to les Allemands (denounced the other, my friend, to the Germans.) They took him away. Gone for five years. Presque mort quand il reviens." (Almost dead when he comes back.) Mais, crois moi, Jack, the other one's a dead man if he stays around here. Paul will kill him. He means it."

Later I learned that this was not an isolated incident. The German occupation brought out the worst aspects of the French national character - especially the willingness of people to betray fellow Frenchmen - their neighbors - to a hated enemy, and to collaborate with that enemy whenever there was some advantage in it. Despicable, but even worse was France's latent anti-Semitism, authorized and given free rein by the Vichy government in obedience to German orders. Thousands of Jewish men, women and children were shipped out under that program, never to return. Very few of the collaborators were ever punished, but among those few that were were the so-called "horizontal collaborators": women who formed liaisons with individual Germans. Newspapers and magazines featured pictures of these unfortunates, stripped naked, their hair shorn, being scourged through the streets as jeering throngs pelted them with garbage.

Any nation has difficulty looking honestly at all aspects of its own history, and France was no exception. In 1949 these scenes from its recent past were still too painful to acknowledge. Better to forget for now, and let time's healing powers cover up the scars.

Chapter Eleven

The Beach Club

Biarritz has several beaches. Not surprisingly, many hours of my free time were spent there. To the north, past the lighthouse and the Palais Hotel is the "Chambre d'Amour" – the "Room of Love" – which I thought was an odd name for a beach, but which I put down to the French ability to see "amour" in almost anything. To the south is the Cote des Basques, another long expanse of sand stretching all the way to the Spanish border at Hendaye. Both of these beaches look out onto the Bay of Biscay, one of the roughest, most treacherous oceans in the world, and the scene of innumerable ship disasters over the centuries. Storms create monster waves, recorded as high as sixty-four feet a few miles further north. Even in good weather a relaxing swim can turn dangerous due to tidal rips and undertows.

Swimming alone one evening on the Cote des Basques, I had a scary experience when I found myself battling a strong offshore current, and unable to get back to the beach. Getting nowhere by opposition, I stopped trying to fight the current and allowed myself to be carried by it parallel to the beach, little by little coming closer until about a quarter of a mile further on I finally made it out onto the sand. The moral: don't swim alone, although I'm not sure what anyone could have done to help.

For these and other reasons, my favorite beach was the one in the middle called "Le Port Vieux" (The Old Port), a tiny strip of sand open at one end to the sea and protected by rocky cliffs on both sides, extending out into the ocean with a light at the end to mark the entrance to the harbor. This natural pier is called "Les Rochers de la Vierge" (the Rocks of the Virgin); in good weather you can walk out to the end. Between these rocky walls the sea reaches inland almost to the town itself, probably the natural port around which Biarritz settled and grew.

Because it was so close to everything, the Old Port beach was seldom deserted. The water was relatively calm, the waves only a gentle swell, a remnant of the surf crashing on the rocks at the entrance. Because of this it was a good beach for children, and there were usually a few of them with toy buckets and shovels playing at the water's edge while their mothers read the latest scandal sheets from Paris.

On one of my free mornings, I had settled in at a sunny spot when a threesome arrived, a young girl, a woman of perhaps thirty and a child of about five. Blankets were laid down, but a large beach umbrella didn't want to open properly. "Pardon, Mme," I said, "Laissez-moi vous aider" (Let me help you), and proceeded to find the catch and opened it up.

"Merci, mille fois, m'sieu," the lady said. (a thousand thanks): "Vous etes Americain?" (Are you American?) I said I was, spending the summer in Biarritz trying to learn French. "But you already speak very well," she said. Not true, but I'd gotten used to hearing polite compliments without believing them. After a few friendly exchanges we each went back to our respective blankets.

Next day they were at the same spot when I arrived with a book of French grammar. "Bon jour, M'sieu," the woman said, and after we had inquired as to each other's health and commented on the weather and the condition of the ocean for bathing she asked, "What are you reading?" When I showed her she laughed. A grammar text on the beach, ah, that is funny, but at the same time admirable. I always heard that Americans love to work – even on the beach."

What could I say? She went on "I must not tease you. That is precisely what I should do with my English – study, study. but I am too lazy."

Before long we were on a friendly basis. Her name was Jacqueline, the child was "Canie," and the girl was Hugette, a sort of governess for the child. They were all from Paris, renting an apartment in Biarritz for the summer. Her husband, Gilbert, would be there also whenever he could get away from his furniture design business. In the days following, before his arrival, Jacqueline augmented my French lessons with vocabulary exercises which were a lot of fun; because of her limited English we had to puzzle out meanings together.

Coming down to the beach a few days later, I saw, added to the group, a dark handsome man with the body of a weight liftter in a skimpy "maillol" (bathing suit). "Cme here, Jack. I want you to meet my husband, Gilbert …Gilbert, this is Jack, an American. He has come to France to learn French."

Over the next two months we were to become very good friends. As this friendship developed, it was as though I had been admitted into a kind of club, made up of young French adults, semi-intellectual, anti-establishment, detached, alienated but not particularly political or left-wing.

Membership was enlarged by the periodical addition of various types who came and went as their jobs permitted. Among themselves they spoke a kind of Parisian street language that most Frenchmen would have had trouble understanding. For me they made a special effort to speak slowly, supplemented with English words here and there.

Gilbert, the intellectual center of this group, was a Jewish entrepreneur, relatively prosperous, employing half a dozen workers in his atelier, turning out handmade creations for an upscale clientele. He considered himself an artist, not the least of his creations being his own body, sculpted and refined by at least one hour of daily workout. Jacqueline also participated in this daily ritual, to achieve a gorgeous figure, glistening with Ambre de Soleil and displayed with only the tiniest of bikinis.

One member was Edouard, a salesman of agricultural products. He was on the road most of the time, dealing with distributors and growers with large estates. Edouard was hyper-intellectual, especially about music – jazz music. He claimed to be able to tell, from just listening to a record, whether there were any black players in the band. A day of dealing with the unimaginative "clods" who were his customers left him frustrated and ready to quit and try almost anything else.

Another club member was Yves, tall, blond and athletic, just returned from two years as a paratrooper in French Indochina, and before that with the French Foreign Legion in Algeria. Not at all intellectual, or talkative, Yves exuded an air of danger, of menace - someone whose personality had been formed in crisis situations.

Also, there was Jacques, a local photographer with artistic ambitions, whom they had gotten to know the previous summer. He longed for the big-city life. He considered Biarritz a cultural backwater, and welcomed the arrival of Gilbert, et al, as an opportunity to plug into the latest trends and café gossip from the center of the world, Paris There were others, but these few were the ones I remember best. The beach was our clubhouse.

Over the summer we lay on the sand, reading, or putting down the books to discuss just about everything that young adults talk about, albeit mostly serious subjects. This group was not particularly interested in sports, nor were they intellectual in any formal sense, just bright young people capable of expressing strong opinions. Mostly, it was the men who talked. Jacqueline stayed in the background with Hugette and Canie.

As an American, I was an object of considerable interest and curiosity. For me, they were a window into postwar French attitudes and culture that I could not have found so easily elsewhere.

I'll let them speak for themselves.

"So what are you Americans going to do, now that you rule the world?" they asked in a teasing way.

"I don't know, what do you want us to do?" I replied.

"We think you should stick around for awhile – your army, that is. No one wants the Russians in here. The Germans were bad enough," said one.

"Yes, send us the army and the Marshall Plan but keep the rest at home: Hollywood, Coca-cola, the whole synthetic culture you Americans live by," added another.

I couldn't let this pass. "You are really mistaken. Hollywood is Hollywood, not America. It's just entertainment, but unfortunately the only side of us you see," I said.

"Maybe," said Edouard, "but underneath all the show biz, I think Hollywood really does express American culture. For instance, the emphasis on youth and beauty, how you love guns, weapons, violence, and the idea that every story has a happy

Picking Up the Pieces

ending – your childish American optimism. That's Hollywood, and these are all aspects of American culture, I think Americans believe in these things."

"OK," I said, "but then why are they so popular over here?"

"Because they are entertaining - childish, but entertaining. Right now we have nothing to compete with you," the photographer replied. "French culture once ruled the world - no more.. The war has left us in a cultural vacuum. It's been a hundred years since you Americans have experienced a war at home. In Europe it's not just the destruction and the killing, but also no theater, no concerts, no film production, avant garde art and books banned – it takes time to recover, if we ever do. Hollywood's fairy tales are just what everybody wants, even though purists like me complain about it."

"I don't know," said Jacques. "Our wines are still pretty good, and relatively cheap. In a few years they could be priceless."

Everyone laughed. "We're not investors. How about a good one to drink right now?"

"I also disagree," said another. "I don't think France is altogether dead culturally. In literature, for example: we have Malraux and Camus. In philosophy, Jean Paul Sartre; his philosophy of "existentialism" has to be taken seriously. And his girlfriend, Simone de Beauvoir – who else is writing about the status of women in the world? Speaking of women, look at our fashion industry. The House of Dior has a hot-shot young genius there who is going to put Paris fashion back on top."

Everyone nodded. His words made them feel better.

But, Mr. Gloom and Doom was not about to give up. "Maybe, we do have a few green shoots starting to come up here and there, but that's just window dressing. Deep down there's a sickness – a malaise – at the very heart of the country that came out in the occupation for all the world to see. Until we get rid of that, all our wine, or our fashion, or our perfumes will not hide the stink."

"OK," I said, "the occupation was a bad time for France, but now all your political parties are promising reform. And De Gaulle was certainly not part of that sickness. Can he lead France out of its problems?"

To which he answered, "That's right, De Gaulle and a few

others were not infected with the disease. Can he lead France out of it? I don't know. For me, De Gaulle represents the past, another age, with his talk of 'la gloire' – the glory days of Napoleon. I don't think he has much understanding of modern problems, or modern solutions, or that he's capable of seeing - or accepting - the fact that there are only two real powers in the world today, America and the Soviet Union."

"Well, what about Europe as a whole?" I asked. "I'm reading that this Marshall Plan is just the first step in a master plan to bring all Europe together with a single currency under a single parliament – only the languages remain different. Is that just a dream? Would you want it?"

Gilbert responded. "You Americans always see your own history as a model for the rest of the world. When your thirteen states came together they had just won their independence from a common enemy. They already spoke a common language. Also they had a common frontier for expansion against another common enemy – the Indians. What do we have in common? Centuries of war, economic competition and big ego politicians."

"Yes," I said. "But doesn't it make sense? Isn't now the time to try?"

"What we don't need at this point is a failed attempt," put in one of the others. "Can you see France and Germany cooperating? Or De Gaulle taking orders from some authority outside of France? This idea of a united Europe has to wait until the older generation dies off."

"You know," I said, "there's a strong anti-colonial movement going on all over the world. I met a few of these young leaders in England at the London School of Economics. They impressed me. Is the colonial empire of France part of that past age of 'la gloire' that De Gaulle is trying to hold onto?"

Yves, the paratrooper, who never talked much, replied, "In Indochina, I never met any leaders, but I can tell you, those little guys are not going to give up, no matter how many of their villages we burn down or how many of them we shoot. They just keep coming back. The more we shoot, the more we lose. We should get out now – out of Algeria also.

"Do you think that will happen?"

"Not a chance, but if it did, I'd like to go back there to live. It's beautiful, and the people too – if you can get to know them."

"Yeah," said another. "For us, we want to get out of here. There's no future here. You know that song, 'Ma Cabane au Canada' – a little cabin in the forest, back to nature – that's for me. Escape, start over."

Later during the month of August Gilbert said to me, "A few of us are going to Lourdes this weekend – you know, where the witch doctors we call priests practice magic on the superstitious boobs that go there in hopes of a miracle. Anyway, we want to see the whole charade up close. It's great entertainment – good for a few laughs. We'll have a lot of fun. Why don't you come along?"

"What are you going to do there?"

"Oh, nothing in particular. Just sit back and enjoy the show – have fun, amuse ourselves."

It so happened that I couldn't go along that time. Even so, I was a bit shocked and appalled at the idea of going to Lourdes – a religious shrine – just to laugh and make fun of cripples and other unfortunates seeking a way out of their misery. "I can't go with you," I said, "but isn't it bad taste to mock people who are suffering like these people must be?"

"We're not mocking them. They're victims of the colossal fraud that is Organized Religion, especially the Roman Catholic Church. These poor fools are being taken advantage of by the church to provide a spectacle – a circus. Since it's a circus, they want an audience. Well, we'll help swell the crowd. You should come along. Where else could you see anything like it?"

I couldn't change my plans, so they took off, leaving Canie and Hugette behind. When we met on the beach a few days later, I asked Gilbert how it had gone. Was it worth the trip?

"Jack," he said, "I'll never laugh at them again. It was a spectacle, but I never imagined it would have such an effect on me – me, a confirmed anti-cleric."

Astounded by this confession, I said, "I don't believe this. You mean you now believe in everything you were laughing at and mocking only a few days ago?" "Not quite," Gilbert replied. "But it was a very moving experience. I could not have imagined it. At least now I can't make jokes about it."

"What caused the big change?" I asked.

"It started the night we got there, after dark. It had begun to rain – hard. A train pulled in, and dozens, maybe hundreds, of people got out, some with crutches, some in wheelchairs, others hobbling or supported by friends or relations. They were given lighted torches, and then this whole mass of people started for the cathedral. It was eerie, the rain pouring down on them in the darkness, lighted only by the smoking torches, some singing, some praying as they moved along. I thought I was back in the middle ages.

Next day, at the pool where they go to be healed by the waters, it was impossible to laugh at so much misery – placing their faith for a cure in a miracle. Even in the church with all the tacky testimonials, walkers, crutches, prostheses – somehow you couldn't laugh at it."

"What about you, Jacqueline?" I asked.

"I'm not ready to confess my sins and start going to mass," she said, "but it did have an effect on me. I understand it better now than I did before. Anyway, no more mockery, no more jokes."

Chapter Twelve

Pamplona

After that, I didn't see them for about ten days during which I too was out of town, in Spain. How that came about is as follows.

Quite unexpectedly, a bit earlier a friend and club-mate from Princeton showed up. I had done my best to find a secluded refuge from touring Americans, but it was bound to be found out. As it was I was glad that the intruder was this person.

His name was Ike Starr, and he came from a distinguished Main Line Philadelphia family. His father had a national reputation in cardiology. He was, not withstanding, a tyrannical despot whose iron rule over the family caused much misery,. Ike was extremely self-conscious and sensitive, blazingly intelligent and musically gifted. His path to success as a concert pianist was abruptly shattered in his early teens when he lost part of his right index finger in an accident.

At Princeton, Ike dazzled all of us who were laboring to acquire a liberal arts education. Ike seemed to have been born with it already intact. Music, art, literature – he knew it all. There was nothing even Princeton could add there, so he majored in the hard sciences, biology and physics. He would keep us up all night explaining how the number of hairs on the back of a man's fingers were influenced by heredity. Classmates like Ike were one of the great dividends of a Princeton education.

So, although I had promised myself to avoid Americans, I was glad to see him. Also, he quickly became a favorite with my beach club confreres. They were forced to revise many of their preconceptions about America and the state of culture in the US as a result of listening to him. As one would expect, he picked up

French in no time at all. (He already knew German upon arrival, but not French.) His fluency in idiomatic French, so quickly mastered, impressed and at the same time discouraged me. I became convinced that I had no real talent for foreign languages, but would keep trying.

About this time, posters began to show up on billboards around town advertising the upcoming Festival de San Fermin, held annually in Pamplona just over the border, capital of the Basque province of Navarro. Who San Fermin was is now more or less beside the point because the festival in his honor is known almost exclusively for its *"encierro"* – the running of the bulls through the streets of the town, ostensibly in pursuit of a crowd of daredevils. Both are on their way to the *"Plaza de Toros"* – the bull ring – where they, the bulls, will be the main act in the afternoon's entertainment.

Having become infected by the Hemingway virus, which attacked many young men of my generation, resulting in a preoccupation with violence and risky adventures, to me this seemed like a good opportunity to find out what the furor was all about. Ever receptive to new experience, Ike was ready to go along.

First, by bus to San Sabastian, and then by train into the Pyrenees. Evidently the word was out, because as we drew closer to Pamplona, at each local stop more and more people boarded the train, entire families bound for a few days holiday. Guitars and bottles of wine made their appearance. Songs competed with the noise of the train, and soon the whole car was rocking along.

Not to be left out, each of us had brought along one of those leather wine containers, which are held at arms length and squeezed so that a jet of wine spurts out, hopefully, and with quite a bit of practice, into your mouth. We had bought these especially for the trip because that was, so we thought, an essential part of the festival macho culture. The "bottles" were new and uncured – we did not understand that curing the leather is essential to making the wine inside fit to drink. The idea of wine sloshing around inside this raw leather "bottle" for a few hours on a hot day might be picturesque, but actually drinking the stuff required great indifference to its taste. The best use for what came out would

Picking Up the Pieces

have been as weed killer. But never mind, we were having a great time and on our way to an even greater one.

The train pulled into Pamplona in the evening, and by the time we had found our ultra-primitive accommodations it was almost dark. Venturing into the center of town, we were immediately swept up in a celebration already well underway.

Two things need to be said about this celebration here at the outset: uno – that it is a 100% Basque National holiday; and dos – that the participants are entirely men. This was a macho affair, at least during the evening revelry and also again in the morning at the running of the bulls. Whether females were kept out of sight for their safety and well-being, I can't say. All I know is that among the boisterous, laughing, drinking, singing, dancing crowd in the streets not a single female was to be seen.

The men and older boys (no young ones) shepherds, down from the surrounding mountains, farmers, mechanics, shopkeepers, and shoemakers from the neighboring towns - all congregated here for this one magnificent blowout, a few days of escape in the company of other men from the hard monotonous labor of the rest the year. And they went at it with an intensity and an energy that tolerated no compromise – you simply could not be indifferent to the spirit of their merrymaking.

This army of revelers had a uniform: they were practically all dressed in white, many wearing black berets, with a red sash or belt tied around the middle. From a distance, this street-scape of white appeared to be pulsating to the music that seemed to come from everywhere: from open windows, doors, and especially from the numerous bars and taverns – music with an insistent Spanish rhythm that had everyone jumping up and down in time, with both arms raised and fingers snapping to the beat.

The men were dancing with one another, facing about three feet apart, looking directly at their partners, laughing, whooping up and down, fingers snapping, turning, and then on to another partner. This was the *"Jota"*, a traditional Spanish dance and rhythm, which to me has always come to symbolize Spain. Its spirit is captured in *Chabrier's "L'Espagne"*; " whenever I hear it I am back there in Pamplona at "*La Fiejo de San Fermin*– the only time in my life I ever enjoyed dancing.

In all this uproar I lost sight of Ike several times, then he would reappear for a moment like a leaf in a cataract only to be swept away again.

Inside one of the bars I found myself at a table with half a dozen deeply sun-dried stocky Basques, all in a high good humor. When they discovered I was an American, one of them jumped behind his chair, and with his forefinger and thumb squeezed off a couple of "shots" in my direction. I pretended to fall mortally wounded, to their great amusement. That was America as far as they were concerned.

Two of them proceeded to stage a mock bullfight. One went into a menacing crouch with his two index fingers at his lowered forehead to simulate horns. The other swept a table cloth from off the table and held it before the "bull," shaking it to invite a charge, then pirouetting into a perfect *"veronicas"* as the "bull" rushed past.

At another bar, I had just gotten out my wallet to pay for a drink when the Basque beside me snatched it up and put it in his pocket. "No, amigo," he said in English. "In Spain you are our guest. Saludo." What a marvelous people. He spoke English because as a young man he had emigrated to the USA, to Idaho, where he had spent the next twenty years herding sheep. With the money thus saved he was able to retire back to Spain, get married and buy a small farm. This, I learned, was common practice among the Basques.

And so it went, night after night, one blurred into another for as long as we were there, one long bacchanal, one indelible memory.

Somewhere along the line we fell in with a trio of young British aristocrats who had driven all the way from England in an open pre-war Rolls Royce touring car. The boys' pedigree matched that of the car. Our purest, oldest ancestral strain alongside your true British blueblood comes off tentative and nouveau in comparison with the Englishman's effortless sense of superiority. These exuded an air of detached amusement as though the entire festival was being staged for their benefit. We were seated at an ordinary café having drinks in between events.

"I say, Nigel, don't you find this aperitif nauseatingly sweet?" said one.

Picking Up the Pieces

"Here," I said, holding out a slice of lemon, "try a squeeze of this to help cut it."

"Cut it? Cut it? Cut what?" He wanted to know.

"Cut the sweetness – the sugar," I explained.

"Oh, I see. You American chaps do have the most original way of expressing yourselves. Cut it …. Cut it. We'll have to remember that one. Right, Nigel?"

It was like the Queen addressing a group of Hutu villagers. It grated on my sensibilities, but Ike found them great companions, just the type we could use more of back in the U.S.

Let me add another complaint while I'm at it. A whole generation of Americans got to know Pamplona and *El Fiejo de San Fermin* from reading "The Sun Also Rises." In my opinion, Hemingway and his coterie of expats were a group of voyeurs, a bit like our English trio, who never managed to get anywhere near, or into, the spirit of the festival. From the novelist's stand-point, a good thing, perhaps, because if he had, the raw vigor and excitement would have run away with his story.

The Festival lasts for a week, and the after dark revels go on night after night until the small hours. The house fronts have no numbers, and all look the same, so finding one's lodging in an impaired condition can be difficult. Even more serious is the fact that the *"encierro"*- the running of the bulls – always takes place promptly at eight the following morning.

Since this is not to be missed, there arises a problem – practically all the potential "runners" are incapacitated, half-asleep, nursing mighty hangovers; many never got to bed at all. Nevertheless valor triumphs over pain, and when the eight-o'clock cannon goes off to signal the start, they are all there, ready to run.

The bulls have been kept in an enclosure by the railroad track. A route has been laid out through the town – about one and a quarter miles, and reinforced with wooden barricades and fencing at street corners – leading from the railroad down to the *Plaza de Toros*. The bulls will run along this route, covering the distance in about ten or fifteen minutes, which is pretty fast considering the dense crowd of men and boys clogging the narrow streets.

At the cannon's boom, the gate opens and four or five bulls are released, led by about the same number of steers, who seem to exert a calming influence on the more excitable bulls, and out they go into the street. The steers, who probably do this job year after year, know the path and the bulls follow along. The steers are bigger than the bulls, with even longer horns but are not considered dangerous. Unlike the bulls, which are almost always black, the steers are of variegated marking, so the runners know which ones to be afraid of.

Actually, fear doesn't seem to enter into it. The whole exercise is a massive display of macho courage, of dare-deviltry, of showing off one's indifference to those terrifying beasts with their needle-tipped horns by running before them and keeping the interval as small as possible. To tell the truth, just running before the bulls does not in itself prove much; the real test is to have the bull actually breathing down your back.

This can happen very easily since the crowd in the streets can move only spasmodically by fits and starts. Where the path is clear and the bulls are catching up, men will throw themselves to the side of the street and lie still while the bulls run by. It's important not to get up too soon because it's always possible that a straggler has been distracted, delayed and by this time, enraged. Not a good position for the runner.

If possible, the bulls keep moving, but in one case I saw the runner decided that the bull was too close. He dodged to one side and flattened himself against a doorway thinking that the bull would keep on going. But it didn't. It stopped and across a space of about six feet regarded the runner with a baleful stare that seemed to say, "Make your peace with God, fool, your time has come."

From my perch on a second story balcony across the narrow street, I was about to avert my eyes from what was going to happen when a miracle occurred! Another runner looking back over his shoulder, saw that the bull had stopped. Taking a tightly-rolled newspaper he darted back and smacked the bull on the nose which caused the bull to forget the man in the doorway and go after the one who had insulted him.

Inevitably among the scurrying crowd, someone would trip, causing others to fall on them, until quite a mass had built up into which the steers and bulls charged headfirst. The pileup at the narrow entrance to the Plaza was just bodies on top of bodies. No matter. Brute force carried the bulls through, into the dark passageway, and then out onto the dazzling sand of the arena.

This early in the morning the stands were only partly occupied by sensation-seekers, there to observe more displays of bravery – or insanity. Sometimes it was hard to tell which. For this entertainment the authorities had allotted about fifteen or twenty minutes during which the bulls were allowed to roam freely about in the amphitheater, while various madmen tried to provoke them to charge, leaping aside at the last moment.

It didn't always succeed. One, I saw, was knocked to the ground. Dazed by the impact, he looked around and started to get back on his feet, unaware that the bull was right behind him. He had just managed to stand when the bull's charge sent him flying. This time he didn't move. While some distracted the bull, others hauled the unconscious body away.

There were any number of such incidents. It was hard to tell if anyone was actually killed or merely injured. To me, they all looked fatal.

Pretty strong stuff for eight-thirty in the morning, with a hangover to top it off. Nothing else happened until four in the afternoon when the main attraction – the bullfight – was scheduled to begin. In between, we mostly went back for bed rest to restore our depleted powers of recuperation – three successive nights of riot and mayhem were beginning to take their toll. Had we been in the mood, there were all kinds of cultural events going on during the day, designed, I suppose, to show the less violent side of Basque civilization: art exhibits, lectures, chamber music, etc. To me, these genteel events had no place there at that time; they sounded a false note; the essence of the festival, and of the Basque personality, was down in the streets and in the corrida.

By four in the afternoon, somewhat restored and primed for action, with our leather wineskins at the ready, Ike and I were among the crowd in a densely packed stadium. Up to now, I have described the night-time festivities and the *encierro* in some detail, since they are not very well known. Bullfighting, on the other hand, has been observed, described and analyzed in such detail that there is little to be added by this highly personal account, so I will simply mention some aspects that surprised and impressed me.

First, the stately pageantry of the event, the solemn brass call of the music, as though summoning the faithful to prayer. Then the glittering entry and parade of the participants around the ring. Finally, the choreographed spectacle itself: A medieval parable in which it is impossible to ignore the religious overtones - a black bull, the incarnation of evil, all powerful against his puny adversary the gorgeously costumed *torero*, wielding the sword of deliverance who will save us from the monster, - all this told in a spectacle of artistry and violence, a ballet with real blood, suffering, and death.

I was astonished by the bulls themselves, some considerably larger or more aggressive – more malevolent – than others, so much so that I, along with the whole stadium, held my breath as the *torero* leaned into that span of horns in what was almost an embrace, and gracefully turned as the beast rushed past.

Before having ever seen a bullfight, as a confirmed animal rights sympathizer my sympathies were all with the bull – the poor animal was being set up for slaughter. All too true. But when actually watching the frail figure of the *torero*, in close combat with the speed, power, and quickness of the bull, instinctively I cheered for the human being, and wished only that he would dispatch the monster before it dispatched him.

I say "him" because most of the *torreros* were male, some scarcely more than boys – Spain's aristocracy of sport; gods, pursued by adoring fans as they and their crews toured from plaza to plaza in city after city across the country during the summer season. But one was a woman, and not a *torero* at all but a "*rejoneador*", meaning that she fought the bull from horseback, descending only at the very end to consummate the kill. This lady was an Argentinian named Conchita Citron. Her skill and willingness to take risks had enabled her to break into this tight circle of champions, and to win acceptance in an entire country of aficionados, although I must admit that a very large share of the credit should have gone to the horse, who normally, must have their eyes covered when in the ring with the bull.

Four or five *encierros* in succession, and four or five bulls every afternoon – and up all night every night – that was it for me, and for Ike too. We slept for most of the train ride back to San Sebastian, and for the next four or five days in Biarritz.

Chapter Thirteen

The Smuggler

Once again, back at the Port Vieux, there had been an addition to our little beach club. This was an attractive young Dutch couple, blond and not yet tanned by the sun. His name was Wim and hers was Kitty. Both spoke excellent English as well as French, and also German. They laughed a lot and made an interesting addition to the group, especially Wim who took nothing seriously. The main purpose in life, he said, was to have a good time, live for the moment and avoid kill-joys and sourpusses who could never be happy anyway. They seemed to belong to a higher echelon of European society which was confirmed for me when I saw them drive off in a very expensive pre-war Delahaye sports car. Just the sort of privileged children you expected to meet on the beach at Biarritz.

But all was not exactly as it appeared. They had stopped off in Biarritz on their way to Portugal and from there to South Africa, but were having such a good time, they decided to postpone leaving for a few days. Within a day or two I learned a bit more about them, mostly from Kitty who liked to talk. Her father was the ambassador from The Netherlands in Paris. She and Wim were eloping. They had run away and hoped to be on the boat to Capetown before their absence was noticed.

"And the car?"

"Oh, that belongs to my aunt. She has several others and will never miss it. When we get to Portugal, we'll sell it for escudos - that's the hardest currency in Europe now - and pay her back."

Also it developed that Wim had been a wartime hero of the resistance in Holland, decorated by the government and idolized

The Smuggler

by the press. I asked him about this.

"Yeah, it was a lot of fun, you know. Fooling them, keeping one step ahead. There are times when I almost miss it," he said.

"But, it must have been a dangerous business. What would have happened if you had been caught?"

"Oh, I did get caught - finally."

"What did they do to you?"

"Well, I had been pretty badly shot up." Here he pulled up his shirt, and showed me a whole line of scars across his mid-section. "So I was put in the hospital to recover so they could hang me as soon as I got well. But I fooled them and escaped. Ha, ha. That was a good one. I heard later that they shot the guard."

"Golly, you were lucky to make such a recovery - I'd say a hundred percent. Are you able to work?" I asked.

"No, I don't really work, not what you would call work anyway." he said.

"Well, I suppose you get a good pension from your government. I mean, they certainly owe it to you."

"Oh, that. Well, it might be enough to cover my bar bills," he replied.

Not having been in Europe long enough to know that it was considered bad form to ask anyone what they did for a living, since many were involved in shady enterprises of one type or another, I asked, "How do you manage to get along without a job?"

"It's simple," he said. "I smuggle - jewels."

My jaw dropped. "Jewels?"

"Yeah, diamonds mostly. I have a source in South Africa. I make the trip twice, sometimes three times a year between Capetown and Antwerp. Good money, easy money." His blue eyes twinkled as he laughed.

"You're certainly addicted to danger. What a life," I said. "Suppose they catch you?"

"Oh, they did - last year."

"But how come you're not in jail?" I asked.

"My wartime resistance record got me off. They determined that I'd been psychologically traumatized, unable to adjust to normal civilian life." He laughed again. "It's a good joke, I think."

Picking Up the Pieces

"Maybe - just so the joke isn't on you. Something like that gets a page in your passport. Every time you cross a border, if they see that page they'll take you apart - your car too."

"That's just it, they won't see it."

"What do you mean?"

"I mean they won't see it because I took a razor and cut it out. Look." He handed me a passport. "Find page thirty-three."

He was right - no page thirty three. Very neatly done. The typical *Douanier* or *Zoll Beamter* would never notice it.

Wim was the real-life embodiment of Hollywood's classic debonair, romantic jewel thief, played by Cary Grant, usually opposite someone like Grace Kelly or Audrey Hepburn, with the French Riviera for scenic background. Biarritz was more than adequate for substitute scenery, and Kitty did quite well in the female lead. The Delahaye added another perfect touch.

So it went, everyone enjoying themselves, when suddenly one day the town was alive with excitement. Big black Citroen police cars were everywhere, with plains clothes officers from Paris. It didn't take them long to find the object of their search, and within minutes the elopement dream of Wim and Kitty came to an end. Wim was charged with kidnapping Kitty - what a laugh - and stealing the aunt's car. Placed in handcuffs, he was driven back to Paris in one of the big Citroens, to stand trial.

Kitty, as the daughter of an ambassador, was given diplomatic immunity, absolved of all complicity in the affair, and whisked back to Holland as an innocent victim, rescued in the nick of time from the clutches of an international criminal.

Back in Paris, the perception of Wim as a criminal quickly fell apart. It was summer, there wasn't much to write about, and once the Parisian tabloids got hold of the story they proceeded to sensationalize it. Wim's wartime resistance heroics were covered at length so that before long the impression grew that he really deserved a medal from the government rather than incarceration for a beautifully romantic escapade. Every day a million housewives wept that such injustices could still go on - "but what can you expect from our politicians?"

On the stand Wim captured the sympathy and affection of the entire courtroom with his jokes, wisecracks, and completely relaxed air, so that the judge repeatedly had to silence the crowd for laughter, applause and other inappropriate behavior.

When the prosecutor asked him why he had stolen the car he said, "I didn't steal it, I just borrowed it for a few days. Besides, you don't elope with a beautiful young girl without a car."

The trial ended in farce and a black eye for the Dutch Embassy, which wished that it had kept the whole matter private and never preferred charges. Wim got a slap on the wrist and was soon a free man. I would love to see him again.

Chapter Fourteen

Virtue Preserved

Under a coppery sun, day by day, summer was melting away. August is the month when most Frenchmen take their vacations. Paris emptied out. The Villa St. Hubert filled up, and blanket space on our little beach dwindled to a few square meters. So we shifted club headquarters to the Cote des Basques, a fifty mile reach of sand stretching from horizon to horizon.

Though still awkward, my French was good enough for undemanding conversational purposes; Jacqueline and I no longer needed a pause to puzzle out every third word.

But it wasn't every day on the beach, especially if it was raining. I packed my fly-fishing gear and the bicycle onto a little train which ran up into the Pyrenees as far as St. Jean Pied de Port and Aux Aldudes. With a sandwich from Mme. Freda, I spent the day wading the stream that cascaded over rocky ledges on its way to the sea, letting the fly drift down into the clear pools. The wild trout weren't easy to come by, but in such a setting it took only one or two to make a perfect day, even better when a couple of times I succeeded in landing a grayling – a cold water fish which had practically disappeared from all but the most remote streams. What a thrill it was to look at that magnificent creature as it lay gasping in my hands, just before I eased it back into the water.

Later in the afternoon, winding back the line and disjointing the rod, I replaced everything on the bike and then proceeded to whistle back down the twenty miles or so to Biarritz without touching the pedals, praying that the brakes would hold.

The combination of sun and sky, with the waves rolling in, and mountain recesses of rushing water and old stone bridges, was a prescription to cure the most tormented soul. And it was certainly curing mine. I can't say that it was a permanent cure, because later during extended stressful periods I suffered from recurrent anxiety attacks. But not once since arriving in Biarritz did I have a single day of that oppressive, obsessive depression that had me in its clutches back in England.

Later that summer, Jacqueline and Gilbert were invited by friends from Paris to join them for a few days at a nudist colony further up the coast. "If we go, will you come along?" They asked me.

"No, I don't think so," I said.

"Why not? You would like our friends," they countered.

"I'm sure I would, but I must keep up my lessons," I answered.

"That didn't keep you from going to Pamplona," said Jacqueline with a laugh. "I think you just don't want to take off your clothes and be seen tout nu. That's it, isn't it? Be honest."

"Well, I suppose so. I'm no believer in nudism. Most of them are ugly and the ones that aren't are just showing off."

"Okay, but it still sounds to me like you are suffering from a cultural problem. You're still in the grip of your American religious traditions. You like our emancipated European attitudes toward tolerance and sex, but only up to a point." This from Gilbert.

"Oh, let him be, cheri," said Jacqueline, then to me, "You can stay here with Hugette and Canie. We'll take our camera and bring back some dirty pictures for you."

It was a role they very much enjoyed playing: the worldly-wise, semi-decadent European sophisticate opposite the confused, naïve American, caught midway between inherited tradition and desire for enlightenment, unable to articulate either the one or the other.

When they returned, it was without pictures; for reasons of privacy, cameras were forbidden. I asked them how it had gone.

"Not bad, I suppose," said Jacqueline. "But naked bodies on the beach are one thing. Sitting around the dinner table, chasing les petits pois on your plate, is quite another – not so attractive. Inside the house people look better with their clothes on."

For a small business owner, Gilbert was able to spend a great deal of time in Biarritz, but occasionally he would be called back to Paris for something that required personal attention. These absences were usually for about a week or ten days. When they occurred, Jacqueline, Hugette, Canie and I, plus whoever else was around, met on the beach. In the evening, Jacqueline sent Hugette back to feed Canie and put him to bed while she and I went to a movie and sometimes had dinner.

At one of these dinners while scanning the menu, she asked if I had ever tried snails - escargots.

"You mean those things I see on the leaves in the garden? I didn't know people ate them."

"Yes, of course," she said. "Broiled in butter and garlic, with a good crusty bread and a glass of wine – that is very French. I'm going to order some for you to try."

When they arrived in their shells, hot and sizzling on an iron plate, in garlicky butter green with minced parsley, the sight and aroma was all it required to make me an instant convert.

"Don't try to pick them up. They're very hot. Use these tongs," she said. "Do they eat these back in America?"

"Never. They would think it degenerate – like a taste for frog's legs. Ever since we heard that they eat them here, some Americans, like the English, call the French "frogs" – kind of a humorous insult."

"Oh, well," she laughed. "What can be done with people like that?"

As part of its summer cultural program, Biarritz staged a film festival – in this case one with an interesting concept: films that had failed commercially – *"Films Maudits"* – but which claimed to have artistic merit. We went to see several categories.

For the most part, I thought they deserved to fail. They were shot in black and white, usually on rainy days - gritty with a strident realism. They dwelt on downbeat, pessimistic themes, designed to show "real life" with shocking scenes of child and animal abuse, spousal cruelty, etc. The combined effect was lack of real depth, two dimensional productions at best. One in particular bothered me: an incestuous relationship between a brutal, cloddish father and a retarded daughter as seen though the eyes of her younger brother. I forget the title.

"How did you like it?" Jacqueline asked.

"Disgusting. It made me sick." I replied.

"Don't you think such things exist, and that writers and filmmakers should show them?"

"Maybe, but those scenes were too strong. They were deliberately designed just for emotional impact."

"What's wrong with that? Maybe in America your emotional defenses are too weak," she replied.

Subsequent films proceeded to further test my tolerance for avant-garde creativity. One whole part of the festival was devoted to "surrealism," featuring films by Bunuel, Dali and others. One of them, *"Le Chien d'Andalous"* (The Andalousian Dog), opened with a scene so shocking that the entire audience gasped in horror. What you saw was the close-up of a human face, filling the screen. Suddenly a hand holding a straight razor appeared and proceeded to slit the eye, so that its liquid interior poured out. It happened so quickly there was no time to avert your eyes. End of scene, and on with the film, which had no apparent connection with that single horrifying episode.

"Were you shocked?" Jacqueline asked.

"More than shocked," I said. "There's a limit to what people can stand. A scene like that will stick in their memory forever – a nightmare."

"Would you have it banned?"

"Yes, I think I would."

"And who decides what should be banned? The church? The film studios? You have a censorship board in America. I understand it is not possible to show even a husband and wife together in bed. I don't think it works very well for you," she said.

She had a point there.

"Also," she went on, "you Americans are always talking about freedom – 'the land of the free'- but in many ways I think we are more free here. At least I would not trade places with you."

Another point for me to think about.

Over the summer I had come to develop an enormous respect and liking for Jacqueline and Gilbert. No subject was out of bounds for discussion, but it wasn't all on an intellectual plane. This openness to and interest in ideas extended to life in general.

Picking Up the Pieces

Good food ranked high in their scale of human pleasures, which of course, could not be separated from good wine of which Gilbert was an expert. It all added up to an aesthetic ideal in which their bodies furnished a visual balance. Every day, no matter where, Gilbert put himself through a routine of conditioning exercises, the result was a sculptured physique. Jacqueline fussed and worried needlessly about her figure which she liked to parade up and down the beach. Both doted on the little boy, Canie. He was nice to have around, affectionate and well-behaved, unlike Christian and Toto back at the Villa St.Hubert.

These were now the last days of August. Next week they would be leaving Biarritz and returning to Paris. Gilbert was already in Paris but would return to help with the move.

At dinner Jacqueline and I killed a bottle of wine then walked up near the lighthouse and sat on a bench overlooking the harbor and down the coast. Further out to the west an occulting light blinked; that would be the northern coast of Spain.

That evening the sea was calm. Neither of us spoke. I took her hand trying to think of a good way to say good-bye, but the words would not come. Unspoken feelings had been building up on both sides for who knows how long, concealed by intellectual diversions and word-play.

"Come, cherie," she said. This is not a good place. Come back with me chez moi ." She got up and took my hand to pull me to my feet. "Come on, Jack. This is a beautiful moment. Quickly, before it passes and we go back to being only half alive."

Still, I sat there. Things were getting back into focus.

"Jacqueline, cherie," I said. "I can't do it. We can't do it."

"You don't want to make love?"

"Of course I want to. You must know that."

"But what does it mean - you can't? Is there something wrong? Are you not well?"

"Oh no. I'm OK. It would be easier if I wasn't."

"Now I really don't understand. You talk in riddles. What's the matter, cherie?"

"It's Gilbert, you, the family. Gilbert - your husband - he's my friend. A good friend. I can't do anything that would make trouble for either him or you."

"Oh, I see now. Oh Jack, you are too amusing, so American.

Down there, in your soul you are still an American puritan. But there is nothing to worry about. There would be no problem, as you fear. That was one thing Gilbert and I agreed to when we married - that we loved, and respected, but did not own, each other. He has his little sweeties from time to time. It's OK with me as long as he doesn't parade them under my nose."

"I guess I understand, but I just don't think I can be so detached. My conscience won't let me. How could I face him next week? You and he have an agreement, but it doesn't include me."

"That is so sweet."

"Please don't be angry with me."

"I'm not. You have found the one reason for turning me down that I can accept without feeling rejected and insulted."

Our goodnight kiss at the door was now just warm, as between two friends of opposite sexes.

When Gilbert returned he said, "Jacqueline tells me she threw herself at you, and you declined the offer."

This direct approach to such a delicate subject had me confused and groping for an answer. "Oh," I replied, "she just had a little too much wine that evening."

"No," he said, "she tells me you turned her down because of me, that going to bed with her, you thought, would spoil our friendship - that I would fly into a jealous rage and challenge you to a duel." Then he laughed heartily.

Still feeling awkward, I said "Well, it's true, I did not want to be the cause of a problem. I like you both too much."

"Dear Jack, my friend. Too bad - you have lost your opportunity. She now feels a bit ashamed of herself and has made me her father confessor, and I have forgiven her - 'Go forth and sin so more,' I said to her."This with another hearty laugh, "Even though, as far as I am concerned, there is nothing to forgive. Mon Dieu, the one thing I cannot stand is hypocrisy."

A week later and they were gone. I was on hand to see them off and helped load suitcases and boxes into one of his company's delivery vans. What marvelous friends! What great memories! Jacqueline held her hand out the window waving a scarf as the van disappeared down the street.

Chapter Fifteen

The Refugee Problem

When it came time to leave Biarritz in October, I was more than ready. The reasons for coming here in the first place were, by and large, satisfied. I could manage French conversation enough to get along and enjoy it without making myself a burden, and without insulting the language of which they were so proud. German was another matter, but with mastery of the grammar in place, I felt that a few months of daily conversation would do for fluency what it had accomplished here for French.

So far as my malaise of depression was concerned, the gloom that had driven me out of England had disappeared, I hoped for good. All in all, that summer of self-indulgence in Lotus Land, in terms of total personal well-being, had to be counted a success.

Also, contributing to this itch to get moving, along with psychological recovery, was my whole sense of purpose for being in Europe. Originally, that had been academic: to get a thesis written, and to be present at the emergence of the socialist welfare state in Britain. That didn't work out, but although there was nothing tangible to show for it, I didn't feel the years in England had been a waste of time, quite the opposite. Still, there remained a sense, if not of failure, at least of non-fulfillment. My conscience was demanding some kind of repayment, of restitution, not just for a failure to deliver but for adding to the debt an entire summer spent mostly in frivolity and the pursuit of pleasure.

From the beginning the plan had been to spend a period of recovery and foreign language immersion in the south of France and then move on to Germany. Now the time had come to put part two of the plan into action. But what, specifically, would that step consist of ? Sitting there on the sands of Biarritz, the idea of launching into the unknown that was postwar Germany without contacts and a place to land - this was a little daunting. Further study might have been an option, but I felt like I wanted to go to work - to accomplish something constructive after so much lying around.

Back in London, at 68 Shepherds Hill, long before the Biarritz escapade, I had made the acquaintance of Joe Noia. Joe was the YMCA official heading up YMCA operations in Germany/Austria, specifically concerned with relief services to displaced persons. At the time he said that if I was interested, they had openings for young people to participate in the program on a "volunteer" basis, meaning junior responsibilities with the YMCA providing food and shelter, but not much else.

At the time, I was not ready to give up on my studies, or on England. Now, many months later, circumstances had changed. Although the offer did not sound glamorous, it did provide an on-site base of operations from which I could observe the enormous scope of US government programs just beginning to realize their full potential, and from there make whatever move seemed appropriate.

I wrote to Joe, indicating my interest in joining his team. His response was immediate: they were prepared to pick me up in Munich on or about December 1st, and take me to a YMCA training center for orientation to the program and possible further reassignment. That gave me time to return to London for a family reunion before once again heading east, this time to Germany.

The sense of anticipation was intense. Even with much of the country in ruins, the late war still reverberated across the world, testimony to the power that Germany had so recently been. That the Nazi regime was evil to its core only intensified that monumentality and its power to fascinate.

Years of classes in European history, then language study and reading had built up a foundation for this new adventure. I had studied German political philosophy, history and government; I had read the German classics: Heine, Goethe and Schiller as well as the works of Thomas Mann, including his two major novels - *"The Magic Mountain,"* and *"Buddenbrooks,"* Finally, there was

Picking Up the Pieces

the experience in London of living among Germans with almost daily conversations and discussions. But for me, music did more than anything to fill out the complete expression of the German mystique - the *uhrquelle* - the wellspring of German national character; from the tiniest Schubert lied, to Wagner's *Gotterdamerung,* the twilight of the Gods, and everything in between. These all had their place as pieces in the psychological puzzle that made up twentieth century Germany. In that moment, I felt almost as though I was entering another world.

This "other world" turned out to have little resemblance to the romantic vision of my academic imagination. To understand this new reality now requires a few pages of historical detail. For that I apologize. On the other hand, the setting for the next few chapters is more readily appreciated if one understands how it came about.

On the ground, what awaited beyond the Rhine were the remains of an upheaval not seen since the end of the Thirty Years War in 1648. First, the unparalleled destruction, and then, streaming through that wreckage, a flood of uprooted peoples left stranded by the cessation of hostilities and the collapse of governmental functions: law, order and basic services. Grating against one another in the flood were every ethnic and racial type from eastern Europe: millions of Jews, Bosnians, Bulgars, Serbs, Balts, Poles, Ukrianians, even Uzbecs from the plains of central Asia. Those who could, walked out of the concentration camps where they had been awaiting death by gassing or by harsh treatment. Still others made up a whole population of "slave laborers" imported by the Nazis to man the German war industry, who now remained in Germany as stateless refugees.

Not surprisingly these victims of wartime violence brought with them a whole set of problems and tensions dating back centuries in addition to the results of their more recent experiences. Many were in bad health, severely undernourished, others were psychologically damaged by years of inhumane treatment, and now by anxiety for the future. Deeper down were the hatreds engendered by religious divisions - Roman Catholic, Greek Catholic, Islam, as well as ethnic rivalries - Serb/Croat, Polish/Ukrainian, Bosnian/Serb, Balt/Russian, etc, etc. And of course, Jews and Gypsies whom no one wanted.

The Refugee Problem

Added to the problem of physical survival was the personal desire of families to be reunited: parents, children, relatives; after years of separation and no communication. where were they? Were they still alive? How to reunite them?

A humanitarian crisis existed, in the spring and summer of 1945. The only agency available to deal with it was the armed forces who did the best they could, even to the extent of sharing their food supplies with the refugees. But this was clearly no solution. With no training or taste for refugee administration, they were unable to handle incidents that became increasingly common.

Within six months of the German surrender, the United Nations Refugee and Relief Agency (UNRRA), working with the armed forces, moved in to create a semblance of order out of environmental chaos. UNRRA's first step was to make some sense out of the heterogeneous mass of humanity. Accordingly, broad categories were established: political prisoners, forced slave laborers, stateless persons, ex-prisoners of war, and of course victims of racial persecution - almost entirely Jews. Added to these were thousands of ethnic Germans living in Eastern Europe, now forced to flee to the west.

Next came the knotty problem of what to do with these "DPs" - displaced persons. As agreed by the occupying powers, the priority was to return as many as possible to their country of origin. A large number were repatriated under this program, but it quickly developed that not all wanted to return. For those, there was no easy solution. An exception was the Jews. Without waiting for formal international approval, an underground system of transportation and relocation had been organized to move Jewish groups from location to location across Europe to embarkation ports in Italy and Greece, and thence by ship to Palestine. This extra-legal system proved to be so efficient that within a few years the number of Jews awaiting resettlement was now a minority, in contrast to others still stuck in the refugee camps and for whom the outlook was not encouraging.

During this early post-war period, it was the UNRRA that provided food, clothing and shelter to those millions of DP's. Shelter was improvised at first, wherever suitable space could be found,: in large houses, hotels, castles - even barns and warehouses.

In one of the greatest population transfers in human history, the UNRRA succeeded in sending most of them back home. By the end of 1945, six million refugees had been repatriated voluntarily. By the summer of 1946, although individuals and families continued to flee from Eastern Europe, the bulk of the problem had been solved. Both the British and American sectors declared a deadline after which no further persons would be accepted under the terms of the DP program.

Meanwhile there remained the problem of those refugees, numbering in the hundreds of thousands, who would not, or could not, return home for fear of persecution. It was therefore essential that a more permanent solution be developed and put into place. But with the transition from hot to cold war, this became increasingly difficult as differences and then open hostility arose between Allied forces and the Soviet Union. Cooperation existed only fitfully, with the DP's a convenient pawn in the struggle. Nevertheless, the great powers succeeded in compromising their differences sufficiently to form a new organization to take over responsibility for the remaining refugees. This was the International Relief Organization, or IRO.

The IRO took over a declining DP population. The easiest cases had been repatriated to their country of origin or had emigrated to Israel, but the hundred of thousands that remained still constituted a formidable challenge. Remaining in war-devastated Europe was not a viable option for these refugees. But for emigration approval, each refugee had to be investigated and certified. Many had no reliable identification or official record. Others were unacceptable because of a past criminal or political history. Health or mental problems could result in denial and permanent classification as "hard core."

Along with the task of certification went that of finding an eventual home in a country willing to take in such a rag-tag group of social outcasts. This enormous undertaking was brought to a successful conclusion by the UN and the allied powers, assisted by non-governmental organizations, or "NGO's,"many of them church sponsored. Among the most active at that time were the

The Refugee Problem

NCWC (National Catholic Welfare Conference), CWS (Church World Services), LWF (Lutheran World Federation), YMCA (Young Men's Christian Association), HIAS (Hebrew Immigrant Aid Society), AJDC (American Joint Distribution Committee), plus others.

Each participating country receiving DP immigration had its own administrative agency to manage selection, processing and transportation. For the US this was the US DP Commission operating under the general supervision and coordination of the IRO, and staffed mostly by political appointees with no prior qualifications or experience.

For the IRO, the task was to house several hundred thousand people until their background investigations were completed, permission to emigrate obtained, and acceptance by the receiving country assured. Mainly this meant furnishing food, clothing, shelter and security until the long process was accomplished. For some unfortunates the long wait did not always mean a happy ending. A history of Nazi party participation or communist activity, chronic disease, mental instability - any of these was enough for rejection. Such "hard core" cases were assigned to special camps for continued retention. The lucky ones approved for emigration were held in a series of "camps" in Germany and Austria.

By 1949, housing of DP's had come a long way since the early days of the UNRRA when anything with four walls and a roof would do. Reduction in numbers of refugees automatically meant a better selection of holding areas through which DP's could move as processing progressed, from initial enrollment to embarkation. At the lowest level of induction, camps were smaller and more numerous, in the western zones of Germany and Austria housing individuals and entire families awaiting clearance. The camps near the North Sea port of Bremerhaven took care of those DP's about to board ship and sail for a new life in a new world.

By 1949, there were about a dozen camps in Germany and Austria where most DP's were concentrated. These were large enough to warrant an IRO administration staff, medical facilities, and the presence of several voluntary agencies carrying out a variety of programs. It was in these camps that DP's were likely to spend the longest stretch of their refugee years, while their all-important paperwork wound its way through the investigation and certification bureaucracy.

The IRO was fortunate in the large number and quality of facilities built only a few years earlier by Germany for its own armed services. Allied occupation forces quickly commandeered the best of these but quite a few remained for the IRO to make use of. They varied widely in appearance. Most were outside town or city limits, some in isolated countryside. While none were luxurious, neither were they below civilized norms. Families were housed together, with reasonable living space for individuals. Movement after dark was restricted; otherwise, people could move about freely.

The psychological damage among DP's resulting from the cumulative effects of war and their prolonged virtual incarceration in the DP camps is not hard to imagine: loss of initiative, loss of the work ethic, creation of a permanent dependency mindset and mental dry rot. That so many preserved the will to become productive citizens upon reaching their eventual destination is cause for wonder.

Chapter Sixteen

Orientation to Refugee Life

At the Munich railroad station I was met by an attractive Swedish lady who introduced herself as Signe Dreijer. The training center to which we were going was her responsibility. I scarcely had time to look around at the much destroyed area of the railroad yards and the twin towers of the Frauenkirche, still standing in the distance when we were loaded into a station wagon and were soon out of the city on the autobahn, headed in a southeast direction to the town of Prien.

Before the war Prien had been a weekend getaway resort for Muncheners for a day's sailing the waters of the Chiemsee - Germany's largest lake - on which the town was situated. They could visit the lake's two islands: the Herreninsel (where the "mad" Bavarian King Ludwig had built the last of his fantasy castles - this one a palace - a scaled down miniature of Versailles. but richer and more elaborate in its details than the original.) Or they could go out to the Fraueninsel. There a monastery of ancient stone buildings takes up most of the island right to the water's edge. The monks - I forget which order - earned a few groschen through the sale of a liqueur they made themselves. For those vacationers remaining onshore, there were small hotels and beer gardens, with a view of the far shore and beyond to where the Wendelstein in the Bavarian Alps reared itself up as a bulwark against the encroaching Austrian Alps to the south.

The Wendelstein, the lake and its islands were still there; otherwise, by 1949 all had changed. Under terms of occupation concluded at the end of the war, Germany was divided into four zones. The British were given responsibilities for the northwest

Orientation to Refugee Life

part of the country and the Ruhr industrial area. The French took over the southwest. The US zone was in the south and west, from Munich to Frankfurt. The Russians got East Germany, more or less up to the point the Red Army had advanced when Germany surrendered. Berlin became a special area under joint occupation - divided into four-power administration. As the saying went - "The Russians got the land; the British got the industry; and the Americans got the scenery."

During the ninety-minute ride from Munich to Prien, Signe provided many of these historical details. She also gave me a rundown on the YMCA program which had some similarities to the War Prisoners Aid program in Britain - sports, free-time activities, and English language instruction. But in fundamental ways it differed from the British model. Here there was no host government or military structure, just the IRO in charge. Then the DP population, although housed in camps, was not a static group, but more like a river of refugees flowing constantly through the camps on their way to final emigration and resettlement. Also, the YMCA was now just one of several voluntary agencies working inside the camps, sharing resources with the others, for the most part peacefully, but not always.

She explained that the "Y" had not yet decided on a permanent assignment for me but would do so in a week or two. Meanwhile, I could help out as needed with her staff, get to know them and become familiar with refugee life in a DP camp.

With this introduction under my belt, we left the autobahn and entered the town of Prien, arriving quickly at a large dilapidated lakeside structure at the edge of town. You could visualize the charm and *gemutlichkeit* of its former existence as a small bourgeois hotel. Now, under gray skies and bare dripping trees it wore a weary, forlorn aspect, neglected and semi-abandoned, like the refugees housed in it. Inside, it was much the same: large, dilapidated rooms, sparsely furnished with cast-off pieces of furniture, creaky floors and moldy walls. My lodgings were on the third floor in a kind of dormitory with a row of iron cots along one side. Compared to this place, the house at 68 Shepherds Hill in London had been luxury itself, even though they both served roughly similar functions - housing visitors come to inspect the

Picking Up the Pieces

YMCA program, and providing temporary quarters for permanent staff as well as transients like myself awaiting further assignment.

The permanent staff consisted of Signe her assistant, a Russian named Vladimir Bilistocki whose wife supervised the kitchen, and two German ex-Luftwaffe types, Meyer and Eschbaum. There was other household help whose names I forget, with whom I had little contact.

It didn't take long to take stock of my surroundings. One of the few tasks assigned to me was to collect the mail at the village post office. There I would often see an elderly gentleman arrive on the same errand. One day, a YMCA staff member who had walked along with me asked if I knew who that person was. Of course, I had no idea. "That's Herr Braun," said my informant. The name didn't register.

"Herr Friedrich Fritz Braun," he explained. "Maybe you would recognize the name Eva Braun. That is her father. He was, they tell me. much respected."

Eva Braun, of course! Hitler's long time mistress, whom he eventually married just before their suicides in the Berlin bunker at the climactic ending of World War II. And to think that this ordinary-looking individual was her father. In moments like this, I felt touched by history - that history was real - real people - some of them still alive, like Herr Braun walking the streets of Prien on his way to get the morning mail. These encounters were to happen again and again during those years in postwar Germany and Austria. They never failed to give me a sense of privilege, when the curtain of recorded history was drawn aside momentarily for me to see, and in some cases speak, with people - some important, some not so - who had been at the center of momentous events.

A trickle of DP's came through the Prien center while I was there. Signe encouraged me to speak with and get to know them - a kind of informal initial orientation program for each of us. Up to this point they had not met many Americans and were eager for first hand information, not colored by official handouts or government propaganda. That was all they had ever known and consequently had come to disbelieve, or at least be intensely suspicious of anything with an official stamp on it. In me, as an individual with no particular status or standing, they might have

Orientation to Refugee Life

felt that here was someone whose information they could trust. Language posed a considerable barrier, but between us we had enough German for a useful dialogue. Most of the DP's in the group had not yet been authorized for a final destination, consequently did not yet know where they were headed: Canada, Australia, or the US seemed the most likely destinations.

So, they asked, given these options, if I were in their situation, where would I prefer to be sent. In trying to answer, my lack of patriotism would have outraged any US politician. I did my best to give an honest reply: that of these three countries, the US was a richer nation, but with the lines between rich and poor now already drawn. Furthermore, as refugee newcomers they would be starting at the bottom with a lot of built-in handicaps. On the other hand Canada and Australia, while not wealthy, were at an earlier stage of both development and opportunity, with many diverse peoples already living there, many of them non-English speaking. All in all, I would rate the alternatives as about even.

Practically all of the questions that followed were along economic lines.

"Will I be able to find a job when I get there?" In the US, yes. A job for you is guaranteed upon arrival.

"Where will we find a place to live?" Same answer.

"I'm a carpenter, should I take my tools with me?" No, your job will provide tools.

"Can my children help me with the work?" At home, yes. Outside employment, only if they are at least sixteen. Younger ones must go to school.

"I don't speak English. Will that be a problem?" A lot depends on your job and where you live, but the ability to speak English is essential if you expect to fit into the community.

"Right now, I'm a stateless person. Do I become a citizen when I am settled in my new country?" Not automatically. There's a formal process for becoming a citizen. Until you complete that you are a resident alien.

"Will I be able to own a car?" Probably. Many working people do - to get to and from work.

So it went, hundreds of questions to which no orientation program could possibly have provided even half the answers or the survival assurances that these people were so sorely in need of. One thing that struck me from these sessions was how few of the questions were political. Considering that almost every person in the room was there as a victim of one oppressive regime or another, I would have expected to hear expressions of concern for guaranteed personal safety and individual rights. If so, they kept it to themselves. Perhaps they were already predisposed to believe that these evils would be left behind with their previous lives in the old Europe, and believed that in the promised land they would be safe and free from an oppressive government.

For new hires like myself, the hotel at Prien was calculated to serve a useful dual purpose: first, orientation and training, although the actual orientation was minimal, and training almost non-existent. Not publicized but more important was the screening function. Volunteers from the US arrived with no concept of postwar life in a DP camp and no experience of living in deprived conditions - miserable housing, poor food, neglect and inefficiency everywhere. For some it was more than culture shock, it was also more than a simple desire to do good could withstand. After a short immersion a few neophytes had had enough of on-site refugee work and returned home, pleased with the sacrifices they had endured. To make the selection process more dependable, a period of several weeks was set aside at the very beginning for newcomers to experience the rough equivalent of what life in a future assignment might be like. This policy only became apparent to me later. At the time I was simply told that they were waiting for a staffing slot in one of the camps to open up.

For the most part, I didn't find this initial trial period too onerous. Yes, the rooms were cold, and yes, the beds were narrow and uncomfortable, and the blankets were threadbare with holes in them. Also, hot water in the morning could be slow in coming, or not come at all. These were all minor inconveniences as far as I was concerned.

Food was something else. I'm not a nutritionist and therefore not certain what caloric intake is necessary to sustain a mildly active adult lifestyle - probably 1,800 - 2,000 calories a day. That was roughly the daily allowance mandated by the IRO for its refugee food program, and followed by the "kitchen" at the

YMCA Prien.

In practice, this worked out as follows:

Breakfast:
- Black coffee, sugar, no cream
- Oatmeal, no cream or milk
- Dark bread, no butter

Lunch:
- Black coffee, sugar, no cream
- A small block of cheese
- Dark bread, no butter

Dinner:
- Black coffee, sugar, no cream
- A bowl of soup with traces of meat and vegetables
- Dark bread, no butter

Not very imaginative, but in keeping with the general surroundings. At first, I didn't mind, but after about a week or ten days I began to feel distinctly undernourished. Day and night-time fantasies began to feature food, orgies of food, memories of long ago holiday dinners, even dishes I used not to like but from which I would be happy to lick the plate. As time went on, I became convinced that I was gradually starving, but I was also resolutely determined not to say anything, and above all not to complain, meanwhile trying to suppress the food fantasies dancing about in my head.

I will go so far as to say that not many Americans, even the poorest, have ever experienced real hunger over any sustained period. They may not always have "enough", or enough of what they like. But to go for weeks on end, subsisting on the bare, statistical caloric minimum is rare in our modern history. For me, this was a unique experience.

After I had been there about two weeks, the need arose to make a trip to Munich for consultation on YMCA business. Signe and Bilostocki, plus two others, would be going. As an afterthought, Signe asked if I would like to come along. Ready for a change of scene, I immediately said that I would. So we all squeezed into the Jeep station wagon and set out.

We had traveled about half an hour when Signe remarked that there was an army (US) snack bar a few miles ahead. Did we want to stop or push on? For everyone in the car, it was a minor question. But not for me. For me it was a life or death issue; if they did not stop, I might not make it to Munich. But with superhuman restraint, I kept these thoughts to myself. After some half-hearted discussion they decided to stop and we went in.

There, right in from of me, were all the goodies I had been fantasizing about: hamburgers, cheeseburgers, greasy french fries with ketchup and relish on the side, deep fried onions, chocolate and sugar coated donuts, and multiple flavors of ice cream, sundaes - even a banana split. All this, and only a few hurried minutes to make a decision. I could easily have spent the day there but contented myself with a cheeseburger and a chocolate milkshake to finish off in the car. Words cannot describe that little meal, so I'll not try.

What I did not know at the time was that I was the only person at the Center actually living on the official IRO ration. For the others, even refugees, the IRO ration provided a nutritional base above and beyond which they had long since managed to add a whole pantry-full of extras from local produce or black market sources. By the time I did find this out, my period of initial trial by starvation was up.

Chapter Seventeen

Making the Best of It

I had arrived in Prien in November. A break in the daily regimen came at Christmas time. I had become friendly with Mr. Bilostocki, the second in command. As part of my "orientation," he undertook to familiarize me with the general area, with tours through the Bavarian Alps in a battered pre-war Tatra - an apparently indestructible car made long ago in Czechoslovakia. I had never before seen snow like this - half buried farm houses, towering snow banks on either side of the road where the plow had cleared a narrow lane, and the Alps on all sides through which we threaded our way over steep mountain passes to isolated mountain valleys and picture-postcard Bavarian villages.

Mr. Bilostocki belonged to the Greek Orthodox Church which had its own theology, rituals, saints and holidays. However, as in the west, Christmas was celebrated as the holiest event in the Christian calendar. It was also a feast day. Even in DP camps, wherever possible it was observed meticulously, including days of advance planning and many hours of preparation. Tradition dictated a feast of twelve courses: one for each of the twelve disciples. Many hands had gone into this multi-stage epic creation, all of whom were gathered around an enlarged improvised table, covered with a white cloth and lighted candles. As the only outsider I felt especially privileged.

One by one the dishes kept coming. I can't begin to remember what they all were, and can't imagine how Mrs. Bilostocki managed to find all of the ingredients that went into them. There was borscht soup; two kinds of fish - pickled herring, and a baked carp; stuffed eggs; cabbage filled pastries; a terrine of duck, and another of chicken livers; potato cakes; a sour cream stroganoff of pork; sauerkraut with liver dumplings, and incongruously for dessert, canned peaches with several kinds of cookies.

On our trips I had a lot of time for conversation with Mr. Bilostocki. He was Ukrainian (at that time still part of the Soviet Union) but had learned German while studying at the University in Kiev. Because of this ability he had been drafted as an interpreter by the invading German army, thereby rendering himself suspect after the war, particularly so to Soviet officialdom as the German army began its retreat. Mr. Bilostocki was a patriotic Ukrainian, but who would believe his story once a wave of retribution swept over the country against anyone suspected of collaboration with the enemy? With these very real fears in mind, he and his wife simply joined the ever-growing mass of persons seeking security in the west.

I asked him whether the invading German Army was as bad as reports had described.

"It was worse than bad," Bilostocki replied. "It was stupid."

"What do you mean?" I asked, to which he answered with a short history lesson in Russian/Ukrainian relations - summarized in my best recollection of his words as follows.

"The Soviet Union is a union in name only, most of the countries in it don't know each other, and those who do in many cases are long-time enemies. They were and are kept together only by force and by fear of what that evil man, Joseph Stalin, would do if anyone dared to raise his head for even a bit of independence. This is especially true of Russia and Ukraine, going back to when the Ukraine was forcibly joined to the Russian Empire. But it was made much worse only twenty years ago when Stalin starved the country into submission. He created a communist-made famine in the Ukraine for failure to deliver our quota of farm products under his so-called Five Year Plan. Millions of people died. It was terrible. Those who survived had nothing but hatred for communist Russia. They wanted only the opportunity for revenge.

"When the German Army arrived in June of 1941 our people looked on them as liberators. We believed they were going to free us from those despots in Moscow. But the Germans didn't seem to understand this, or if they did they did not want our outstretched hands. In line with their ridiculous racial theories, to the Germans we Ukrainians were an inferior race, Slavs, not as low as the Jews perhaps, but still only fit to be slave labor under Aryan masters. In every way, they treated us like dirt, so that after awhile our people said, they're no better than the communists - maybe even worse - we may as well stay loyal to the country and fight the invaders.

"So we did fight them, in the army and more and more with the partisan guerillas. This defection was decisive. Had Germany taken advantage of the boiling hatred in the Ukraine for the Communists, they would have won the war on the eastern front, defeated Russia, and forced a negotiated peace with the west."

I was to hear similar opinions expressed later on by other DP's. It simply reinforced my conviction of how stupid Hitler's racial theories were, and how his grandiose dreams of a German Third Reich with its master race, ruling over eastern Europe's millions of Slavic serfs was a fantasy that never could have succeeded. But at that time, Nazi ideology was blinded by racial arrogance, and no one dared speak up in the name of simple realism. After all, the Nazis believed there was no problem that force couldn't handle.

In addition to Mr. Bilostocki, there were the other two staff members, Meyer and Eschbaum, whose first names I've forgotten, but with whom I got on a friendly basis during my weeks in Prien. Both were ex-Luftwaffe, rugged outdoor types about ten years older than I, As a result of their work in the YMCA program, both could speak a little English.

At least enough English for a bridge game which took place most evenings. Sometimes a fourth was made up by a young Czech ex-pilot who had escaped from the continent to fly fighter aircraft for the RAF. At other times, the fourth was supplied by an old (60 plus) Pole, part of a group of DP's passing through.

This old Pole, Josef Walewski, deserves a book all to himself. As you can imagine, during those years in Germany and Austria I heard a lot of war stories, but almost none equaled his own tale of the ferocity, ruthlessness and ultimately despair as to the fate of so many, even those who managed to live through it. He and his wife lived in Warsaw where he worked in city administration. Bombed out of their apartment in the first days of the war, they eked out an existence under the iron heel of German occupiers, worsened after

June 1941 when Hitler's attack on the Soviet Union occurred. In May and June of 1943, they watched helplessly the suppression of the Jewish Ghetto and subsequent obliteration of its entire population, some 40,000 Jews. Walewski was not Jewish, but along with most of his friends, he joined the Polish Underground, which was having some success against the Germans in other Polish cities, particularly as the tide of the war turned.

By early August 1944 Red Armies were just across the Vistula River at the edge of the city. Under its leader, General Borowski, the Polish Underground struck at the occupation. At first, the Germans taken by surprise things went well. The Poles confidently expected help from the Russians whom they had aided on previous occasions, and could not understand it when this help was not immediately forthcoming.

During all of August and into September a battle of unparalleled viciousness raged in the city, no prisoners taken on either side, wounded burned alive by the Germans. In this desperate resistance, Walewski commanded diversionary operations. That is, when a strike was planned against an enemy objective, Walewski, with a handful of men, would stage a fake attack elsewhere to draw off defending troops. In this suicidal tactic he was greatly helped by his previous experience. As a city administrator he had access to all of the utility records and maps of roads, streets, alleys, passageways, buildings, warehouses, factories, even sewers. The sewers were especially valuable. The Germans had succeeded in dividing the Polish forces; above ground movement became almost impossible. Using this network of sewers, resistance fighters could not only coordinate forces, but show up in unexpected places. In that type of guerilla warfare surprise is everything. However, ingenuity and resourcefulness could go only so far. The Germans brought in heavy artillery and tanks. Whole buildings were demolished and burned to get at the few guerillas hiding inside; any civilians were considered "collateral damage."

Meanwhile, the Russians still held back in a cynical act of great power politics. To the masters in the Kremlin post-war control over Poland was a primary objective. A Polish underground resistance army fighting German occupiers would be just as likely to fight Russians. Here was an opportunity to get rid of them both. So the Red Army stood still as the slaughter across the river continued.

In September, a limited number of women and children were allowed out of the city, Walewski's wife among them. In another few weeks the insurrection collapsed, most of the original force dead. By this time, with defeat staring them in the face, the Germans were too busy trying to save themselves to take retribution on the remaining population. Walewski survived but never saw his wife again.

War experiences seldom interrupted our bridge games. In fact, we seldom discussed the war. Walewski's story came out one afternoon over a cup of black coffee as part of a casual conversation. Everyone had his or her story - some, terrible. Nothing special in that, so most of them went untold.

Chapter Eighteen

Bad Aibling

Just after the first of January came word of my new YMCA assignment. It took only about ten minutes for me to pack up, and within an hour we had arrived at our destination, only about forty miles away, just outside the village of Bad Aibling. There, on about twenty acres of snow covered fields in a former Luftwaffe facility, consisting of a nondescript collection of buildings, the IRO had set up a "Children's Village," meaning that it was devoted to the care of refugee children, mostly orphans, who had lost or became separated from their parents during the war and its aftermath. In total there were perhaps a few hundred inhabitants, along with about twenty to thirty IRO staff and volunteer agency workers like myself.

The Bad Aibling camp was called a "Children's Village" appropriately, since it was the only refugee facility devoted primarily to the care of children. These ranged from toddlers on up to teenagers, although there were also a few babies - newborns - since the DP population did not stop reproducing itself simply because normal care facilities were not available.

Child care took the form of organized "family" units by which each orphan was consigned to the care of a DP couple who functioned as foster parents for which they received special privileges. Therefore, although a Children's Village – in name, there were actually three of four times as many adults as children within the total population.

Heading up the IRO administrative staff was one Doug Dean, a 40-year old Australian. The rest of the IRO team comprised international social workers, all young women, many from

Scandinavia and the low countries, and a medical doctor from Belgium plus several nurses who seldom appeared outside of the infirmary section. Vol Agency personnel were there from the American Friends Service Committee (Quakers, who occupied themselves with "family" issues) along with a Yugoslav Roman Catholic priest, the HIAS (Hebrew Immigrant Aid Society), and the ORT who taught job skills.

I represented the YMCA. We had our own small building, but large enough for an office/conference room, a classroom and an open area fitted out as a gym and basketball court. Upon arrival I, as the new director, was introduced to everyone by the outgoing director who took the opportunity to explain the YMCA program. It wasn't much: mainly English classes, sports and a small library of books scrounged from any source, mostly army issue paperbacks.

For such a small operation we had a more than adequate staff comprising entirely DP's. There was a husband/wife team from the Baltic states: Mr. and Mrs. Brazdis. He really ran the program, and she managed office functions, including bookkeeping and petty cash. There was another husband/wife team, Mr. and Mrs. Gulbis, Hungarians, who had previously operated a dance studio. Every so often they staged a social evening in the gym, including music and dancing. Our English teacher was a local German woman, Frau Schultz, chosen because none of the DP's had enough English to qualify. Sports for women was the domain of a pretty Czech girl, Irena Kankova, who had been a skating star back home. There was no men's sports leader. That had been managed by the previous director, until his departure.

There was one other person, a young Hungarian named Lazlo Wachtler. He had no official position, but spoke German, a bit of English, and liked to hang around the YMCA office. As time went on, he became useful in keeping me informed through a daily briefing of gossip and rumor as to what was actually going on in the camp. For example, I learned that I had been sent to Bad Aibling to replace the previous director because he had become romantically involved with the skating star, frowned on by the YMCA as inappropriate for a married man and role model leader. I could easily empathize with the temptation, and at the same time understand the implied warning.

As far as my work went, I had very little to do. Mr. Brazdis and his wife were in total control. Brazdis was tall, of authoritative presence, and spoke all the languages important to DP work: Russian, Polish, Serbocroatian, German, English and, of course, his native Baltic tongue. Incredible, this talent Eastern Europeans have for mastering a variety of languages. He could have run an entire country efficiently. His wife made up the other half of this formidable duo. Short, plump, blonde, cheerful and with a head for detail, she was the ideal administrative assistant.

Under their supervision, Frau Schultz conducted her English lessons with Teutonic efficiency, trying to cope with conditions beyond anyone's control which made real learning almost impossible. Class populations were constantly shifting as new arrivals entered and older inmates moved on to their next destination. Nor was there any common language for translation purposes. German was about the best choice. Finally, a good percentage of DP's in the class were functionally illiterate, making both texts and chalkboards useless.

From time to time I sat in on the class, but it seemed that I was a disruptive force because, when I was there, all the DP's wanted was information about where they were going, which at this point no one knew. Very politely, Frau Schultz made it clear that she could manage her class very well without me, thank you. So I left her to her own methods.

For many of the reasons cited above, our small library struggled to fulfill its mission. Mrs. Brazdis acted as librarian, but even her administrative skills could not control what books arrived - a miscellaneous, grab-bag of cast-off titles mostly in English - or those that left, vanished along with the reader to his/her next destination. Reluctantly, I concluded that the library, like the English lessons, was a well-meaning gesture, but to be useful had to be re-organized from the ground up.

That left sports. Girls' sports, mainly volleyball and ping-pong, were conducted by Irena Kankova with considerable success. She was a natural athlete, high-spirited, and loved sports. Her name and reputation made her widely known, admired, and a natural leader. Men's sports were another story. To begin with, I was not well suited for this part of the program. Competitive sports had never held the least interest for me. All through school I avoided them whenever I could, and played poorly when I couldn't. I had no team spirit or will to win, and thought anyone who did was childish and somewhat retarded. A worse coach or team leader could scarcely be imagined.

To this unpromising start, add the fact that it was winter, and the DP's themselves were not interested in sports, sunk in a general mood of pessimism, defeatism and inertia, the product of years spent in camps. When their minds did open up it was to worry for what might lay in the future.

Facilities for a sports program left much to be desired. The gym was too small for a real basketball game. In any case there was just one basket, and most of the open space was occupied by two ping-pong tables that had to be removed for volleyball. Outside, snow covered the fields; there was no pond or accessible body of water for skating. Our equipment locker held a miscellany of useless gear: a baseball bat and ball and an American type football which no one had the faintest idea how to use. Also there were several pair of boxing gloves. When these first arrived, I was told, there had been organized boxing matches. But they had to be discontinued because they quickly became bouts of national rivalry - of national honor - Russians vs. Ukrainians, Ukrainians vs. Poles, Serbs vs. Croats, and so on. The passions thus aroused, especially by a good match, threatened the communal peace of the camp, so after several bad experiences the idea was abandoned.

However, the sports program was not a total failure. The women's portion went well, and as previously mentioned, ping-pong was a success, especially with the younger element, while the older ones liked to watch. Because of this popularity the two tables were kept up most of the time, and taken away only when a volleyball game was scheduled.

However, the real success was with parlor games, especially chess. Some battered boards were there when I arrived, and I was successful in getting a few more. These kept people occupied for long periods, especially the older men, and were more in keeping with the sedentary lifestyle of the camp. Chess was the game of choice, but Parcheesi and checkers had their adherents. There was also often a German card game called Skat going on in one corner accompanied by groans and shouts of triumph according to the fortunes of the players.

In the camp there was one group that I tried very hard to reach out to and bring in to these activities, but without much success. This was a group, really a gang, of teenage hoodlums - orphans from the storm, strays picked up off the streets and given shelter here at Bad Aibling because there was no other place to put them. They were growing up deeply alienated, uneducated, with no sense of purpose and no prospects for the future. As guaranteed social problems, they were wanted by no country The IRO with all its other problems had not been able to integrate these youngsters into the German educational system - which did not want them either - or to establish its own program because of the relatively small numbers involved.

There were both girls and boys, some as old as 16-17. Keeping them apart in well-supervised activity proved to be almost impossible. The boys had formed themselves into a "club," and the IRO administration had made available a room where they could hang out and plan all sorts of deviltry, which was the one thing they liked to do and which required no encouragement from above. This included sneaking girls in after hours, most of whom were completely cooperative, if not actually complicit. It also included stealing anything that was not closely guarded. Light bulbs, wiring, plumbing fixtures, automobile parts, etc.. were all fair game. At that time such items were still scarce in the German economy. .

They had a leader whose name was Halemba. "General Halemba" they called him in fun, but also out of fear and respect. I got to know Halemba in an effort to help them to keep their club room which was always in danger of being taken away, and also to use their club as a vehicle for whatever activities I could devise. From the beginning it was clear that he was their leader and spokesman, and that if you wanted to gain their attention, and possible participation, it had to be through him.

Neither then, nor seldom in later life, have I ever met a more commanding personality, a natural leader in effortless control over his subjects. There was nothing in his appearance to suggest the intangible power he exercised over his group, neither athletic prowess nor appearance of strength. He was sixteen or seventeen years old, of less than medium height, slightly built with sandy hair and an unhealthy sallow complexion. But his most impressive feature was his eyes: cold, gray, remote, expressionless even when he was smiling. His manner was unconsciously authoritative. Without his ever saying so, you were meant to understand that you were dealing with an equal, so different from the usual obsequiousness displayed by most of the other DP's in dealing with administrative staff. Unlike them he was totally self-possessed and at ease.

At our first meeting he sat down, crossed his legs, offered me a cigarette - declined - then lighted one himself, in itself a gesture of power and independence since almost no one ever actually smoked a cigarette - they had become a kind of artificial currency, a medium of exchange.

Our interview went more or less as follows.

"What I understand, Mister Jack" - all the other DP's called me Mr. Barwick - "you are interested to start games here. I don't know, maybe ping-pong, volleyball - what else? It is winter outside. We don't have much place for games." He spoke quite good English.

"Yes," I said. "I think we could get a second net for basketball. Get everyone participating, we have enough people to form several teams in each of these sports. It would be fun - you know, friendly competition, maybe even compete against the other DP camps."

"What means this 'compete'?" He asked.

"It means to play against another player, or one team against another team to see who wins. Like any game, when it's all done one is the champion, the big winner. All in fun, of course."

"What does the 'big winner' win?"

"Not much, usually. Maybe a ribbon, whatever we could afford."

"A ribbon? That's all? Why not money, or cigarettes, or something interesting? Maybe people would bet on who would win."

"No, no. The YMCA would never go for that. Our purpose is a

Picking Up the Pieces

healthy life for everyone, and that means activity, exercise, helping your body build a strong heart, bones, muscles, and the best way to do that is through sports."

"To me, I can't see the big difference between that and hard work. Except in hard work, you get paid."

"Yes, well there's a big difference, but it's hard to explain." This kid was beginning to tie me in knots.

"Also, Mister Jack, these 'teams' you say - are the Bad Aibling boys all one team, or do they play as single people, like just Rolf or Ludwig, or me?"

"It could be both. It depends on the game. In the beginning it would be here with small teams. Later on, if we played against other DP camps, Bad Aibling would have its own team."

"So for now all our boys would play against me and against each other, yes?"

"Yes, but as friends."

"Oh, I see. Against me, and against each other. That does not have a good sound to me. It is against what we feel. All of us have many bad experiences out in the world. But now we are together. We have our room where I can go to and be among friends who are just like me, and who I can trust. For the first time, and who knows for how long.

"So now, Mister Jack, you want to start up - you call it a 'competition' where we all play against each other. Why would we want to do that?"

I could see that I was no match debating this uneducated leader and politician. My cause was clearly going down to defeat in the face of cogent arguments. Best to close on a note of friendly exchange and keep the lines of communication open.

"OK, Halemba" - he used only one name - "I understand. I'll do all I can to help you keep that room. You can help yourself by not letting your boys do anything stupid. But think about the sports idea. Come spring, and nice weather your boys will want to go out. A sports program would make that much easier."

Halemba nodded. "Okay, Mister Jack. You help us, now I help you."

"You help me, how?"

"Mister Jack, you are not smoking, right? And you are not

selling your cigarettes, I know."

I had to admit this was true, mainly because I didn't know how to go about it.

"And your liquor allowance - whiskey, brandy. - are you drinking it?"

"No, I don't even buy it."

"Mister Jack, I make business in all these things, coffee too. You buy in the PX once a week. I pay you two, three, five times what you pay. I pay better than anyone here because of my connections. They sell in Czechoslovakia. Highest prices there. Everyone get rich. Do we have a deal?" Clearly, he was a master salesman as well as a natural leader.

"Well, Halemba, I appreciate the offer, but there's no way I can do it. The "Y" would never go for that."

"They don't have to know. Everyone here sell their allowances. Some with me. I like to do you a favor too. Do we agree?"

"No. Not now, probably never. We'll just say no for now. But let's keep talking."

Halemba nodded. "Okay, we talk about it."

He and I developed a relationship of mutual tolerance based on an understanding of the other's situation. The next time Halemba came to see me, he had with him a little boy of Asiatic appearance. A very cute kid.

"This is my new friend, Goripov. He is an Uzbec. He come in last week. No mother, no father. Gori, you say hello to Mister Jack."

"Hewo, Meezr Zek", said Goripov, trying to smile.

"They give him a new mother and father here. Both are no good. They only do it for the money. I don't like what I see and what I hear. Too much like my own life."

"How do you mean?"

"I too am - how you say - no mother, no father?"

"Orphan."

"Orphan, yes, since maybe seven, eight years. Both dead in the bombing. The Germans, soldiers, they find me in the street and I go with them. Near the end they are captured by the Americans - so, what the hell, now I am with the Americans, like a pet dog. Nice guys though. The sergeant wants to take me back home with him. I would like that, but the UNRRA grabs me, and since then I'm here in the camps."

"What can you do for Goripov?"

"Make him feel he has some real friends. Learn to speak German. Maybe even some English. Teach him the ropes, we would watch out for him, see that he isn't beaten or harmed."

The two were frequent callers at the YMCA office. It was touching - children taking care of children, their trust in adults destroyed. Whenever I saw Halemba, Goripov was always with him.

Chapter Nineteen

Religious Zeal A Problem

In line with its non-sectarian relief mission, the IRO tried to avoid any appearance of religious participation or favoritism. The voluntary agencies, most of which were of a religious nature or church sponsored, had to conform to this policy as a condition of being allowed to participate in its program. This caused no problem for the YMCA where the evangelical mission had long ago been relegated to a minor role by the emergence of strictly humanitarian services, and by the controversy that always seemed to be present wherever aggressive proselytizing was pursued.

Unlike the larger DP camps, there was no provision for formal religious services at Bad Aibling. Larger inmate populations could justify the presence of rabbis and priests to hold regular services and preside over ceremonies. At Bad Aibling there was only one priest, and he was restricted to a role more in line with family counseling - a role which he regularly violated by aggressive and conspicuous observances of holy day rites and ceremonies.

Nevertheless, with small exceptions, this policy of "live and let live" worked well. Religious opportunities were not uppermost in the minds of the refugees, who were far more concerned for their immediate future here on earth. Unfortunately, not everyone got the message.

Enter Chuck Hunsicker and his wife, Lorie. Chuck and Lorie were a young couple from the Midwest, taking a year off from studies at the Moody Bible Institute in Chicago to see the world, and if possible do good along the way. As he explained to me, "Lorie and I want to learn all we can, and see if there's a way we can help in the great work you're doing here in the short time we have - just a week before we go on to Salzburg."

"What would you like to do here?" I asked.

"Mainly, meet some of these refugees. Get a feel for their problems and hopes. Maybe talk to some of the staff, understand how the place is run."

Chuck did most of the talking. He was clean-cut, well-trimmed and scrubbed, with an ingratiating smile. He exuded warm feelings of idealism and friendship, but also a sense of naiveté - of innocence, even simple-mindedness. Lorie sat there quietly, nodding from time to time. Next to them I was feeling old and cynical.

"Well, Chuck, I'm here to learn too. After a month I know less than I did at the beginning. Maybe you can do better in only a week. I can set up some interviews for you with staff people, including ours. For the DP's, just introduce yourself. Mr. Wachtler here can go along to help with the languages. Do you have any German?"

"No, I'm afraid not."

"Well, good luck. Let me know how it's going."

First reports after a day or two were disconcerting. When I asked the Swedish social workers for their opinions, they laughed. "Just a waste of someone's money. They're babes in the woods wandering around Europe. They should be in a tour bus."

The Quaker girl who dealt with family supervision was also unimpressed. "He seemed less interested in how we manage family arrangements and problems than in their spiritual life. He kept turning the conversation to religion. Why did you ever bring him over here?"

Wachtler reported the same tendency - to make religion the point of every conversation whenever an opportunity offered itself.

Chuck's own appraisal reflected a mixed picture. "There's a lot of opportunity here for anyone with energy and the right message, but I didn't get the feeling that the administrators were taking advantage, or were even aware of it. They struck me as a bunch of governmental bureaucrats - technicians, spouting a lot of social dogma and officialese. There's potential here, but you have to shake the dust off and reach out to people in a personal way. To

Picking Up the Pieces

take advantage of the few days I have left, I'd like to help in two ways, and incidentally help the Y's program.

"First - don't laugh - Lorie and I would put on a barn dance tomorrow night. Your Mr. Gulbis tells me that is dance night anyway - a perfect fit. Our barn dance is something like a square dance, only easier for beginners - fun, simple, a nice way to introduce strangers to some of our American customs. What do you say? Lorie and I are both callers, and I've got the music if you can supply a record player."

What could I say? It seemed harmless.

"Then," he went on, "with them now warmed up, I'd like to hold a small meeting, but open to all, the next night. I've prepared a brief talk called 'The Road Ahead,' kind of catchy title for people in their situation. OK?"

He had already outlined this plan to Mr. Brazdis who said it was alright with him, if I also approved. So I said yes, but to keep it free from anything that sounded like religion. Chuck agreed.

When I spoke to Gulbis, our dance teacher, about the dance, he said that Chuck implied that I had already approved and that all that remained was planning and details. It began to seem that our friend Chuck was a bit of an operator. Gulbis had no knowledge of square dancing and was not enthusiastic about interrupting the planned program subject, which was to have been "The Tango," but he agreed to function as MC and Impresario.

The next evening about forty people showed up, mostly out of curiosity, including a few teenagers and a dozen or so elderly women. Chuck and Lorie were wearing cowboy hats and western check shirts and vests when they stood up in the front of the gym which had been cleared of ping-pong tables, with chairs set along the side.

Chuck delivered a short speech which Wachtler translated in which he, Chuck, made the following points:
- Everyone likes to dance
- Every country has its own distinctive folk dances
- There is no better way to make friends or get to know new neighbors

Chuck then called for eight volunteers. No one came forward. After much persuasion, assisted by Gulbis, seven timid volunteers ventured forward, and one was recruited from the YMCA staff. With that, our hard-used phonograph was put to work playing the records that Chuck and Lorie had brought. Chuck alternated between explaining the movements and singing the words while Lorie joined the group to demonstrate. The audience was urged to clap along with the rhythm. "I've got my own method," he said. "It uses some old American tunes, music and words. OK now, ready.

> "Here we go round and round:
> She'll be comin' round the mountain when she comes.
> Swing your partners,
> She'll be comin' round the mountain when she comes,
> All together ….."

What resulted was mass confusion. The only part that went well was the clapping, several dancers were under the impression that they were also supposed to clap. Not everyone stayed with the rhythm. There were false starts, wrong turns, collisions.

"Come on now, folks. Watch Lorie. Do what she does. Don't mind mistakes. Everyone makes mistakes. OK - now again."

> "Flies in the buttermilk, shoo fly, shoo.
> Flies in the buttermilk, shoo fly, shoo.
> Flies in the buttermilk, shoo fly, shoo.
> Skip to my Lou, my darlin"

At the side, an elderly woman asked Mrs. Gulbis, "What he singing?"

"I don't know. I think flies in buttermilk. He wants them to go away."

"Flies in buttermilk? What kind of song is that? Do they have flies in their milk over there?"

One dancer was clearly never going to get it and was excused in favor of a replacement whose courage to come forward was bolstered by several shots of slivovitz and being pushed by his friends. Once there, he stood, foolishly tipsy, laughing at nothing in particular. When Lorie took his arm to pull him into line, he fell, taking her down with him. His friends howled with laughter.

So did the audience.

As a demonstration of America folk culture, the barn dance was not going well. The plan had been that the original group of eight dancers would serve as a model demonstration for the audience from which other groups of eight would be added until the whole floor was covered with dancers. At least that was the plan. But now almost an hour had passed. Several more attempts had seen little improvement, when Mr. Gulbis as dancing master and impresario decided to take matters into his own hands. Stepping to the front of the room, he effusively thanked the Hunsickers for this "interesting contribution to our understanding of American dance," and then announced that the rest of the evening would be devoted to the Tango.

Chuck concealed his disappointment manfully but rationalized it as follows: "These people are so down in the dumps they just don't have the joyful spirit for an evening of wholesome fun. Maybe I can bring a message of uplift to them in my talk tomorrow night."

His talk, which went on for about half an hour, was a thinly disguised sermon, basically an elaboration of the following points:"

- America was built by pioneers
- You are pioneers facing an unknown road ahead
- Along this road you will need help from friends, and strength and dedication of spirit.
- For help, your church will be your best friend
- Strength and dedication of spirit lie in Jesus Christ and his message of hope

When he had finished, to my surprise, he pulled a sheaf of pamphlets from a briefcase and passed them out to the audience which numbered about thirty people.

"And now," he said, "how about some questions?"

Given the nature of his talk, members of the audience hardly knew what questions to ask.

"Will I have to work on Sunday?"

"How can the Church help?"

"Does the Church run the schools?"

"Suppose I get sick and can't work?" In   trying   to   answer

Religious Zeal A Problem

these questions, Chuck showed how unfamiliar he was with the legal aspects of immigration, or with the role churches in the US were actually playing in the refugee program. When he could not give a forthright answer he turned the issue back to something like "God helps those who help themselves."

At the end he said, "Now I would like to offer up a prayer for all of you, for God's mercy and loving kindness in your journey on the road ahead."

Even he could see that reaction to his talk was at best lukewarm. The uplift he had promised failed to get off the ground. Many pamphlets were left lying on the seats where they had been passed out. He couldn't conceal his frustration when we talked about it afterward.

"I'm not used to speaking where I have to go through an interpreter. It puts my timing off. Just when I get going, the interpreter breaks in. Anyway, I think we got through to a few of them. Three came up afterward with more questions that ought to get a follow-up. I have their names, here they are. Just a friendly talk, Jack, that's all. If I were here I'd be glad to do it - but what's your opinion?"

"If you want to know, I think you stepped over the line."

"What line?"

"The line between helping people and trying to convert them - in this case, between orientation and pushing a religious point of view. Under the terms of the IRO charter, we're not allowed to do that. This whole operation was set up to solve a problem of six million refugees who needed new homes. All kinds of people and organizations have joined in that effort and have agreed to put aside their religious differences to get the job done without being distracted by the areas where they didn't agree - particularly in the area of religion."

"OK, but the C in YMCA stands for Christian. As Christians, we're obligated to 'be a light unto the world.' I'm overwhelmed when I think of the opportunity you have here, a captive audience of hundreds of people looking for a new life, in here all day long with nothing else to do. Excuse me, Jack. I don't mean to criticize the work you're doing, but it seems to me like a fraction of what you could do. I'm not talking about conducting baptisms or anything like that, but maybe quiet prayer meetings - informal, you know, when you feel the opportunity is there? What do you say?"

"I say I think it would get me and the YMCA kicked out of here."

"But don't you think it's right?" "Not if it harms the work that I believe in, and that I was brought here to do."

"Well, if you believe that there's no room in that work for the Christian message, I don't know. It seems you have come a long way from your family roots, Jack. I understand your father was a minister at one time when they really preached the gospel."

He looked deeply into my eyes. "Jack, I really do want to be your friend, and all this advice is given purely in the spirit of fellowship. I would just like to spend a minute or two with you in prayer. Let's hold hands."

I didn't want to hold hands, I didn't want to pray. This guy was beginning to get to me in a big way. After only a few days, he was my self-styled "best friend." And after only a few days, with little or no preparation, he was ready and eager to tell all of us how to run our business. Just under that veneer of humility ("I'm here to learn") was another layer - one of aggression, fortified by faith and sanctified from above, uninterested in and indifferent to consequences. Also beneath that exterior of homespun simplicity was the duplicitous skill of a master manipulator. "Be cunning as the serpent," says the Bible. The strange thing in all this was that I don't think he had the slightest self-awareness: of being manipulative, duplicitous or of acting immorally. Other people did these things, not him.

Shortly after Chuck and Lorie carried their crusade on into Austria, the real life consequences to us in Bad Aibling were made all too apparent. At the monthly staff meeting, the Roman Catholic priest launched a vicious attack on the YMCA program, and by implication on the IRO for allowing violations of its policies of non-sectarianism.

This particular priest, Father Angelo, was a singularly unattractive individual: young and energetic, with a perpetual combative stance. In him, the religious wars of the sixteenth century were still burning. All Protestants were heretics, their

Religious Zeal A Problem

dogma evil, and their organizations unsanctified missions of sin. The fact that he was universally disliked and shunned by the camp staff members made him all the more zealous in his complaints, mostly about trivialities.

His attack at our staff meeting, therefore, came as no great surprise, except in its intensity, an accumulation of resentments for perceived slights and lack of support.

I'll try to summarize his indictment as follows:

"The IRO program is a failure in its treatment of religious organizations that are here to serve the legitimate spiritual needs of their DP membership. It is a failure for severely restricting the functions of the Roman Catholic priesthood, while at the same time tolerating the openly evangelistic activities of Protestant organizations, particularly the YMCA. We have just had a clear example of the YMCA infiltrating missionaries disguised as tourists for the purpose of seducing people to its faith - people at a vulnerable point in their lives when false messages can appear to offer hope. The techniques these missionaries use are clever - entertainment, dancing, to draw people in; meetings supposed to offer information which are no more than Protestant sermons; and pamphlets pushing the same message, advising them to join a Protestant church if they want to get ahead in their new home.

"This is intolerable from our point of view - this IRO toleration, even encouragement, of open Protestant evangelical policies. But I am not surprised. It is but one more instance of how the YMCA helps in this effort. For a long time we know the YMCA has been operating a youth program here - a 'Club,' with its own room, which has become a nest of immorality, and which undermines our efforts to teach moral values. We do not like to lose our young people to a poorly supervised youth program, which is actually just a recruitment device. This recruitment has no age limits. Just recently it recruited a little Uzbec boy, eight years old. He has now become the protégé of one of the gang leaders and no longer listens to his parents,"

"These are a few of my criticisms, but I am tired of complaining, only to watch time go by while the whole situation becomes worse. Therefore, this time I shall make a formal complaint to my superiors and through them to IRO headquarters in Geneva." "Those are pretty strong words, Father," said Doug Dean after a long silence during which all the staff members looked at one another in shocked surprise, and I tried to think of what I would say in response.

He continued: "As far as the IRO goes, we don't condone religious favoritism. As a matter of fact, we've had to warn you once or twice. And I don't think there's religious recruitment going on - friendship and normal association doesn't imply a religious motive, much less recruitment. It's natural for young people to want to be together, and having their own room makes it easier for us to see what's going on, even if rules are broken from time to time."

"Joan, you're the Quaker representative with responsibility for our family program. What do you think?"

Joan Aitken spoke slowly. "I wouldn't be honest if I said there were no problems. There are, and there always will be when you're dealing with an unassimilated, traumatized migrant population, with no real community institutions or support. But taking that into account, I think we do about as well as can be expected."

"Thank you Joan," said Dean, then turning to me: "Apparently what triggered this perception by Father Angelo, Jack, was this recent visit by Hunsicker and his wife. I was not present at either the dance or his meeting, but from what I heard, they were both failures. Is that so?"

"Very much so. The dance was a joke."

"As far as active religious proselytizing went, would you consider Hunsicker an evangelist - actively promoting his brand of Christianity?" Dean asked.

"Well, he certainly went over the line, in my opinion." I replied.

"But how did he get in here? Why would the YMCA sponsor someone like that?"

"I don't know, but I'm sure the YMCA didn't sponsor him. He was a freelancer. I don't think Munich knew what he was up to. They seemed like good people who only wanted to help. The barn dance - well, that seemed harmless to me. And his meeting was supposed to be an orientation talk. The pamphlets were a big surprise. After a day or so I began to feel he didn't fully understand the situation here and how we operated. I warned him to be careful, but he wasn't listening."

"Jack, Hunsicker is gone. There's nothing we can do about him. I'm more concerned about the YMCA and its program. We're glad to have you here and wouldn't want unauthorized activities to spoil that - or give grounds for complaints."

"Thank you, Doug. I think this person slipped through the cracks. I'll give Munich a full report, and promise to be more careful myself."

Dean then addressed the priest. "Father, you heard Jack's explanation. I believe him. This was a one-time failure of our policy on sectarian favoritism. We apologize to you for that, and will be more careful to catch any similar possibility."

Then to the room at large: "How do you all feel? Is this something we can handle ourselves, or does it need to go higher?"

The opinion was general. "No, it's our problem. We can deal with it."

"Father, I like to think that as a family group here we are capable of dealing with any day-to-day problem that may arise. If we agree on our goals, the rest can be managed, and I do believe we are in agreement on goals. So I would suggest that we keep this as an internal problem, and not take it upstairs to higher authority - either church or IRO. They have enough to worry about. I ask you, Father, can we keep this for now among ourselves?"

Father Angelo remained obdurate. "For years I am hearing the same thing, getting the same answers. Always promises and nothing changes. I can see that I have no hope with the IRO. You talk about agreement on goals. I don't think we have agreement of goals. So I shall not complain again to the IRO since it is quite hopeless. But I will write to my Bishop from whom I am sure to get a better hearing than is given to me here." And with that he marched out of the room.

Chapter Twenty

Background To Danger

Because of its role as a "Children's Village" Bad Aibling got more than its share of visiting dignitaries, politicians, church officials and ordinary civilians - well wishers of all sorts. Along with the photo-ops, most of them got the guided tour, a session with Doug Dean, and an overview of IRO administration for the camp. They departed with words of praise, satisfied with their new knowledge of the DP program and its beneficial results.

What they did not know was that they were seeing only part of the picture - the surface - and beneath this surface lay another whole layer of camp government, one run by the DP's themselves.

Quite a few weeks passed before I became aware that this arrangement existed. It was Wachtler who first provided a few details. We were discussing our Mr. Brazdis. I remarked how impressive a gentleman he was, and what a waste of talent that someone so able and gifted had been uprooted from his native community where he had been someone of importance, and was now serving in a job far below his real capabilities.

"Not as far as you might think," said Wachtler.

"I don't mean to trivialize what he does for us here in the YMCA program, only that I think he is capable of so much more," I hastened to add.

"You would be surprised if you knew how much more he actually does," Wachtler replied.

"What do you mean?"

"Well, I don't know if I ought to be the one to tell you," said Wachtler. "But there's a lot goes on here in this camp that doesn't meet the eye."

"Like what?"

"Like the way the camp is run. On top is the IRO: Doug Dean and all his social workers, plus you folks in the vol agencies. That's the part that everybody sees. But the DP's have another - I guess you could call it - government, a board or council that handles problems or situations that come up among the DP's themselves. Problems the IRO couldn't really handle. Of course, all this is kept secret, very hush-hush. Nobody talks about it openly, so I can understand how you wouldn't know about it. But I think it's good if you do know about it, only don't act as if you do. I'm telling you all this in confidence. Okay?"

"Sure, I'll not say a word. It all sounds very mysterious, but I suppose it wouldn't be there if it wasn't necessary."

"Yes, as far as I know, every camp has a similar underground organization. Yeah, it's kept out of sight. Even we don't know what goes on in those secret meetings, or who the actual members are."

"How does Brazdis fit in?"

"He's the head man. There are others, not many. I'm not sure how many, or who they are, but I've got a good idea. They act in secret, but only on complaints between DP's, and what they say goes."

"Can they enforce their decisions?"

"I guess so, because the system works. A warning is usually all it takes. These people are about to emigrate. They don't want anything to go wrong. Any threat or even an anonymous denunciation could hold them up for years while it is investigated. I don't say that's what happens, it doesn't have to. Just the possibility is enough." After this conversation I looked at Brazdis with increased respect. He seemed like a person who could gain and maintain the trust of the people around him to do the right thing. But I never asked him about it, or gave any sign of knowing about his undercover role. Things might have gone along without this undercover role becoming a factor in the YMCA operation. Then things changed. Here I must interrupt my story to provide a bit of essential historical background.

At the four-power negotiations at the conclusion of hostilities in 1945 the victorious allies met to decide how the occupied territories in Germany and Austria would be administered. There was a great deal of wrangling and accusations of acting in bad faith - not to be wondered at since the cold war was already well under way. Mutual suspicion was rife. No motive went unquestioned, and none more so than the assertion by the Soviet Union that all of the Eastern European refugees were the remnants of the Nazi slave labor masses forcibly brought into Germany for work in the armament industry. There is no question that many were just that, but there is every reason to question the Soviet claim that all of these refugees wanted nothing so much as to return to their country of origin, for most the USSR.

Where this was the case, many were quickly repatriated. However, there remained hundreds of thousands of others who did not want to return. Some were anti-communist; some were simply fearful of returning to an unpredictable tyranny; many, if not most, wanted a better life somewhere in the west.

Given the spectrum of motivation, it is hard to understand the extreme measures the Soviets employed to reclaim this native group. To implement their repatriation program, the Soviets set up "repatriation centers" in major cities in the western zones of occupation out of which they operated with relative independence; at least it seemed the Allied powers did little to curb the excesses that soon became apparent.

Normal publicity for repatriation, including information meetings and interviews to help individuals decide for themselves, were all acceptable. What was not acceptable were the kidnappings - forced repatriations that began shortly after the program got underway. More and more it began to appear that the Soviets were after individual refugees: politicians? labor leaders? technical experts- who could tell? All one knew was that from time,to time a refugee would disappear, and then another, and another. Their disappearances created an enormous cloud of uncertainty and fear within the camps. No one knew who would be next - or why.

These Soviet repatriation centers looked the part: usually a large gloomy building, in poor repair with a red flag flying on top. To persuade refugees to return, the Russians publicized frequent information meetings held there, but no DP dreamed of ever setting foot inside - it would have been like entering Lubyanka prison. So the Soviets concluded, "If they won't come to us, we'll go to them, wherever they are."

Actually, the Russians did not do all of the kidnappings themselves. A large number of abductions, I was told, were carried out by a gang of thugs from eastern Europe under the leadership of one Benno Blum. Quite possibly other agents were involved. In payment for its services the gang was rewarded with the protected cigarette smuggling concession into Czechoslovakia, amounting to a virtual monopoly.

From time to time small changes took place in the YMCA staff roster as individuals moved on and replacements were added. One of these additions appeared in my office with no warning, having just been driven up from Salzburg where there was a large DP camp and a YMCA presence. The IRO said he had worked with the "Y" in Salzburg, so he was turned over to me to find something for him to do while he awaited further transfer.

At first sight he was a singularly unattractive person: about thirty years of age, with thinning hair and a pockmarked face, short, and wearing a green leather coat which came down to his knees. His manner was relaxed, at ease, and to my surprise, his English was good enough to be understood, so that it was not necessary to speak in German. The history that he told me was sketchy but similar to many others I'd heard. He was Polish, from Lvov, drafted into the Polish army in 1939. He managed to escape after its quick defeat, but was picked up and shipped to a munitions factory in Czechoslovakia where he worked during the war years making fuses for explosives. He declared himself to be a devout Catholic and anti-Communist, interrupting his tale to show me a religious medal which he wore around his neck. When the Red Army advanced into Czechoslovakia and partisan resistance groups came out of hiding bent on revenge, because he had worked for the Germans he decided to seek safety in Austria. He applied and was admitted in the DP program, but because he had no documentation things had moved slowly. He was hopeful that his transfer here indicated a speed-up in processing. His great ambition, he said, was to go to the USA, to Buffalo, New York, where an uncle had settled. He hoped the uncle was still there.

It was hard to see why Wladislaw Warschauer had been sent to Bad Aibling. He was not an orphan, and had no children with him. There was no real need for him here, and as far as the YMCA program went, I was at a loss to figure out how to keep him usefully employed. We already had more staff than we really needed. Finally, the idea came to me to assign him to Frau Schultz's English classes to work with individual students, explaining the meaning of forms and documents, and helping them to read and understand commonplace signs and directions. Predictably, Frau Schultz took this as a negative commentary on her own teaching methods and sulked for days with a long face and an air of resignation to unmerited interference. Gradually, however, she began to see how it complemented her classes and its practical usefulness. I heard her explain to visitors how she had conceived the idea and enlarged the original program to include Warschauer and his tutorials.

For a time it appeared we had made the best of a bad job. Things were going well in the English classes. Warschauer and I had little communication; there was no apparent need for it. Then disquieting rumors were brought to my attention, first by Wachtler, always up on the latest rumor or whiff of gossip.

"People in camp are talking about our boy Warschauer," he said.

"Why? What's he done?" I asked.

"It's not so much what he's done as who he is," Wachtler replied.

"He's just a Polish DP on his way through just like thousands of others."

"That might be, Jack. It also might be that he was deliberately sent here as an informer."

"An informer?" This was hard to believe. "An informer for whom? For what?" I wanted to know.

Here I must interrupt my story once again to fill in important historical background. Abduction of targeted DP's by the Soviets, or by their associates the Benno Blum gang, was a highly organized operation. They did not want to abduct the wrong person. Even worse, they did not want a planned attempt to go wrong, to misfire as many often did. When these failures occurred, the effects were to worsen relationships and cooperation at the Four-Power Command level and also to send a wave of fear and apprehension through the camps already trembling in dread.

To guarantee results, and to make sure they had the right person in their sights, an advance team of spies was formed to infiltrate the camps, mingling with the great mass of DP's, posing as just another semi-anonymous refugee. The commonplace lack of documentation made such infiltration relatively easy. Catching these spies was much more difficult. Once inside the camp, the informer had to operate with the utmost care; first, in identifying the targeted individual, and then getting word out together with a workable plan for the "snatch." Not at all easy, which explains why there were so many abortive attempts.

Organized and staffed as it was, a real counter intelligence operation was outside the IRO's mission and resources. The army had its own counter-intelligence operatives, but no presence, secret or otherwise, in the camps. As a result, the problem of spy-catching in the camps by default fell to the DP's themselves, with neither direction nor encouragement from above. Separating suspicion from certainty was almost impossible, especially given the age-old hatreds between different ethnicities or nationalities. A denunciation of one DP by another could easily be the result of personal or inherited animosities - who could tell? Mistakes were made. In some DP camps, it was not at all unusual for the IRO to find the corpse of a murdered inmate lying outside the camp perimeter in the early morning. Who was guilty? Very hard to say. But one thing was certain: that the kidnapping spies were actively at work at their murderous trade inside the camps.

I had heard these informer stories before, but always associated them with what went on in the larger camps. I had trouble believing that anything like this was possible in our little community.

"Do you really believe that a kidnapping is possible here?" I asked.

"Who knows? We have always to be suspicious," Wachtler replied.

"Do they think Warschauer could be one of these informers?"

"Many do, but they're ready to believe anything about

anybody. Personally, I'm not sure."

"What has been done to make people suspicious?" I asked.

"Well, he doesn't seem to fit in. He keeps to himself except in the English classes. There, he does teach some English, but he also spends a lot of time asking people all sorts of questions about their backgrounds - you know, previous jobs, education, where they lived, associations. Much more questioning than would be normal, especially since he doesn't tell us anything about himself. Also, they don't like his spending all that time in Czechoslovakia and that he speaks such good Czech. Some of the kidnapping gangs have their base there."

"Well, I'll say something to him about sticking to the point in the English classes,
but -"

"No, don't do that please." Wachtler interrupted. "We want him to do whatever he wants to do - not feel he's being watched. Please, not to say anything."

"All right. I get your point. But I still feel this is all exaggerated. Fear can easily turn into hysteria, especially in this situation."

"Jack, you're new here, if you will excuse my saying so. I mean no offense. But you have much to learn. I would be very pleased for you to meet one of the refugees here in Bad Aibling. I think you will find him interesting."

Chapter Twenty-One

High Drama Intrigue

This person of interest turned out to be one Count Bninski who came to the office with a young woman introduced as his daughter, although Wachtler later said that no one believed that. The two had been refugees since fleeing Poland, and were now awaiting orders to proceed to the embarkation camp in Bremen. Meanwhile, she worked in the infirmary.

After some preliminary chit chat, Wachtler said, "Herr Bninski, Mr. Barwick believes that DP's have little reason to fear abduction here in Bad Aibling, and that we should not allow ourselves to become hysterical over small suspicions that could easily turn out to be baseless. Am I correct in saying this, Jack?"

"More or less," I replied, anxious to get on with it and hear what Bninski had to say.

"OK, good. Now, Herr Bninski if you would be so kind as to tell Mr. Barwick of your own experiences and why you are here in Bad Aibling."

"Yes I should be most happy to oblige." And with that Bninski launched into his tale of terror and intrigue, the gist of which was that he had escaped two attempts at capture, both times in Vienna, in the American Zone. The first attempt came in the early morning just as he stepped out the door of his apartment building. Two men grabbed both arms and tried to force him through the open door of a waiting car. He succeeded in breaking free and getting back into the building and shutting the locked door. The second time occurred at night in the entertainment district. A stranger stopped him to ask the time and used that moment to cover his face with a cloth soaked in chloroform while two other men seized his legs

High Drama Intrigue

just as a car pulled up with the door open. In the melee, his daughter held fast to his coat, screaming. People stopped to look. The abductors tried to say that their victim was ill and they were taking him to the hospital, but his daughter kept screaming "Helfe, helfe - entfuhring." The noise had quickly attracted more people so that the few seconds critical for success were gone, and the kidnappers fled.

Even the American Zone was dangerous. Bninski knew he had to get out of Vienna and decided to apply for DP status. The IRO headquarters where applications were made and processed was in the Schwarzenberger Platz which unfortunately was situated just inside the Russian Zone. As a choice for the IRO location, it was terrible. DP's were afraid to go there - Bninski as well, even in broad daylight. But he decided to risk it. Because of his history, Bninski and his daughter were given priority status and flown out of Vienna, across the Russian Zone of Austria to Linz, just over the Enns River. The Russian Zone began on the other side - much too close for Bninski. He wanted to get as far to the west as he could. After much negotiation, both he and his daughter were temporarily directed to Bad Aibling, largely because Bad Aibling needed help in the infirmary, and she had been a licensed medical technician.

"My goodness, what a story!" I was most impressed. "And is it now OK for you? Do you still feel threatened - in danger?"

"Always," he replied. "I never go out unless I have to. I know they want me and have not given up."

"Why do they want you?" I asked. "Do you know?"

"I have a good idea," he said, and pulled a box containing several photo prints out of his briefcase. The prints were quite clear and showed what looked like army barracks set among pine trees with soldiers walking around or in small formations.

"Why are these important? They all look pretty ordinary to me," I said.

"Maybe to you," Bninski replied. "But not to Soviet Intelligence. You could not be expected to know, but this is a camp in the Katyn Forest in Poland. Those soldiers in the foreground are Russians in Russian uniforms. Those in view in the rear are Polish officers, lined up, waiting to be taken away and shot. The Katyn Forest Massacre - perhaps you have heard of it."

Of course I had. The Katyn Forest Massacre - an incident of bitter dispute between Germany and Russia over an atrocity committed in Poland at the very beginning of World War II. At that time the Polish army had been quickly defeated by the Germans. Remnants in that part of Poland invaded by Russia were quickly seized, incarcerated and, along with a miscellaneous group of civilians, were taken to the Katyn Forest in the extreme eastern part of Poland, where they were shot and thrown into a mass grave. This burial site immediately became the subject of mutual recriminations between Nazi Germany and Stalinist Russia. Each accused the other of committing a dastardly act. The struggle was still going on and one could easily believe either country to be guilty. Evidence that would have settled the issue was lacking, which put a premium on anything that would decide the questions of guilt one way or the other. Hence, the value of Bninski's pictures.

"So as long as you have these pictures in your possession, you feel yourself to be in danger?" I asked.

"Absolutely - yes."

"Even here in Bad Aibling?"

"Not as bad as Vienna, but their people are everywhere. They move about freely, right here in the American Zone, operating with the full knowledge of the authorities. So, yes - definitely. I do feel threatened. I almost never go out, and when I do it is always with a group, and I keep close to them."

"And your daughter?" "The same."

Good night! I felt as though I had suddenly landed in the middle of a Graham Greene novel of terror and intrigue, like Joseph Cotton in that movie, "*The Third Man*", which I had seen back in London. Now here I was up to my ears in the real thing.

When we were alone I asked Wachtler, "so you think Waschauer is here to put the finger on Bninski?"

"Not necessarily just Bninski. These people work from a list of 'most wanted.' Bninski would definitely be one, but there could be others. The fact that there doesn't seem to be a fixed pattern whom they grab makes everyone nervous. Each one thinks, 'It could be me.' "

Not long after that, on his own initiative Warschauer came to the YMCA office. In answer to my questions, he said that the English classes were going well and that he and Frau Schultz were on good terms. "But that is not why I am here to see you, Mr. Barwick," he said. And then there followed this ominous conversation.

"Oh. well, how can I help you?" I asked.

"It is that yesterday they put another one in my room - a new one. Slivic is his name. And I think he is crazy," he replied.

"What do you mean, crazy?"

"Well, back home he is a carpenter, and he bring all his tools with him, in a big box. And he look at me kind of funny. And he say, 'These good tools.' Then he take out a big hammer and he say 'This a good hammer - good for lots of things,' and then he show me an ice pick and he say, "This little guy, he good for lots of things too. They are my friends. My tools - where I go they go,' he say.

"Mr. Barwick, this Slivic not right. He make me very nervous. He talk to himself. I tell you in Jesus name, I am afraid of him. Can you do something for me?"

I said I would try, but that room assignments are made by camp administration, and I generally have no part in it. But I promised that I would try.

So I did. I saw Doug Dean a day or two later but he was not particularly encouraging. "If we took all the crazies out of here, there wouldn't be anyone left in the camp. Besides, Slivic has the right to keep the tools of his trade with him. I don't want to interfere in room assignments unless it's a clear danger or a compassionate case."

"Who actually made the room assignment?" I asked.

"That's Loukie's job but she always consults with Brazdis to make sure there's no conflict."

"So you're saying that Brazdis had a part in the assignment?"

"Definitely. He recommended it. We trust his judgment in cases like this."

Warshaeur took the bad news without comment, his head down, looking at the floor. But this was definitely not the same man who had arrived in my office only a few weeks ago. Then, he

Picking Up the Pieces

had been calm, composed, confidant. Now he was all nerves, restless in his chair, his eyes darting from one corner of the room to another, with jerky animated gestures as he spoke - someone, it seemed, under a great strain.

When I told Wachtler that Brazdis had engineered the room assignment, he only smiled with a knowing air. Later he came back to the office, shaking his head. "The rumor is that there is more to Warschauer's story than we knew. We have contacts in the Salzburg camp. When we asked them about Warschauer they said he acted suspicious there too - he had a big interest in people's background. Also, he was absent from the camp for long periods. The Soviet Repatriation Mission is located just down the road there toward Hellbrun. They think he might have been brought into Austria that way and was working under their direction."

That same day the Belgian infirmary physician, Dr. Louis Favre, called me. "Anything special going on over there at the YMCA?" he asked.

"Not especially." I replied. "Why do you ask?"

"Your chap, Warschauer - Wladislas Warschauer - has been in twice to see me. The man is a nervous wreck. I wouldn't be surprised if he had some kind of a nervous collapse. The first time I gave him something to calm his nerves, but he came back saying he was completely unable to sleep, hadn't slept in a week. He even said he was afraid to go to sleep. Weird. So I wondered if there was anything in his work that could be a cause."

"No, Louie, nothing over here to explain it," I lied.

"Well, most of these people have seen enough to drive anyone crazy. I may increase his dosage of sleeping medication. I'd appreciate it if you kept an eye on him and let me know if there's any more trouble - if things get more serious."

"Certainly, Louie. I appreciate your interest."

Things had now reached a point where I was genuinely concerned about what to do. What was my role in all this? I felt like a cork bobbing about on the surface of waters with deep, dangerous currents. Was this all a manufactured intrigue - people's overheated imaginations? Or were those real flesh and blood threats? And what should I do with the little bit of knowledge that was in my possession? Above all, I didn't want to see the YMCA program damaged by whatever might happen. Did that mean taking my little tale to Doug Dean and the IRO, and probably get laughed out of the room as a naïve alarmist? That idea was not appealing. If only I had someone with understanding and mature judgment with whom it was possible to discuss the situation. That should have been Brazdis, but now I felt that he was a major player in the whole conspiracy. Increasingly, I felt that the pace of events was accelerating and that we were moving rapidly toward some sort of a climax.

Two days later Warschauer again came to the office, for the second time a completely different person. Instead of restless movement, shifting body positions and wild gestures, he was now slow to move and with muddled speech. His eyes, when he raised his head to look at me, seemed unfocused. His mood was one of total dejection, as though he had fought a battle, lost, and had given up. At the same time, what I could see was not too hard to explain: Dr. Favre had done exactly what he said he was going to do - given him a stronger dose of medication to help him sleep. It was as simple as that, I persuaded myself.

"Mr. Barwick, would it be all right - I like to be excused from the English class for a day or two? I don't feel good. I can't sleep. At the infirmary they say it sleep I need. But I can't do that in my room. Slivic is always there."

"Yeah, sure. I can't help with the sleeping, but I can tell Frau Schultz not to expect you for a few days."

I was still sitting there trying to think my way through this sinister scenario when there was a knock, and Wachtler walked in and sat down.

"I think we are coming to an end of our *schauspiel* - our little drama," he said.

"An end - what kind of end?" I asked. "I assume you're talking about the person who just left."

"About Warschauer, yes. He didn't look very good. Did not answer my greeting. Well, he will have his chance to explain everything."

"How is that?" I asked. "Explain everything to whom?"

"They are going to put him on trial. The whole thing is very

Picking Up the Pieces

secret. All we have now is rumor. No one knows when. We don't even know who, but everyone assumes it will be Brazdis and his wife plus one or two others. It will be DP justice - fast, efficient. A lot more than he would get back where he comes from."

"Suppose he's found guilty, what will happen to him?"

"He'll never see the sun come up."

"And if he's innocent?"

"He can't run. Here in a DP camp just to be accused is about the same as guilty in peoples' minds. These rumors that brought him to trial will follow him wherever he's sent. Some fanatic could easily decide to take matters into his own hands."

"My God, Laszlo, this is awful. Even if he's guilty, I can't just stand by and act as if I don't know what's going on. Just the thought of that guy Slivic gives me the creeps. I have no doubt why he was put in Warschauer's room. I feel I must take this upstairs."

"Jack, take my advice, don't do it. You have nothing to go on except what I've told you in confidence, and I'll deny everything. So will everyone else. You'll look like a fool and do yourself and the YMCA a lot of harm. I like you and don't want to see you get hurt."

Of course he was right. But to sit there and do nothing with someone's life possibly in the balance was almost more than I could bear. Fortunately, the suspense abruptly ended.

I had just gotten to my desk the following morning when Wachtler arrived. "It's over," he said.

"The trial you mean?" He nodded. "What happened?" I asked.

"The version I get is that they think he is guilty of being a Soviet spy, but there is no conclusive evidence, at least not enough to warrant punishment. But they told him it would be best if he left the camp, even if he had to get out of the DP program."

"Where is Warschauer now?"

"He stayed away from his room all day yesterday and never went back last night after the trial. He's left the camp for sure. I think his handlers pulled him. He could have gone out hidden in the five o'clock laundry pick-up. It's so early because we have same day service. Yeah, I think they waited til the last minute for a verdict, and then pulled him. The whole thing looks planned to me. He's not out there today, just wandering the streets of Bad Aibling, you can be sure."

"So you think he was guilty?"

"I wasn't sure at first, but I am now."

A dozen unanswered questions were whirling around in my head. "I don't quite see why he didn't run away. There was always a good chance of being found guilty, and he was obviously terrified of Slivic - said so himself. Why not just take off?"

"Because he was just as terrified of the people he was working for as he was of vigilantes here in the camp. And they wanted him to stay, right up to the end. Poor devil, they were probably holding a wife, a child, a girlfriend hostage back in Prague. You do what we say, or else, my friend. These are very bad people, Jack."

I had not thought of that angle. Poor bastard, I actually began to pity him. Then another thought intruded. "If you're right, Lazlo, this was a planned operation that went on for several months. He must have been reporting in from time to time, and receiving orders - any idea on how they communicated?"

"I do, but you'll not want to hear it."

"Of course, I do."

"I think Halemba and his boys were the go-betweens. Selling the cigarettes, liquor, coffee, nylons, and so forth was all part of the payoff. Again, it's just a suspicion, a plausibility - I can't prove it. The trouble is that by the time you can prove it, it's too late."

The last left me stunned. The more I thought about this whole episode the more confused I became. Here at Bad Aibling, my little YMCA program had developed into the core of an international criminal conspiracy with peoples' lives hanging in the balance. An employee a DP Soviet spy, English lessons perverted to personal information gathering methods, a youth program for smugglers and criminal couriers, and by popular acquiescence, my chief administrator the head of a clandestine vigilante kangaroo court with powers of life and death. It was all totally unbelievable. And at the end, I was no clearer in my mind as to what I could have done about it than I was before.

I had plenty of time to think about it on the train traveling up to Bremen two days later. A new set of orders had just arrived authorizing my transfer to the Embarkation Center, Lager Grohn, to be in charge of the DP Orientation Program located there.

Chapter Twenty-Two

Camp Grohn

The train trip from Munich to Bremen lasted most of the night. Dawn disclosed a different landscape once we had passed through the Harz mountains into the North German plain of Lower Saxony: Flat pastures, interlaced by small waterways, stretched to the horizon, with great half-timbered farmhouses and outbuildings at intervals to claim ownership. Instead of snow-covered Alps, masses of wind driven North Sea clouds filled the sky.

The contrast between Bad Aibling and the DP camps at Lager (Camp) Grohn was just as striking as the landscape - fittingly so, since Grohn was the end of the European part of the DP experience, the embarkation point from which refugees would sail to take up new lives in Canada, Australia, or the US. Apart from the Jews, most of whom had gone earlier, every DP leaving Europe would pass through Camp Grohn in Bremen.

My first impressions of Camp Grohn was that this could not be a DP camp. I could easily have imagined myself back in the USA: modern brick buildings, well tended lawns, trees, and shrubbery, with convenient sidewalks criscrossing the open spaces, beside perfectly maintained roads. Not a sign of deterioration or of bomb damage, perhaps because the facility was located on the outskirts of Bremen whose center had been bombed heavily. Like Bad Aibling, Grohn had been a Luftwaffe installation, but one more dedicated to housing personnel, so that the impression it created was that of a larger modern institutional complex capable of accommodating thousands of people. Compared to the quonset huts, flimsy shacks and tents that passed for troop housing in the US during World War II, Lager Grohn went beyond any GI's service experience.

Also, for its postwar role in the DP operation, Grohn was an ideal choice. All the tributaries of the great river of refugees along which the DP's progressed, through dozens of camps, finally came together at Grohn, The actual port from which they would set sail was at Bremerhaven, about forty miles distant. Meanwhile, they would be housed at Grohn until final administrative details could be taken care of: security, health check, transportation, etc.

Here I must correct an earlier misstatement. There were actually two DP camps at the embarkation center: Grohn, and Tirpitz, a smaller camp a few miles to the south. The YMCA conducted its program in both locations under two leaders, with more attention given to Grohn. Tirpitz was only a shabby collection of dormitories plus an administration building.

Because all of the functions took place in one general area, including the dramatic scene of shipboard transfer, and because of its image of modern twentieth century efficiency, Lager Grohn quickly became the preferred destination for visiting dignitaries. In a one day visit, they could learn what they needed to know about the DP program, and take back to their church, club or political base an enthusiastic report of what they had seen. The IRO administration never lost sight of its public relations mission, which translated directly into widespread popular confidence that the program was well run, and its supporting dollars well spent.

Administratively, Camp Grohn was Bad Aibling multiplied by ten. The lower camps had been no more than holding pens for housing masses of refugees while an attempt was made to determine whether these individuals were all legitimate applicants, or if hiding among them were criminals, Nazi party activists, and communist subversives. This task of separating the sheep from the goats was centralized in Berlin at the Berlin Documents Center, or BDC as it was commonly referred to. At the BDC, an enormous trove of information had been assembled from every conceivable source: local and military records, court proceedings, employment data, newspapers, a mixture of verified as well as "raw" or unverified allegations. Not ideal, perhaps, but remarkable considering the magnitude of the task and the difficulty of collecting information in a dozen different languages, going back into the prewar years. This "BDC check" was a crucial step in obtaining "clearance." and one from which appeal was almost impossible. No reason was given for denial since the BDC did not want to reveal its sources. Once clearance had been granted, it was simply a matter of managing the flow of refugees in the pipeline as they arrived at Grohn, and then coordinating that incoming population with the arrival and departure of ships to their final destination.

Because the feeder camps had little administrative responsibility, the IRO staffs there were relatively limited, just large enough to take care of small, transient populations. At Grohn, processing entered its terminal stage, certifying that all previous steps had been complied with, including a final physical examination. Three large administrative groups were in charge of managing this complex step. As in Bad Aibling, there was the IRO with overall responsibility, and a staff to grind out the details. Then came the Vol Agencies, including several who had not been present in Bad Aibling: Church World Service, the National Catholic Welfare Conference (NCWC), Hebrew Immigrant Aid Society (HIAS) and others, each with a substantial staff.

All through the emigration process, the role of the Vol Agencies - especially the churches - was extremely important. It was they who organized and managed what would happen to the DP's once they reached their country of destination. I was not familiar with how this transpired in Canada or Australia, but in the US it was primarily local church groups who located an availible sponsor. This could be an organization or individual who was willing to guarantee housing and employment to a DP emigrant for a period of at least one year. It also meant, sight-unseen, in collaboration with their overseas representative, finding a reasonable matchup between the individual DP and an available job in the US. Everything else in the whole DP program was simple preparation for this crucial final step.

The third group in this process was the US Displaced Persons Commission (DPC) which had offices throughout Germany and Austria, but not at Bad Aibling. The DPC had been formed by the US Congress under the Displaced Persons Act of 1948 to supervise and coordinate the flow of refugees and their eventual resettlement in the US. This meant working closely with the IRO and the Vol Agencies at all stages of the process. It also meant sole responsibility for security clearances. It was the Displaced Persons Commission that operated the Berlin Documents Center (BDC), working closely with various allied intelligence sources.

Considering that this massive administrative apparatus had been created from scratch in the chaotic years after 1945, it is a tribute to the spirit of western international cooperation and United Nations leadership that made success possible - and not just senior UN leadership, but also the quality of its mid-level management at regional and local sites. To this, add the volunteers that staffed Vol Agencies activities: mostly young persons such as myself - inexperienced, unprofessional, naïve, but skillfully placed alongside DP's with administrative talent, to form energetic, competent teams.

For the USDP Commission, a mixed judgment is necessary. The trouble went back to the Act of Congress which created it. With so much of major international importance going on at the time, creation of the DP Act itself received little attention, and the top level appointments scant oversight. The entire project was seen as one of moral obligation, but not involving national security, which automatically meant third priority status. Members of Congress were given the task of appointing DPC personnel - in other words, a job bonanza for loyal political supporters, no prior education or experience necessary. The result was a stream of relatives, sons of relatives, job seekers and hangers on of every description. But also intermixed with this tacky lot, in about equal proportions, were persons of genuine quality and ability, having arrived there more or less by accident. That it all worked as well as it did was a minor miracle.

The people who made all this happen - IRO staff, DP Commission personnel, and Vol Agencies - were housed together in the Bremen Hotel, a two story brick structure spread out in a parklike setting on the edge of the city. Surrounded by tennis courts, a swimming pool and other recreational facilities, the Bremen hotel was more like a resort than a typical commercial hotel. It stood in total contrast to the city center where whole burned out sections still remained from the allied bombing raids.

Other than a curiosity visit, there was little incentive to go downtown. Life at the Bremen Hotel organized itself into a kind of ghetto existence: privileged international personnel almost completely separated from the local German community, very much like an embassy or diplomatic enclave. There was no obvious hostility or bad feelings between the two groups, just that they existed in parallel universes.

For the international group, it was work all day, Monday through Friday, regular business hours, then play at night and on weekends, with local hires to cook, wash dishes, make beds and clean rooms; then cocktails at the end of the day, dinner usually with the few friends, and from time to time organized parties. In case boredom set in, there were side trips down into the Harz mountains or to resorts up on the Baltic sea. The irony in all this is that back home Americans believed that those who opted for foreign service did so at great personal sacrifice if not actual danger. The Iron Curtain was less than a hundred miles to the east.

The YMCA program to which I was assigned as assistant to the leader - an Esthonian DP named Ed Manniko - was a more polished version of what we had in Bad Aiblling. Emphasis was now on what life would be like in a totally new environment as well as the obligations and responsibilities of US citizenship, and along with that the ability to communicate in English. This meant English classes and an orientation program. Both responsibilities were assigned to the YMCA.

The English classes, each with its own teacher, were under the direction of Frau Koenig - the mirror image of Frau Schultz - who managed her domain with great attention to the rules of grammar, and was totally unreceptive to any outside ideas or suggestions, which were ignored or dismissed as "interference."

Orientation was aimed at reinforcing the goals of the DP Act as legislated by Congress. Two of these goals were: (1) Dispersion and (2) Self-sufficiency. "Dispersion" meant avoiding the tendency of immigrant groups to clot together in big cities to form ethnic enclaves. By and large, this had been the history of 19th and 20th century US immigration. Therefore, an intensive effort was made to find DP sponsorship all across the country, especially away from large urban population centers. As we have just seen, the churches played a key role in this. But it was also important to minimize "culture shock" so that the new arrival not feel totally isolated and unable to relate to the new environment..

"Self-sufficiency" meant ensuring that incoming DP's would not become welfare cases or public charges. To this end, each individual or head of household was guaranteed a job to last at least twelve months. This was a tricky area legally, since any American worker is free to leave his employer for whatever reason, and in the case of DP's any agreement was not enforceable. So the matter was left to each individual DP as a "moral obligation." along with the veiled threat that leaving one's employer constituted a violation of the agreement and could pose a threat to one's alien status.

Implementing the goals were classes, posters, brochures, and official-looking letters covering:
- Your rights and responsibilities as an alien
- Your path to American citizenship
- Employment and job security
- Sponsorship and housing
- Community resources

The centerpiece and showcase of the orientation program was a large (6'x 8') scale model of an American supermarket, constructed with meticulous attention to detail by a master craftsman whose name unfortunately went unrecorded. Each section was carefully labeled: produce, canned goods, meat, housewares, frozen-foods, etc., etc. This miniature cathedral of commerce seemed to excite more curiosity than admiration - it was too far removed from the DP's actual experience, which even in the best of times had consisted only of a small local market, the butcher, the baker, etc. This supermarket model may not have made a clear impression on the DP's, but as an expression of national pride it did wonders for visiting Americans. As much as a single display could, it encapsulated the material side of everything America had to offer, and as such was an instant success, tangible proof that American tax dollars for the orientation program were being well spent.

All this, of course, was simply buildup to emigration. As the fateful day moved ever closer, emigrant tensions visibly increased.

In many cases, after so many years, there were still unresolved issues of health or security awaiting final clearance. When it was finally granted at the last minute, their relief was overwhelming. When clearance was denied, as it was from time to time, the impact was catastrophic. Especially heart-rending was the situation of families traveling together, often including three generations. Not untypical was the dilemma created at the final health examination when x-rays revealed lung spots in an aged grandparent - clearance automatically denied. What to do? After enduring so much, to have come to this - it was bureaucratic cruelty compounded.

Those with clearance were given twenty-four hour notice, time to g baggage organized and personal gear assembled for the short rail journey downriver to Bremerhaven where one or more ships were tied up at the wharf. The loaded train pulled up on tracks directly next to the ships, with excited faces crowding the windows. At a given signal, unloading began, forming a long line of individuals next to the train. Each person wore a large identification tag - no exceptions, small children as well as adults. A gangway led from the wharf up to the ships rail. In the line people strained, listening for their boarding numbers as they were called out. One by one they moved up to the foot of the gangway where a sailor in uniform checkedtheir ID tag, and then up to the rail where another sailor did acondcheck.From there, they disappeared into the ship's interior to begin a new chapter in thejourney that had brought them this far.

Chapter Twenty-Three

Mae Ballou

Presiding - I should say, "reigning" - over our little group at Grohn was a most unlikely individual. Whereas we were in our twenties and thirties, she - a woman - was in her early seventies. Whereas we were mostly liberal indoctrinees, children of the New Deal years, she was a society clubwoman from the midwestern steel and iron industrial aristocracy. And she looked the part: an imposing figure, with white carefully coiffed upswept hair and pince-nez eyeglasses that helped her survey the world with an attitude of equal parts good humor and old-fashioned scorn, but in which the good humor always prevailed, and the scorn was mostly for theatrical effect.

Her name was Mae Ballou, nee Cosgrove, and how she happened to be at Camp Grohn is an interesting story in itself. The Cosgroves were immigrant Irish, landing in Braddock, Pennsylvania just about the time Andrew Carnegie was looking for a few big men to run his steel mills then rising on the banks of the Monongahela River. In no time the elder Cosgrove became shop foreman, plant superintendent, and finally an officer in what was by then the US Steel Corporation. His two sons - Mae's brothers - followed as pillars of the Pittsburgh banking establishment, one later as chairman of Continental Oil. Meanwhile, Mae married the CEO of the Cleveland Light Rail Transportation Company, Clarence Ballou, a handsome but balding young Irishman. Lacking hair, he was then and forever afterward known in the family as "Curly."

Mae Ballou spent the depression and wartime years in the role of Cleveland society clubwoman and hostess: arranging charity balls, dances and debutante parties, playing bridge in the afternoon, with little awareness of life outside her immediate circle, to say nothing of the world beyond. Never well educated - "not really necessary" - she absorbed the rules, rumors and prejudices of a plutocracy only one generation removed from its Irish roots. But there was still a lot of old Ireland in her - down to earth, warm, fun-loving and deeply religious.

In 1947 "Curly" Ballou dropped dead of a heart attack, leaving a wife still brimming over with energy and love of life. Alone in an empty house, she found that her old society routine suddenly had little appeal.

Enter Monsignor Ryan, a transformative figure who could see beneath artifice into the real person beneath; a man who could recognize underutilized talents and energy, and knew how these could be used by his Church to the benefit of all concerned. The Roman Catholic Church in the US was at that very moment developing its response to the refugee emergency in Europe and passage of the DP Act in the US. A relief program was to be set up as part of the National Catholic Welfare Conference (NCWC) with offices and personnel in Europe to help prepare DP's for emigration. It was necessary to find people capable of representing the Church and managing each overseas office. Looking at Mae Ballou, Msgr. Ryan saw a potentially great ambassador for the Church, and persuaded his superiors to offer her a job in Germany at Bremen.

When I arrived, she had already become a center of attraction, drawing people to her effortlessly and exerting an influence throughout the camp far above and beyond her actual official position. All this was done through sheer force of personality; she had no conscious management or administrative skills, and wisely left that part of the job to an assistant. Her role resembled that of the famed Washington hostess of the period, Pearl Mesta, whose parlor had become the meeting place for diverse persons and opinions where, despite political differences, everyone had a good time.

Mae Ballou's Irish heritage contained an ability to talk to anyone, high or low, as equals, born out of the fact that only one generation separated her from centuries of poverty. This, plus a genial, sunny personality, prevented her from becoming the formidable grande dame that her appearance suggested.

It was a case of the right person in the right job - a job that above all required large feelings of compassion and human sympathy - qualities easy to lose as one grew overburdened by the never-ending procession of hopeless cases. To Mae, each of these became a crusade; and she battled officialdom on all sides: the DP Commission, the IRO, even her own Church, to see that wrongs were righted, and rights not ignored.

There was one case involving an extremely attractive Russian girl traveling with family. Her misfortune happened to be a gorgeous face and figure which had attracted the attention of practically every man in the camp, including me. Under such pressure even the strongest resolve can bend, and the poor girl found herself to be pregnant. When, at the final health check, this condition was discovered, her clearance was denied and her name removed from the embarkation roles. Bad enough, but an unsympathetic DP Commission clerk added the phrase "moral turpitude" to the file. Now, all hope of ever joining her family in the US was gone, not just now, but forever.

At this point, Mae Ballou entered the fray, threatening to hold up dozens of cases, if this situation was not corrected. A devout faith of Catholic teachings and dogma were no impediment where issues of human frailty and compassion were concerned. Only by her promise to take the whole issue to another level did the DPC agree to drop the moral turpitude issue, and sweet Svetlana was permitted to sail.

As I have said, Mae Ballou's gregarious nature and open friendly personality made her the ruling social presence at the Bremen Hotel, sometimes in her room, or in the bar at the end of the day. It was a free-floating circle, joined by anyone in need of a drink or convivial conversation. It included a group of four or five young men from the IRO, others from the DPC and myself from the YMCA. Women were not excluded, and from time to time would join in, but the regulars were young men. As one might have guessed, Mae Ballou liked young men. Having them around made her feel young again - as if she needed it - the Queen and her coterie of courtiers, trading news, gossip, stories, opinions and discussing issues of the day.

There were plenty of those at that time. Under the aegis of the United Nations, the US had just declared war on North Korea. Not far from where we sat, the Soviets had blockaded Berlin, and the Allied airlift flew day and night to sustain the city. And yet here, only a few miles removed from the very epicenter of the Cold War, there was no fear, no sense of crisis, no talk of emergency evacuation. Headlines in the newspapers found no echo in the bar of the Bremen Hotel.

What did turn discussion into animated debate was politics, also the issues raised by big business, particularly as it had evolved in US manufacturing and heavy industry. This was a sensitive subject. Pittsburgh and its steel mills symbolized industrial capitalism, the source of Mae's family's wealth and that of all of her friends, as well as of the entire region. To Mae, the steel mills were cathedrals of a secular religion; detractors were all heretics: socialists and anarchists or college graduates misled by too much education, meaning those of us seated at the table who ventured to raise questions.

Her deepest wrath was reserved for labor unions - "A bunch of good-for-nothings who want to tear down what others have sacrificed to build up." From there the discussion went as follows:

"But Mae, why shouldn't workers get a living wage and some protection against business downturns?"

"Because the average worker likes what he has. This is all caused by a bunch of outside troublemakers - union organizers who come in only to get things stirred up."

"Well, if the average worker is so content, why do they join unions? And why do the owners do all they can to prevent union elections?"

"Owners don't want to see a great industry go to rack and ruin for a bunch of empty promises that these agitators hold out just to put themselves in power. They have no idea how to run a big steel plant, much less an industry. It's power they want."

"OK, but what's wrong with sharing power? After all, workers make a big contribution to the success of the business. Why shouldn't they have at least some say in how the business is run?"

Mae was a staunch defender of the status quo. But when she

ran out of arguments, or wearied of the exchange, she would retort, "Stuff and nonsense." Or - "When you boys have had a chance to grow up, you'll understand what I'm saying" - always with a twinkle in her eye and a good humored laugh.

At this point, in the interests of providing a complete portrait, honesty compels me to concede that Mae Ballou had one small weakness where class diistinctions were concerned. She was in no sense a money snob, or a family snob, or a society snob, although she had the credentials for all of these. No, her particular weakness emerged in the presence of old world aristocracy, even minor aristocracy, of which there were a great many floating around at this time. A "Von" preceding the family name always earned a few points of special consideration, a "Baron" - a few more. "Count," or "Graf," was definitely worth special accommodation, even inconvenience, while "Furst" or "Furstin" - prince or princess - deserved a major effort.

One day a note arrived requesting Mae Ballou to do the honor of taking tea with His Royal Highness Prince Louis Ferdinand and his wife Princess Kyra, who were then living in a Bremen suburb not far from the hotel. Mae Ballou, that hardened society hostess, was nervous as a schoolgirl on her first date at this prospect of tea with actual European royalty. Prince Louis Ferdinand was the younger son of the late Kaiser Wilhelm II, last of the Hohenzollern emperors, who could arguably be accused of starting World War I. Princess Kyra was a Romanoff in the direct royal line, niece of Czar Nicholas II, executed by the Bolsheviks in 1918. "How should I address them?" Mae wanted to know.

Properly tutored by monarchist sympathizers in the camp, she managed to spend a very enjoyable afternoon. Her spontaneous naturalness - just what Europeans liked about Americans - helped take the edge of stiffness and formality off the occasion. "I think it would have been a little stuffy if I hadn't been there," was her own appraisal. Apparently they thought so too, because a short time later she was invited for an afternoon of bridge.

With a lifetime of bridge-playing behind her, it should come as no surprise that Mae Ballou was an excellent player, good enough to hold her own in any but professional circles. At any rate, the afternoon was a success, and the invitation was followed by others. On one of these occasions a critical invitee had dropped out, and Princess Kyra asked Mae Ballou to bring a bridge-playing friend, so she asked me. By this time she had become very blasé about hobnobbing with royalty, but feeling very much out of my league, I voiced my concerns.

"Oh, don't give it a thought. They're just like anyone else, and your game is more than good enough."

I wouldn't say that they were just like anyone else, but my bridge game didn't disgrace me. There were just the four of us around a game table that was a permanent fixture in the drawing room which looked out through French doors onto a garden. A uniformed maid served coffee. Princess Kyra, a large full-figured woman of upper middle age, seemed a little remote, but Prince Louis Ferdinand took special pains to include me in the conversation. He didn't say so, but if it had been up to him there never would have been war between Germany and the United States. Back in the 20s or early 30s he had lived in the US as a junior employee of the Ford Motor Company, and the result was a lifelong enthusiasm for America and all things American. He was full of questions, many about Detroit and car manufacture - about which I could say very little - but also about Princeton and opportunities for Germans to study there.

On the other side of the room stood a grand piano on which were arranged family portraits in silver frames. Two dominated the group: one of Kaiser Wilhelm II, and the other of Czar Nicholas II, both in full court dress. As I looked at these silent portraits from the recent past, I could not but think of the enormous role these two had played in World War I and the Russian Revolution.

It was another of those moments that occurred from time to time during my years in Europe when history took human form and seemed to be right in the room with me.

Chapter Twenty-Four

Count Potocki

This story of Prince Louis Ferdinand and Princess Kyra brings up the whole subject of monarchism, royalty and nobility which, in the 1950's, still figured as issues in Europe. I was to meet quite a few individuals from this caste, some very ordinary, others quite colorful. The following account may explain why they are no longer in positions of power and influence.

A few pages back, I mentioned that there were two DP Camps in the Bremen area: Grohn and Tirpitz, of which Tirpitz (named after the admiral who created the German navy) was the smaller. The YMCA had decided to operate a program in both camps, each with its own staff. When the time came to pick a leader for the Tirpitz camp program, there didn't seem to be anyone from the DP population who had the necessary qualifications. At that time there was a large percentage of Poles passing through. There was also present and available one Count Potocki and his wife. The count had been a large landowner in prewar Poland, and the Potocki name was traceable through centuries of Polish history. Because of his name and the prestige it carried, the YMCA assumed that he, and by inference the program, would command immediate respect among the DP population.

The trouble was that the count's exalted position in Poland represented not just nobility, but carried over into the Roman Catholic Church, the state religion of Poland, in which he occupied an important position, symbolic of the tie between the nobility and the church. It was questionable for such an important Roman Catholic figure to accept a position in a Protestant quasi-religious organization. On the other hand, it was a paying position, completely secular in its duties, and a way of providing a small income to the now destitute and impoverished count. For this to happen, however, permission had to be granted at the very highest level of the Church - i.e. the Pope. So a petition was drafted and sent to Rome where it was duly considered and approved.

The count took up his duties at Tirpitz but continued to live with his wife in a special apartment that had been assigned to him at Grohn. I visited them there from time to time, and soon became as close a friend as such transient relationships permitted. Clinging to custom, they would invite me for drinks, and I always arrived with a bottle of brandy - he liked Courvoisier - and left it behind on departure.

The count was a handsome man of upper middle age, about six feet tall with patrician features but just a hint of weakness in them. His hands were unusually fine, with long aristocratic fingers and manicured nails. One had the impression that he was very proud of them, as he poured drinks or lit a cigarette in a long enameled holder. He affected an ancient smoking jacket with a tasseled belt and an open shirt with an ascot.

The Countess was a study in contrasts: a peasant type, square jawed, iron gray hair, and steel gray eyes. No hint of weakness here.

Conversation with the count and the countess was not easy, not because they were haughty or uncommunicative - quite the contrary - but because it consisted almost entirely of trivialities: camp gossip and such snippets of scandal from the outside world as reached these remote parts, best if the scandal involved royalty or great wealth.

Is the Queen Consort of England carrying on an affair with a prominent Anglican churchman? Was Prince Philip the best choice as a husband for Queen Elizabeth? Is it true that the heir to the Krupp fortune is homosexual?

Such speculations went on at great length and in great detail. After a few glasses, the mood warmed up, and the count produced an album of photographs with pictures of the family properties back in Poland. There were several, each more enormous than the last: vast, sprawling estates on thousands of acres. When I asked about managing them, he said that he had never been actively involved in the managerial details; they had someone who attended to that. The purpose of the estate, apparently, was to produce an income to support his and the countess's life in the capitals of Europe and his interest in art.

Another glass of brandy and talk turned to their plans for the future. "I don't think America is the place for Elena and me," he said, indicating the countess. "You Americans are too materialistic. Always business, business, business. Old families must fight to keep from being taxed to death and from losing lands and homes where they lived for generations."

"Yes," said the countess. "America is too big, like an immature, adolescent boy, still growing up, with no time for refinement or culture."

I protested that we did have writers and painters the equal of any in the world.

"Come, come now, Jack," replied the count. "You may have them some day, but not now, and not for a long time. Those of your writers I've read are just provincial story-tellers, not by any means universal literary figures. The same goes for music - it's just folk music. Poetry also. Dance, ballet, that doesn't even exist. No, Jack, where art and culture do exist in America is only in one or two big cities, particularly New York, and I couldn't bear to live there in the midst of all that noise."

"Well, where would you like to live?" I asked.

"We're thinking, maybe Estoril, in Portugal. We have friends there. It's a beautiful place and a wonderful climate," he said.

To fill in his description, Estoril, after World War II, had become the favorite landing spot for European aristocracy dispersed by the upheavals of the period. It now formed an enclave all its own where these often still wealhy refugees could reminisce, free from any danger of further expatriation. This was because Portugal remained under the one-man rule of the dictator Salazar, who, along with Franco in Spain, kept the Iberian peninsula free from the pollution of liberal ideas.

"You are probably wondering how we could manage even to entertain such grand ideas," said the countess. "Would you like to know how we will do it?"

"I would," I said, because the question had arisen in my mind.

"Just a minute. I show you," she said mysteriously, and went out of the room.

When she returned she was carrying a small chamois bag. Carefully moving aside glasses and other objects on the coffee table, she loosened the tie on the little bag and poured out a cascade of precious stones, mostly diamonds, including some very large ones, although there were a few emeralds, sapphires and rubies buried in the pile. I knew nothing about the value of jewels, but it seemed to be easily a king's ransom.

"Well, what do you think? Is it not beautiful?" Elena demanded, her face flushed with pleasure and her eyes sparkling.

She stirred them around with a forefinger so that a few hidden below came up to the top. "I shall hate to give them up. This is all that remains of our past life."

The count turned out to be a total failure in his new job. The idea that it was a job demanding dedication and leadership, and not an honorific position conferred on him as personal recognition, seemed not to have occurred to him. The YMCA program became his mini-estate where he reigned as a feudal overlord. His secretary became the estate manager, in effect the real program director. Neither sports nor English classes held any interest for the Count, and these now ran only fitfully with no direction from above.

But there was one area to which he devoted his entire interest and enthusiasm; that was art. Never mind that art education was near the bottom of everyone's priorities. He saw latent skills and talent among the DP population, only waiting to be developed. Everyone, he believed, had the power of self-expression, if only given encouragement and an environment in which this could emerge.

So, while basketballs, volleyballs, and ping-pong paddles gathered dust, orders were placed for easels, oil paints, watercolors, brushes of all types, sculpting clay, tools, etc.. Most of these orders were made on his own initiative, outside the normal requisitioning and approval system. Our first indication of such irregularity came when a bill arrived from the supplier - usually a local German firm.

As these mounted up, our director, Ed Manniko, became more

Picking Up the Pieces

and more frustrated. Finally, upon receiving an invoice for one hundred camels' hair paint brushes of various sizes, he exploded. "I don't know what the hell is going on down there," he said. "It's got to stop, even if we have to get rid of that crazy monkey."

But, just as hiring the count had been difficult, getting rid of him proved even more so. Repeated requests from Manniko to YMCA headquarters in Bad Kissingen came back counseling patience and closer supervision.

Meanwhile, Count Potocki's art program continued with increased participation - even to the point of an organized exhibition, "Kunst der Fluchtlinge" (refugee art). It consisted of about 40 or 50 items, including oil paintings on canvas, several water colors and charcoal sketches; sculpture was represented by a tangle of polished tree branches, also by a figure made from Maxwell House coffee cans. Manniko very reluctantly agreed to have the exhibit shown at Grohn, where it received generally favorable comments.

As time went on, the situation at Tirpitz became clearly out of control. After many exchanges, YMCA headquarters agreed to send its deputy director up for a conference to see if there was some way to bring the errant count into compliance. He, however, did not see it that way, but rather as an opportunity to show off his art program to higher authority - to persons of taste and culture, positioned well above his unsympathetic boss.

"I am delighted," he said. "We will all sit down over drinks, and they will see for themselves what I have done."

When our visiting delegation arrived, his secretary said that the count was with his art class, but that we should go in. We did. It was a large room formerly used as a gym. Now most of the space was taken up by twenty or so "artists" at work: some with easels and oil paints, others with sketch pads and charcoal or water colors. A few were sculpting figures from lumps of clay. But all were working from the same model, which was the count himself, seated on a dais in the center of the room, holding a noble, idealistic pose, head raised, tilted back, with his eyes fixed on a corner of the room. Without changing position even slightly, he acknowledged our presence.

"Just five more minutes, gentlemen. Forgive my holding this

pose, but these artists are not yet sufficiently advanced to work from memory, or using their imagination. That will come. Meanwhile, feel free to look around and observe their interest in what they are doing, even if the results need my help. Just a few more minutes, and we can move into my office."

If the count had expected an educated aesthete from Bad Kissingen sent to review the program with a sympathetic eye, he had to be disappointed. The deputy director who arrived was a gregarious six-foot-six Lithuanian, a former all-Europe basketball star, named Puzinauskas. "Puzy" had been raised from grade-school in YMCA programs, which did not include art. But in addition to being an athlete, Puzy was a diplomat. Without making any commitments, he soothed the count's ruffled feelings and any possible suspicion that the real purpose of the visit was the elimination of the program and himself. No sign that this would happen emerged during our office conference. Instead good feelings prevailed to the extent that the count produced a bottle of Schnapps, and we all drank a toast "to success."

Back at Grohn, the mood was totally different. Manniko led off. "All right, Puzi. Now you've seen it. Does that look like a YMCA program to you? Tell me, how do we get rid of this guy?"

"OK, Ed. I agree. But a mistake was made back there at the beginning, and we're to some degree stuck with it, way up, at the very top, where big names in the Y and the Catholics are concerned to show how well they can work together."

"Yeah, but Potocki is totally out of line."

"Not totally, Ed. Who are you and I to say that art can't be part of our YMCA program? There are folks who give Potocki credit for bringing it in, and who want to see it encouraged in other camps. There are a lot of reasons to be careful here."

"So where does that leave us?"

"Let's let it rest for now. I have some ideas, and there are people I need to talk to who I'm sure can help. OK?"

"If it was anyone but you, Puzi, I'd say no," said Manniko. "I'm sure you'll try. If it doesn't work out, then I'm going to get my own emigration date moved up."

The opposite is what actually happened. Somewhere inside the bureaucratic hierarchies of three organizations, the Roman

Catholic Church, the YMCA, and the USDP Commission, strings were pulled, deals were made, and when the smoke cleared, it was the Count and Countess Potocki whose emigration dates were moved up. The Tripitz program was left to the tender mercies of Ed Manniko, a loss from which European art quickly recovered.

I had left Grohn by that time, but was later surprised to learn that the Count and Countess Potocki did not go to Estoril. I was amazed to hear that instead they had decided to go to Ethiopia, to Addis Ababa, realm of Haile Selassie, the "Conquering Lion of Judah," almost the last of the world's emperors. It was not altogether unfitting that their search for an aristocratic, autocratic kingdom should have brought them this far from Western civilization - a journey back in time.

Chapter Twenty-Five

Occupation Oddities

Up to this point, a succession of interesting characters and stories has almost taken over my narration; and although an attempt has been made to set the DP refugee movement in its historical context, I have not provided the on-site framework within which it took place, that is the occupation of Germany itself.

From a distance it was easy to overlook, but on the spot evidence of the occupation was everywhere. The army requisitioned and assigned living quarters; it set up commissaries and PX's for food and supplies; printed scrip money and gasoline coupons; established recreation areas, and hotels; and wrote laws - even those for hunting and fishing - etc. This wall of privilege was as complete as the victors wanted to make it, with the deliberate purpose of forcing the German people to experience at first hand and personally the humiliating consequences of losing a war, which they themselves had started, and heartily approved of as long as they were winning.

Nevertheless, in contrast, it was also a model occupation, particularly in the British and American Zones. The Nuremberg trials had punished the guilty, no more was needed. In the French Zone, howevr, where French administrators had actually lived through a German occupation, the desire of revenge was more evident; and in the Russian Zone, for all practical purposes, the result was the creation of a separate country, The German Democratic Republic.

My experience was a fairly narrow one: mainly with the DP refugees, the IRO and the DP Commission - no direct relations with German officialdom, and very little with the German people themselves. Nevertheless, one incident illustrates the concern occupation authorities had for German individual rights.

For transportation I had been assigned a little Fiat Doppelino station wagon: a cute, diminutive bug of a car, too weak for the unlimited autobahn speeds, or even capable of inflicting much damage in case of an accident, but a practical vehicle for the times.

I used it for getting around town and occasionally for a longer trip. One day I had driven into the city center and was progressing at moderate speed along a busy street when with no warning a child - a little girl of about ten years - darted out from between two parked cars and into the right front fender of my Fiat. It was a real question as to whether the car struck the child, or the child ran into the car. Probably both. In any case, it was all so sudden I never got my foot on the brake.

I stopped the car and ran to where she was lying. Fortunately she had suffered only shock and bruises. Her mother was present, and together we brought her to a nearby physician, where I remained long enough to hear him declare the child able to return home with her mother, under her own power, after which I filed a report with the military authorities, including the names of several witnesses.

Now here is the point: the concern occupation authorities had that people at all times were to be fully protected, and that no harm come to any German citizen at the hand of any occupation member - civilian or military. Applicable law stated that any case of physical injury to a German national involving an occupation member automatically demanded a full investigation, followed by a courtroom trial. So the process now unfolded in a case that in the US would probably not even have merited a report.

Its final act found me in an occupation courtroom, with an American prosecutor, but no jury, and a presiding American judge. I was accused of "negligent operation of a motor vehicle with resulting injury to one Annamarie Schimmel." The prosecutor was a habitué of the Bremen Hotel bar, and we had had many drinks together. But on the day of the trial, one would never have suspected that we had ever seen each other before. In fact, his demeanor was positively antagonistic as he conducted an accusatory cross-examination. Since courtroom procedures did not provide for a defense attorney, I began to worry for my future. Fortunately, the investigation and police report set forth the circumstances clearly enough so that when I was asked to rise and stand before him, the judge said, "Given the facts of this incident, as determined by a full investigation, I have no alternative but to find John H. Barwick innocent of all charges."

When he asked for further comment, the girl's mother rose and said she was not satisfied, that I did not even come back to visit the child, and that some kind of compensation was in order to assuage pain and suffering. The judge dismissed her complaint with few words.

It was now 1950, five years since the war ended, and in those years Germany had made huge progress economically. From 1946 to 1950 German industrial production increased by more than 300%. Signs of this could be seen on all sides, but most drastically in the cleanup taking place in the bombed out centers of the large cities, where removal of the debris had to occur before rebuilding could begin.

Enter the Canterbury Corporation, which as far as I could see consisted of two young American men and not much more. It did not appear that they had any real office; the Bremen Hotel bar was where they spent most of their time and from which they managed the activities of the corporation. So what was this mysterious business? It was all out in the open. They made no secret of it. The Canterbury Corporation contracted with local labor sources to go into the bombed out parts of the city and remove the steel and iron beams and girders from the fallen structures. These were then assembled for rail shipment to steel mills in Belgium, refashioned to new building specs, and then shipped back to Germany. A small part of the capital seed money was put up by the Canterbury Corporation, but the greater part of the cost was borne by German building firms, using reconstruction funds and Marshall Plan money.

Brilliant! I thought, as I tried mentally to calculate the millions these two were earning simply by being facilitating agents - in the right place at the right time, knowing how to recognize an opportunity and then acting on it. That never would have occurred

Occupation Oddities

to me.

As the occupation went on, more and more authority was transferred back to the German police. American MP's were still in evidence, but local law and traffic enforcement was handed over to the Germans. In areas where speed limits applied, you could easily get a speeding ticket from a German officer. Many American victims had trouble adjusting to this transfer of authority. "Who do you think won the war anyway?" All that got them was the added charge of obstructing an officer in the performance of his duties. This return of authority did a great deal to restore German pride and self-respect without a corresponding return of the old arrogance, and fear that a uniform used to command. Nevertheless there was a certain love of authority the Germans associate with certified position and a uniform, as the following incident shows.

Blood sports - hunting, fishing, etc. - in Europe, unlike the US, have a centuries old history of privilege, reserved for nobility and the upper classes or owners of large estates. There, the animal population was monitored and guarded by professional gamekeepers as a sporting resource, to be enjoyed by the owner and his friends. Conforming to its policies of democratic egalitarianism and the destruction of laws whose sole raison d'etre was maintenance of class distinctions and privilege, the allied authorities reserved hunting and fishing rights only for occupation personnel. A minor humiliation, but one felt keenly in some quarters. In any case, impact of the new restrictions was small; a few soldiers hunted and fished, but by 1950 many had gone home. As law enforcement responsibilities were transferred to German civilian government, in addition to traffic cops there were now also game wardens.

Very few of the civilian occupation personnel had any interest in hunting and fishing, but among those who did, other than myself, was Leon Schertler, an official with the DP Commission. Like most hunting and fishing addicts, he was born to it, among the lakes and woods of Minnesota. He and I shared this addiction and made forays into the lakes, ponds and drainage ditches that dotted the North German landscape around Bremen, where the standard catch was *"hecht"* - pike - some of exceptional size.

One day we heard of a small lake, not far away, locally known for its amusement park, but which we were told also contained pike of enormous size, so we decided to give it a try. At the last moment, Leon tossed a shotgun into the back seat of the car. "Who knows," he said. "We might scare up a few ducks."

The sky was cloudy and calm, the sun just rising through a thick mist at the edge of the lake. A hour or so of casting from our canoe along the shoreline and to the edge of weed patches had yielded not a single strike. Just then a flight of pintails flew in and circled overhead preparatory to landing. Leon dropped his rod, grabbed the shotgun, and squeezed off two rounds. One duck fell, landing close by in the brush along the shore.

We nosed the canoes into the rocks along the lake and were just about to get out, when a figure dressed in a gray uniform and a military style cap materialized out of the bushes. Very official looking.

"Kommen sie hier, bei mir," he commanded.

Unthinkingly we did as he said.

"Jetzt, zeichon sie mir ihre ausweis papiere --- papers," he said.

I was just at the point of reaching for my wallet when I thought, "Who does this guy think he is?" I hadn't helped to invade France in '44 just to be ordered around by some petty official trying out his new authority to see if it fit.

"Wait a moment," I said to Leon, then to the German, "Ja, vielleicht (perhaps). Aber zurerst missen sie uns zeigen ihre offizielle genchmigung. Ich kenne sie gar nichts. (You must first show me your official authorization. I don't know you.")

With that, his whole demeanor underwent a drastic change. The air of not-to-be-questioned authority fell away, to be replaced by one of apologetic confusion. I finally understood what he was trying to say, which was that he had left his official ID and appointment papers *"zu haus."* And that he had not meant to offend us. In fact, we were most welcome to fish in his lake, he would be glad to help us. His only desire was to prevent unlawful poachers from ruining the sport for gentlemen such as ourselves, etc., etc.

Maybe so. But my gut impression was that he had had total confidence in the ability of the uniform to intimidate us. He knew perfectly well that we were not German poachers. And when that authority was questioned and found lacking, he didn't know what to do. For that generation of Germans, I think this little incident had meaning. Winston Churchill once said, "The Germans are either at your knees or at your throat."

However, I can't resist including another little story, one also dealing with the pretenses of position, but this time with an American focus. In a number of places I have noted the constant stream of visitors in Germany to "inspect," and otherwise to inform themselves about the DP program which was still front page news in the American press. They were of all types: politicians, aspiring politicians, religious leaders, and a few oddball types representing no particular constituency.

One of these was a black athlete named Herman Halliday - a basketball player, more than six and a half feet tall, recently retired and now active in some sort of national physical fitness program. His trip was sponsored by the government as a goodwill gesture, although the purpose of his visit was not clear to me.

At any rate, Mr. Halliday was making the rounds for a series of photo-ops: playing basketball with DP children, scoring a free throw, otherwise spreading the word about the good life awaiting refugees once they arrived in the US. He made a convincing picture in his tan gabardine suit, dark skin, flashing a white smile. Admirers crowded around wherever he was, in various ways letting him know how welcome he was, and how totally free from any prejudice they all were.

The party had arrived at the foyer of the Bremen Hotel and paused for a moment. Mr. Halliday stood there smiling, awaiting the cue for his next appearance.

At that moment a small Army "brat" (defined as "a pestilential species, the offspring of US service personnel, to be found mostly in and around US bases") - one of these of about five or six years emerged from the group and stood directly in front of Mr. Holliday, who thought this was another staged photo-op.

"Mister," the little boy said, "are you a nigger?"

There was a momentary hush, then a gasp from the crowd. Mr. Halliday stood transfixed, as though he had just received an assassin's bullet. Then he exploded.

"You bad boy. Who taught you that? Did your daddy teach you that? You need a good spanking. You hear me? You're a bad boy!"

The child, startled at this outburst, began to cry. His mother rushed out to snatch him back into the group which was buzzing with disbelief at what had just happened. Mr. Halliday's handlers gathered around him with soothing words and expressions of horror that such things, although completely untypical, were still possible.

"Please don't take this personally, Mr. Halliday," one of them entreated. "The child didn't know what he was saying."

"I don't care if he didn't. The little bastard needs a good beating - beat some of that racist shit out of him." Still agitated, Mr. Halliday was led away, and the accompanying crowd had now disappeared.

There was a lot to reflect on in this incident, just as there had been with the German game warden.

One aspect of the occupation, previously noted, was that American civilian employees' standard of living far exceeded that for the same work had they been doing in the US. To this disparity were added all sorts of fringe benefits, including one illegal at the time but for the most part, tolerated or at least enforced erratically and with half-hearted effort. This was the resale of goods from the Army PX's and commissaries intended for their personal use.

In terms of the national economy, concern would have been with currency values, raw and manufactured goods shipments, and the balance of payments. At the individual level, it manifested itself in terms of items that could be bought at artificially low, government-fixed prices in the Army PX's and commissaries, and then easily resold to an eager crowd of German middlemen for distribution into the German economy. For the most part, these items were cigarettes, but also coffee, nylons, and liquor. This array was more than enough to add a substantial amount to the average civilian employee's income. Selling was ridiculously easy, and you could make a 900% profit from your weekly ration.

Good enough - or bad enough, depending on your point of view. What was harder to understand was that the law placed no restrictions on goods imported by US occupation personnel through the Army Post Office. And as far as I could see, no attempt was made to determine if these items were actually, as claimed, "solely for personal use."

This huge loophole in the system opened the door for a new class of entrepreneur - by day, a civilian worker for the Army or the DP Commission, in the off-hours an unlicensed large-scale importer and reseller of black market goods.

I wondered why the practice was tolerated. Both the German government and Allied authorities had to know about it - in detail. It was so open. Why didn't they crack down? The best I could figure was that the black market functioned as a safety valve, permitting the import of just enough "luxury" goods to appease demand, at astronomical prices, but without disrupting the rest of the German economy. As thus constituted, it did not expand into mass shipments - freight cars, etc. Scale was limited to Post Office regulations, and what the trunk or back seat of a car would hold. Nor did the items involved go far beyond normal retail household goods. As far as I know, these quasi-civilian retailers never got involved in gasoline or pharmaceuticals.

Even so, they could make a lot of money. I had no contact with Army civilian employees, so I cannot speak for them, but the DP Commission had filled its ranks with more than a few job-seekers from county and state politics, adept at fleecing public treasuries. As political boss Croker once said, "I seen my opportunity, and I took it."

I became particularly friendly with such a one - I'll call him "Harry" - nominated for the DP Commission by his congressman from the Buffalo, New York area. The hours he spent by day processing DP's only took away from his real job at night.

One evening I had come to his room for a drink. He was busy in the kitchen, so I went to hang my coat up in the hall closet. I opened the door but had to immediately close it again to keep boxes stacked from floor to ceiling from falling out.

"What is all that?" I asked.

"Oh, the usual," he said. "Mostly coffee, but some nylons too."

"Who buys it?"

"I've had a wholesaler in town, but too many people are getting into the act with him, so it's worth the trouble to drive a few miles

Picking Up the Pieces

further out. It's easy, and it's legal, as long as you don't get caught selling it."

I rode along out with him one night. Just outside of Bremen we came to a stop. The German police had set up a road block, and cars were backed up for a considerable distance.

"Shit," said Harry. "Wait for me just a minute."

He pulled around the line of cars and went to the side of the road where several police officers were gathered. When he came back, a guard pulled aside the barrier and we drove through.

With a perfectly straight face, Harry said, "That roadblock - that's how they catch those black marketers."

"Yeah," I said, "too close for me, what did you say to them?"

"All I had to do was show them a card, certifying me with Army G2 / Criminal Investigation. I have a buddy there. Actually, I do help them now and then when he has an inquiry involving one of our cases."

During the months I was in Bremen, Harry had commissioned a fifty-foot sailing yacht being built in a shipyard in Finland. He left some time after I did, sailing the boat back to the US with assistance from the builder. I heard the boat was valued at $100,000.

It didn't always work out that well for smugglers. Shortly after my trip with Harry, I was on my way to Salzburg, and had stopped at the border crossing at Freilassing manned by an American soldiers. I had gone inside to fill out some forms for myself and the car at the Sergeant's desk. He was explaining something about vehicle registration to me when there was a sharp bang, like an auto backfire, to which we paid no attention. A minute or two later a voice over the squawk box said, "Hey. Sarge."

"Yeah," the Sergeant said without taking his eyes off the paper.

"You know that national we caught with a car full of contraband cigarettes?"

"What about him?"

"He's dead. Just shot himself while I was moving the boxes."

"Dead, huh? Well, don't let him get away."

Then, to me. "You're OK to go. I gotta get back there before they tell anybody else." Typical Army black humor.

These few snapshots of experience under the occupation, both narrow and untypical, should not obscure the fact that it was the most successful occupation in history, and the same can be said of our administration in Japan. A peace treaty was still three or four years in the future, but the foundations were being laid for a century of German/American friendship. The Berlin airlift, the Marshall Plan, and the threat of communist aggression in the east helped cement this foundation into a solid block on which the German people felt they could rely. It made possible the "economic miracle" of Germany - already well under way, the future reunification of the country and its eventual integration into the European Union.

Chapter Twenty-Six

Salzburg

That unfortunate incident at the autobahn Frielassing border crossing occurred as I was traveling from Bremen to Salzburg. The reason for this trip was that I had just switched employers, from the YMCA to the DP Commission, from a private voluntary organization to the federal government. Although the auspices were different, the nature of the work itself remained practically the same, but with a new title of "Orientation Officer for Allied Zones, Austria". The YMCA was already in Salzburg with a program for Austria. I would be working independently but collaborating with them as a team, helping to fund and carry out the program. The YMCA chief had an office in Salzburg, whereas my immediate DPC superior was located in Frankfurt. For administrative support I would be attached to the DPC in Salzburg, but my actual work site would be Camp Hellbrunn on the eastern edge of the city.

Making this shift to the DPC was not difficult. The transition itself was minimal. Although I liked and admired the work the YMCA was doing in Europe, I had no real identification with the Y itself. With a highly secular outlook, and far from being a practicing Christian, I always felt like a whore in church when the message became too evangelical. As a government agency, the DPC made such considerations irrelevant; despite shortcomings, it was doing an outstanding job of moving large numbers of refugees to the US without divine assistance.

On another level, there were significant differences - mainly material. As a government employee, I now had a government salary - the first real paycheck I had ever received excluding the wartime years, which didn't count. I don't remember how much it was - probably in the $4000 - $4500 range, modest, but with a living allowance of $100/month added, more than enough.

As orientation officer, almost all my work was out at the Salzburg DP camp, but administrative consultations at times required my presence at HQ in town. The actual head of our local DP office was a remote presence with whom I had almost no contact. When and as need arose, my go-to was his second in command, a young man, product of Andover and Yale, only about a year older than I. This background and the fact that his father was a person of consequence in Washington, conferred on him an extra notch of authority, so that he appeared to be and acted as if he were in sole charge. However, the way the work was organized prevented our having much to do with each other, and we existed in a mutually agreeable arm's length relationship.

Most of the staff was made up of clerical workers - "analysts," I believe they were called - a level above secretarial or administrative, who checked case data on refugees as they came and went. These were all females in their thirties and forties. Back in the US they would have been typical secretaries in ordinary businesses, but here in Austria they enjoyed a status undreamed of at home. The housing, allowances and privileges had all gone to their heads as a sustained delusion in which they imagined themselves to be remarkable people, fit only to socialize among themselves in a pecking order that completely ignored Austrians and demeaned lower level administrative types. In this mutual admiration society they got along quite well with one another. Disagreements, when they arose, had to do with whom was to be assigned a Buick for travel, or who would have to make do with a less prestigious Chevrolet. As a model for social organization, this one left a lot to be desired; as a machine for processing refugees, it worked very well.

Without a car, my first two weeks in Salzburg were restricted to whatever I could manage on foot. That was fine with me since the DPC offices were at one end of the old city, and my hotel at the other, not more than a half-mile walk through one of the finest historical cityscapes in all Europe - by the Franciskaner Church, the cathedral, the Mozartplatz, directly under the towering presence of the fortress or, alternately, via the Getreidegasse with its elaborate wrought iron shop signs, where not much had changed over the centuries.

Since nothing but the best would do for US occupation personnel, the DPC had arranged rooms for me at the Goldener Hirsch hotel, the epitome of medieval hostelry: low, vaulted ceilings, wooden chairs/tables, whitewashed walls covered with trophy horn racks, and at the small, deeply recessed windows, woven curtains to soften the effect. And great bunches of flowers everywhere - the authentic Austrian peasant culture: rough, and at the same time, elegant - handcrafted, nothing mass-produced.

Walking around London carried one back overwhelmingly into the nineteenth century, with earlier outcroppings visible here and there. The old city of Salzburg, at that time still unspoiled, moved the journey back another two or three hundred years. Exploring Salzburg in the autumn sunshine, I found myself more and more drawn into the feeling of the place: steep, forested mountains at the edge of town, a rushing river through the center and a cluster of medieval buildings and churches huddled under the massive battlements of the fortress above.

It was the beginning of a love affair between me and a country; between me and its villages, lakes, rivers, valleys and mountains; between me and its people, their art, their architecture and their music. As I got to know Austria better, this affinity only deepened so that I could understand and overlook its weaknesses, its shallowness and love of pleasure, with occasional lapses into decadence and cruelty. It was a land one loved, but did not necessarily admire. As in most love affairs, sentiment ruled.

Money at that time and in that place went a long way, so that despite my modest salary I was able to do what everyone does upon receiving a promotion and a raise in pay - that is, run out and buy a new car.

Living in Biarritz had exposed me to both the virtues and eccentricities of French automobiles. I don't know why it is, but the French seem incapable of making a car that conforms to the prevailing concept of what a car ought to be. It probably has to do with the fact that for many years most automobiles were designed and manufactured for the American market, and for driving conditions very different from those in Europe. With almost no automotive representation in the US, France was free to indulge its taste for quirky design, plus a few radical innovations. This uniqueness was entirely acceptable to me; a car was a personal statement, and the last thing I wanted was what everyone else had. All things considered, a French car would do very nicely.

The *"voiture"* that had caught my fancy was the Citroen; a car that certainly didn't look like any other. For one thing they were all painted black. As Henry Ford once said about his model T, "You can have any color you want, as long as it's black."

The Citroen's front end did bear a certain resemblance to a 1934 Ford, but there all similarity ended. The Citroen was low slung with a wide front wheel road stance, and the installation of front wheel drive. Inside, the innovation created an unprecedented amount of space by eliminating the transmission and drive shaft hump, both front and back, so that there was now loads of room, missing up to then for legs and feet. Missing also was the floor mounted gearshift. Instead, the gearshift was a lever protruding from the dashboard just to the right of the steering wheel. Very good so far. However, what would have been useful was power-assisted steering. Unfortunately this development still lay a few years in the future, so that all that added weight up front required added steering leverage at the wheel - in other words a truck-sized wheel of at least fifteen inches in diameter.

Compared to standard rear-wheel-driven vehicles, results on the road were spectacular, especially in alpine terrain: climbing icy snow-covered slopes, or navigating curves without the need for braking. The car pulled itself into and around corners, maintaining a constant speed, and the driving wheels up front eliminated the dangerous tendency of the car to "fish-tail" on hard braking with consequent loss of control.

The Citroen of that era came in two models: the "eleven" and the "fifteen." I loved the fifteen, with its more powerful engine, favored by all the police forces in France, but it was a real six passenger car, not a practical solution for my more limited needs, so I opted for the eleven - perfect for four people, although I would mostly be driving it alone.

Salzburg at that time had a Citroen dealership where I placed my order, and a few days later I was informed that the car had arrived. There she stood in the parking lot, all new car shine and smells. It was my first new car purchase, and my heart nearly burst with pride of ownership as I handed over a check for about a thousand dollars - I forget exactly how much - to the pleased dealer.

But there were still details to take care of. I had to arrange for special license plates, identifying the vehicle as belonging to a member of the occupation, and the "Carnet de Passage" that went with them, so that I could travel around Europe and cross borders with a minimum of bureaucratic hassle. There was also the matter of looks. If the car was to be a personal statement, black didn't seem to be the right color. After much thought, I decided on the gray-green tone much favored by the German military for both uniforms and vehicles. That change immediately gave the car a more cheerful aspect, but I wanted still more. Those improvements were to add a pair of fog lights up front, and a roof rack for baggage on top.

The car now looked ready for any and all travel requirements. I couldn't have been happier, walking around, looking at it up close and from every angle, wiping away any trace of dust that had settled on its mirror-like exterior.

Newly mobile, I was now able to turn my attention to the pleasant problem of finding a place to live. As was usual with me, I wanted to have as little to do with Americans as possible, and therefore dismissed housing reserved for occupation personnel. The Old Town was attractive, but like the newer part on the other side of the Salzach River, it was hard to find anything with a garage. So, on weekends, I started to explore the hinterland, looking for something not more than half an hour from town. (There were so few cars on the road at that time that traffic delays were unknown). A few miles outside of town, Anif looked good, particularly a genuine castle with several apartments, but almost non-existent plumbing. Even so, I was seriously tempted, but decided to look a bit further. South along the Salzach was Hallein, also with a castle, unfortunately at that time unrestored. The town, walled in east and west by towering mountains lay in shadow for most of the day, and with the rushing river and the frowning battlement of the castle, presented a gloomy aspect. I decided to

Salzburg

continue my search.

So it was that a two-lane road led me to Mondsee, a village situated on a lake of the same name, about twenty minutes southeast of Salzburg. The autobahn which now runs from Salzburg to Vienna grazes the edge of Mondsee, but was then not yet built, so that the village and its lake were quite isolated from commercial, tourist, and military bustle.

I had not yet heard the term Salzkammergut, designating the sub-alpine region of lakes and picturesque villages, famed for its scenery and, after Vienna, Austria's primary tourist attraction. Mondsee was at the edge of this tourist paradise, but remained strangely untouched by it, separated from the more famous Wolfgangsee by a mountain barrier and the Scharfling Pass. The town centered around an open plaza with a beautiful church at one end and a small *schloss* (palace) along one side, both in need of repair. On the other side of the plaza stood a row of typical village buildings - low pitched roofs, whitewashed facades with flowering window boxes and massive doors. It was a quiet town. The few tourist hotels there were located further out along the lake. Every Sunday morning after church the villagers gathered around an oom-pah band which played cheerful marches and Austrian favorites.

I was responding to an ad which specified "Lakeside chalet. Living room, bedroom, kitchen and bath. Balcony. Furnished." In reality, it was a second floor apartment, with its own entrance reached via a stairway on one side. The lake was across the road directly in front, and a hill covered with fruit trees rose at the rear. Both outside and in, the style was traditional Austrian, highlighted by an old-fashioned "kachelofen" (ceramic stove) in the living room, with a bench built around three sides. The entire building had been designed by the present owner, a retired architect named Feichtinger. He and his wife continued to live on the ground floor while renting the more desirable second floor for extra income.

It didn't take me ten seconds to make a decision. The place was perfect, the view spectacular, the semi-isolation just what I had in mind, and at the right price. I checked out of the Goldener Hirsch and moved in the next day.

Chapter Twenty-Seven

Camp Hellbrun

The road to Camp Hellbrun ran out of town in the direction of Schloss Hellbrun, an 18th century palace after which the camp was named, although any similarity began and ended with the name. Even then, the schloss and its gardens were a major tourist attraction, one of the many magnificent leftovers of Austria's golden age. As an income producer for local tourism, the schloss was well maintained in all its former glory.

Not so the camp, which did not figure in any of the elaborate brochures meant to entice tourists to visit the city. A collection of ramshackle buildings, it lay just out of sight off the main road. These unpainted, weather beaten, one-story structures gave the impression of a former fourth class military installation, or a holding pen during the forced importation of eastern European slave laborers. It now served a similar purpose but toward more idealistic ends. Passable in summer, the unpaved road to Hellbrun became an icy obstacle course in winter and a muddy track in spring.

. Along the way, on the right hand side, stood an isolated mansion of gloomy, forbidding aspect, much in need of refurbishing, over which waved a red flag with the insignia of the Soviet Union. This was the much feared Russian repatriation mission, the center for planning and carrying out seizures and forced repatriation back to the USSR. Its proximity was a cause of great concern to the camp's inmates - nothing could induce them to venture outside the camp, or to walk the short distance into town.

Approaching Camp Hellbrun, one's nostrils were assailed by

an odor which I came to associate with eastern European villages in general and with DP camps in particular. It was a complex stink compounded of rancid cooking fat, fried cabbage, uncollected garbage, and a lack of sanitation. It hung heavily over the camp like a blanket, especially on overcast days with no wind to carry the fumes away.

My office was in a kind of administration building, large, with pieces of cast-off furniture and a coal stove in the corner which worked so well we had to keep the door open. The telephone was connected, and we were ready to roll. As I said, the DPC might not be your cup of tea, but they were efficient.

In this case, efficiency meant getting orientation information out to as many DP's as possible, both at Camp Hellbrun and to the smaller camps in both the American and British Occupation Zones of Austria - there were no refugee camps in the French Zone. The DPC program involved the usual distribution of printed information kits and posters, occasional film showings (where projection equipment was available), personal lectures, Q/A sessions, and English lessons.

It also meant working cooperatively with the YMCA very much as we had done at Camp Grohn, except that now I was on the other side of the fence. On the YMCA side were two individuals, both women: Nan Thompson and Juliana Van Doering. Thompson was in charge of all YMCA activities in Austria. Her office was downtown where the IRO was located. I never understood exactly what she did and had very little contact with her. Working under her was Van Doering, directly supervising the YMCA program at the refugee camp level, especially at camp Hellbrun, her base of operations. Our working relationship was extremely ambiguous, except that the DPC ordered and paid for anything having to do with orientation, including English teachers.

How we shared our day-to-day activities was pretty much left up to us, but in general she dealt with program specifics while I provided administrative support and personal participation when needed.

"Julie," as she liked to be called, was a Dutch citizen, a large woman, tall, heavily built, about thirty-five or forty years old, not particularly attractive with buck teeth, an unhealthy complexion and hair, cut short. Nor did she do much to improve on what nature had given her: no makeup, of course, looking uncombed and dressed with total indifference to appearance, usually a heavy sweater with men's trousers tucked into work boots. A Dutch tulip she certainly was not. Nicotine stained fingers from a pack-a-day cigarette habit completes the picture.

Not quite. I am also obliged to mention that Julie was completely without charm; tactless and direct to the point of rudeness, indifferent to even the minor social niceties and pleasantries that lubricate working relationships. She almost never smiled, and when she did it was a mere facial contortion, made consciously without warmth or feeling. Almost everything she said seemed designed to put you on the defensive, to make you feel inadequate. Needless to say, a sense of humor was nowhere to be found. It didn't take me long to wonder if all these unattractive mannerisms were her way of dealing with the world in general, of whether they were reserved for me in particular.

All this was somewhat redeemed by a razor-sharp intellect and an intense dedication to the job - to her work in the YMCA program. In fact, this seemed to be her whole life. Whereas I tended to keep normal business hours, anxious to get back to my little chalet at Mondsee, Julie never left the camp - no outside social life at all, not even with the IRO multinationals. Such friendships as she had were with individual refugees, all the more intense since she immersed herself in their lives, in the details of their troubles and tribulations. This was only too easy to do; troubles were what they loved to talk about, given a few hours and a sympathetic ear.

Our contacts were completely businesslike, because from the very beginning it was clear she wanted it that way. My efforts to get our relationship on a more personal basis were either ignored of brushed aside. However, one time early on I did manage to find her in a more communicative mood.

I began by congratulating her on her command of English which she spoke perfectly with a slight upper class inflection.

"Well that is the product of three years at a Quaker girls boarding school in England," she said.

"Did you continue your studies in England?" I asked.

"No, I took a degree at the Sorbonne afterward, just before the war broke out."

"What did you study?"

"Cultural anthropology. I have a graduate degree in that."

"Cultural anthropology, that seems a long way from what you're doing now," I said.

"Not as far as you might think, but for five years during the war it was not possible to continue that pursuit. So I stayed home with the family and tried to last out the occupation."

"Yes, it must have been terrible. I've read about it."

"Well it was much worse that anything you might have read," she replied.

"How do you feel about Germany now? The Germans, I mean."

"At first, I hated them. For a long time. Then I began to see that the German people had been misled, hypnotized into doing things they could not have imagined. They were Hitler's first victims - none more that the Austrians."

"And now, here you are working to repair some of the damage that was left behind - right?"

"Yes, it's a mission with me, to try to help, as much as I can, all these broken lives you see around here."

"But how did you come to work with the YMCA?"

"Because here I can work directly with people, down at the one-on-one level, no office, no desk, no office politics, no one looking over my shoulder. I can do what seems to me to be right, and at the same time feel I'm meeting a real need."

For Julie, this was a long speech. I had never heard her say half so much. "Well, it's quite a sacrifice you're making," I said.

"If it is, I don't feel it. Low pay? Discomfort? These are bourgeois values that mean nothing to me."

"Are you religious?" I asked.

"Religious?" And she laughed, a rare thing. "You might say I'm socially religious - a belief in human beings. But God and Jesus, churches, and all the fol-de-rol that goes into it. No thanks."

"What does your family think about your work here?" I asked.

"My family," she laughed again. "My family thinks I'm crazy.

Too bad I'm an only child. They have a lot of money and they're getting old. As an unmarried woman, their fear is that I will give the whole family fortune away once they're out of the picture. Who knows, maybe I would."

As far as the job went, I was neither fish nor fowl. My day-to-day work in semi-isolation at the Hellbrun refugee camp kept me outside the American "golden ghetto." It had little impact on the primary DPC mission, and few persons at HQ understood my role in the process, or cared to learn. As a result, I was regarded by them with a certain amount of suspicion, as being not totally American. Nor did I help the problem by wearing knee-length lederhosen, heavy knee-hi stockings, rough peasant-type shoes and a checked shirt. To complete this costume, I had acquired a green "*jaeger*" type Austrian hat decorated with the traditional "gamsbart" (chamois hair) decorative plume. To make matters worse, I insisted on wearing this ridiculous get-up not just at the camp, but even during official calls at the downtown HQS. Little wonder they didn't know what to make of me. The settled opinion was that I had "gone native," and in a way I had.

Chapter Twenty-Eight

A Difficult Journey in Winter

Julie and I continued our somewhat strained working arrangement as the golden days of October gave way to endless rain in November. The road to Hellbrun turned to mud, the camp buildings sagged and dripped. Inside, the orientation program went on as before. My job was ridiculously easy, the more so since, except for administration support, Julie was firmly in charge, and had no intention of changing that, or of sharing responsibility. She regarded me as her assistant, and an unneeded one at that. In fact, one day she said, "I really don't see why they sent you here. It hasn't done any harm, but neither has it added anything we couldn't have done ourselves."

I was going to reply, but before I could, she went on, "Oh well, if that's the way you Americans want to throw away your money, go ahead. But it's a great shame to see such a waste." Any reply would have led to a full scale altercation; in fact, I'm not sure she wasn't looking for one, so I ignored it and kept my mouth shut.

About two weeks into December my boss in Frankfurt, Gussie Mayerson, decided that I should become more familiar with the outlying parts of the DP operation in Austria, particularly the camps in Graz and Klagenfurt, which were in the British Zone. From the DP's standpoint, it would also be a good idea for them to become more aware of the role America was playing in the resettlement process; better still if that were in the person of a living, breathing American, something almost none of them had ever seen.

I agreed wholeheartedly. In addition, it would be a chance to visit provinces of Austria - Steiermark and Carinthia - for which I might never have another opportunity. But when I relayed this proposal to Julie, she hesitated. "Yes," she said. "It is a good idea - but," and the "but" was that she was unalterably opposed to the idea of letting me go down there alone to play around in her empire. As an excuse for delay, she said she wanted to talk to Nan Thompson to make sure that it was all set up properly. After the discussion the proposal had become a trip to be made by the two of us. Her own visit to the region was overdue; she could introduce me properly to the people on site, and a joint appearance by both representatives would show how well the YMCA and the DPC were working together. All true, but I privately suspected that Nan had told her she had no choice in the matter; the DPC connection was too important - if it wanted me to go down there, then that is what would be done.

So it was that about nine o'clock on a Monday morning we headed out of Salzburg in Julie's overloaded Hillman Minx, a small, stylish English car, well suited to the country lanes and byways of Olde England but totally impractical for Austria. Our destination was Graz, in the southeastern corner, and a DP camp in the vicinity.

Normally, this would have been a trip of about five or six hours, so we expected to arrive sometime in the afternoon. Our route led south along the Salzach, then turned east, through Radstadt and along the upper Enns River valley, with the massive bulk of the Dachstein hidden in clouds on our left and the Niedertauren Alps on our right.

So far, so good. Then as we went through Schladming it started to snow, tiny, wind-driven flakes sweeping across the road - worrisome because we had not consulted a weather report, and the worst leg of the journey lay ahead, negotiating the pass over the Niedertauren Alps, then down into Leoben and Graz.

As we progressed over near empty roads, the snowfall increased. We decided not to stop for lunch but to keep going in the hope of arriving in Graz while there was still daylight. But the storm - which is what it now was - was coming out of the east, head-on into the headlights which we were forced to use as the afternoon darkened. Our speed slowed to no more than forty miles an hour. Visibility was now reduced to just a few feet of whirling

Picking Up the Pieces

snow in front of the car. By good fortune, one of the giant Alpine snow plows, with a seven-foot plow blade, had passed through not far ahead of us, so we were following on a partially cleared road. Even so, there were several inches of new snow there. I didn't want to think what would happen if we were to meet an oncoming vehicle. The cleared track was just as wide as the plow blade, with walls of snow on either side.

We were now well into the mountains. The angle of climb was becoming steadily steeper, and the pass still ahead. As the snow deepened, the little Hillman struggled to maintain traction, but it was a losing battle, and our rate of climb slowed even further. I cursed inwardly that we had not made this trip in my Citroen instead of this Hillman, which was just about the most impractical car possible for these conditions, with its small wheels and weak engine.

Neither of us had spoken for some time, a tense silence prevailing, when Julie suddenly said, "I know this pass, and we're not going to make it with things as they are. Fortunately, I have a set of snow chains in the boot. It won't take long to put them on. Frankly, there's no choice." I had to agree.

Unloading the boot, filled to capacity with miscellaneous cargo, was a matter of minutes to get to the car jack and the chains.

"Have you ever mounted chains on a car?" Julie asked.

I was forced to admit that I hadn't. In fact, I had never even changed a wheel. The need had never come up. Nevertheless, it was embarrassing to admit it.

"I thought as much," she said in her usual superior manner. "Well, you can make yourself useful by holding the light while I take care of it." And she handed me a large flashlight.

I felt like a total idiot, standing there like a surgeon's assistant, while the operation went on, which it did, and in a short while we were once more underway.

She was right, we never would have made it without those chains. (It was a lesson to me. Afterward I went out and bought a set myself.) Even so, our speed slowed further to just a crawl as the road twisted and turned, doubling back on itself every few hundred feet, steeper and steeper to what I felt was at least twenty-five or thirty degrees of incline. The top of the pass was just ahead. "Come on, baby," I said to myself and to the straining Hillman. Five minutes later we were over it and on the downgrade. I heaved a huge sigh of relief as the tension began to evaporate.

It was now late afternoon, but dark as midnight. Not too bad, we could still be in Graz for dinner. Nevertheless, we had to exercise even more caution descending than we had on the way up; the grade was just as steep, the curves unending and just as dangerous. But still no traffic, thank God for that. Things were just beginning to seem almost normal when a loud slapping sound came from the rear, followed by the squeal and screech of tortured metal.

God in heaven, what now? This trip had the curse of the Almighty on it. One look, and it was obvious what had happened. The right rear chain had come off, and a closer look revealed that it had wrapped itself tightly around the axle of the car.

"Nothing for it," said Julia climbing back up from underneath. "I'll have to see if I can't somehow loosen the chain so we can get it out. I'm going to need that tire iron." Back into the boot. The tire iron, of course, was at the very bottom, and with it in hand, Julie prepared to crawl underneath the car.

"Not this time, Julie," I said, handing her the light. "It's my turn." I was determined not to endure a second humiliation. I guess my resolve was so apparent that she handed me the tire iron without a word. Pushing aside enough snow to create working room, I was eventually able to loosen one broken strand of the chain and pull it around the axle. From there, the rest unwound easily.

"I don't think we should drive with chains on just one wheel. Let's take the other one off." Julie said. So we did. No chains, but at least we were now on the downgrade.

Two hours later we were in Graz.

The dining room at the hotel was nearly deserted. A bottle of Lagrein Kreutzer (a locally available red wine from South Tyrol), and a dinner of roast goose with red cabbage and potato dumplings had done a great deal to make Julie's mood almost jovial. This transformation had been helped by our waitress, an attractive college-age girl, in whom Julie appeared to take an extraordinary

Picking Up the Pieces

interest.

"We do appreciate such excellent service so late in the evening," said Julie to the girl in German. "What is your name, please?"

"Lieselotte," said the girl smiling as she began to remove the dishes.

"Do you work here all day?" asked Julie.

"No, only in the evening. During the day I am helping to restore the inside of our church - the windows, the woodwork, even some of the paintings. It has not been done since before the war."

"Why, that is fascinating," said Julie. "So interesting. I would love to hear more about it ….Tell me, Lieselotte, is it possible to order a nightcap - like a demi-bouteile of sweet wine - Tokai, perhaps - sent up to the room?"

"Yes, with pleasure," the girl answered.

"Excellent," said Julie. "Then I would like to order that, with two glasses, if you please, to room 104. And Lieselotte, one glass is for you, I would be so happy if you could visit for a few minutes to tell me more about your restoration work at the church."

At this, Lieselotte, appeared somewhat confused, and cast a wondering glance in my direction.

"Oh, don't worry about Jack. He has his own room and says he wants to go to bed immediately after dinner." I nodded even though I had said no such thing. "It would be just you and me Lieselotte, and only for one nice drink," urged Julie. "Please say you will."

The girl continued to look uncertain. "It is very kind of you," she said. "Maybe I can. I will see." And with that she hurried off to the kitchen.

"What a sweet girl," said Julie on our way upstairs. "I hope you put a big tip on the check."

Next morning at breakfast, I asked how the visit had gone.

"Very disappointing," said Julie. "Apparently Room Service is not part of her domain, so they sent someone else up with the wine. I was quite annoyed. Even a little place like this has its bureaucracy."

At the camp, a few miles out of town, we unloaded the car. In addition to the usual supplies, there were a number of small packages, gift-wrapped as if for Christmas.

"What are these?" I asked, holding one up.

"Just a little something for the staff: Dutch chocolates and mocha coffee from Arabia, things unknown here for more than two years. I always try to bring something along whenever I come."

Such a thing would never have occurred to me. I was genuinely impressed at this act of kindness. "That is very generous of you," I said.

"They are my family," she replied simply.

The camp was a small-scale replica of Hellbrun, although many of its shortcomings were hidden under a foot of snow. Once inside, we were welcomed like visiting royalty. The entire reception had a highly personal quality. I was introduced to the camp leader and his various assistants, and during our "business" meeting we were served tea and cookies.

After that we sat in on one of their English classes, and following that a general meeting for all the refugees in the camp, about a hundred. Through all this, Julie made quite clear that it was her show, her stage; she was the emcee, and I was the guest "act," a visiting performer on road tour. It was especially annoying when I had to deliver my set speech on what they could expect from this point on, including embarkation and getting settled in the US. My German was far from fluent, but it was at least equal to the demands of the simple narration I had in mind as well as the Q/A period to follow. Julie insisted on acting as interpreter - interrupting to translate everything as I went along. It had the effect of breaking up the natural flow and destroying any sense of spontaneity. But, as I say, it was her show.

We left early in the afternoon. The objective was to reach Klagenfurt by evening, which was reasonable now that the snow had stopped. There were no mountain passes and the roads were clear. Compared to what we had been through the day before, it was relaxing: sunshine on a snowy landscape, picturesque villages, churches, and roadside shrines.

Conversation in the car was all business, but at dinner in Klagenfurt that evening, after her third cigarette, Julie said, "Tell

Picking Up the Pieces

me a bit about your father's work in England with German war prisoners. I've heard it was most successful."

So I did, at some length, since she seemed genuinely interested.

When I finished, she said, "Very impressive. Why didn't you get involved with that?"

I explained that it was too late, the program was already winding down. Besides, I wanted to get over to Germany where the whole process of reconstruction was going on. My immediate objective was to be part of that, in some sort of government job.

"And the YMCA - that was mainly a means of getting over here. Is that right? Was your father helpful in getting you a job here with the YMCA?" she asked.

When I admitted to that, she pushed on. "So now you have your government job. What now? Will you make refugees a lifetime work?"

"No, not at all. My real goal is not particularly humanitarian. I want to join the State Department as a Foreign Service Officer. All those other jobs are stepping stones in that direction," I answered.

These off-hand responses, to what seemed more and more like an interrogation, were given carelessly in an almost flippant manner. I never liked portentous, solemn, self-glorifying speeches or moral commitment. Even if such sentiments were deeply held, I preferred to conceal them.

"I must say," Julie said, "it seems a great shame that, working here with refugees and in a position to do some real good, you would prefer to climb the bureaucratic ladder - just like any other opportunist. But you know how I feel about bureaucracies - any kind: government, business, church - they're all the same. You wind up executing other people's orders, whether you agree with them or not. Not for me, but if that's what you want ..."

It was an exchange that could have gone on forever, so I let this last remark pass. To me it was just a casual conversation. I had no reason to think that even a casual conversation could bear unforeseen consequences. Such an extended exchange was made possible by the fact that our waiter, this time a young man - no nubile, twenty-something to distract Julie.

Nothing of particular interest took place during our visit to the Klagenfurt camp. It was a replay of the day before. We had one

A Difficult Journey in Winter

high pass to surmount on the long drive from Villach up to Salzburg, but we did it in clear weather over newly plowed roads. I had been gone four days and was glad to get back to my cozy chalet and the gentle warmth of its kachelofen.

Chapter Twenty-Nine

Fishing and Racism

Spring arrived mid-May. Buds burst into bloom on the apple trees behind the house, and Frau Feichtinger set out her flowering window boxes all around.

As it always does, the coming of spring turns my thoughts to trout - when the air is warm, but the water cold, with insects venturing out into the sunlight, and small birds darting from the streamside brush to catch them. It was time to get out the rod, oil the reel, check the line and leaders, and also the boots for possible leaks. I didn't know whether my collection of flies and nymphs from America would work in European water, but I was ready to find out.

Trout fishing in Austria at that time was the high point of any fly-fisherman's dream. To begin with, the scenery was spectacular, in any direction a picture-postcard view: snow capped peaks above lush valleys and forests, a church spire poking up here and there. Then, you had it all to yourself. As noted earlier, fishing was reserved for occupation personnel, but not many took advantage of it. Also, during the war years, Germany and Austria were too busy waging war to be distracted by such non-essential frivolity as trout fishing. So the waters were, in a sense, virgin waters, ready for action.

There was one more appealing aspect to the experience of fly-fishing in Austria, as contrasted with America. Back in the US, I was always getting up at three in the morning to be in the water by five, just at dawn with mist rising off the water. Beautiful, but still a sacrifice - only half a night's sleep, and no breakfast. These few early morning hours were usually a productive period, but by nine or ten the fish seemed to have had enough of sport, and action dropped off, to resume at the end of the day and on into dusk until it was too late to see the fly.

In Austria the fish were more civilized. You could arrive at the stream as late as eight or nine, well-fed and rested, to find the fish waiting for you. Even across the middle of the day, when at home you might as well enjoy a nap, they were there and still interested.

Maybe it's because in the Alps the water is colder, only a few miles further up still ice and snow into summer. The valleys were places of beauty. That spring I fished around Golling and Abtenau and later on, in the waters tumbling down from the Dachstein, that massive block of solid stone the size of the average US county. There were times when I drove the car so far up the mountain that uncleared avalanches - common in late spring - still lay across the road, and I could go no further.

At these heights the rivers that ran out of the Dachstein glacier were a milky, greenish color, not crystal clear, but semi-opaque from the rock dust the ice had ground out of the stone. It ran so fast and at such depth that wading was out of the question, flies too. I couldn't imagine insect life at that altitude, not that a fish could see them even if there were any.

So I decided to try a spinner. I always carried both sets of tackle with me: fly-casting and spinning. It was a glorious Sunday morning in early June - warm in the sunshine, but the wind coming down off the mountain had a cold edge to it. Standing on a rock I flicked a small brass spinner across the stream, reeling quickly as the current swept it along. Two more casts, then a solid strike. At first I thought my lure had snagged in the rocks, but this illusion was quickly dispelled as the fish rocketed first upstream and then headed down. Now I was fighting both the fish and the current. Thank goodness both rod and lines were not of the ultra-light variety, usual for small stream trout fishing; this was a strong fish. Gradually I worked him in, getting an occasional glimpse as he came closer to the surface, the sun flashing on his sides. One last rush and he lay, held by a taut line, on top of the water. Because the rock on which I was standing was several feet above the stream and my landing net had only a short handle, it was not easy to keep a grip on the rod and, kneeling, reach down for the

Picking Up the Pieces

fish. And I didn't want him to get rested. But on the third try I had him in the net and away from the water. A beautiful brown-trout, smaller than I had thought, about fifteen or sixteen inches. Even so, he did not fit into my fishing basket.

More casts, but no more fish. Time to move on. Time also for lunch. Then I remembered a bit down the road I had passed a gasthaus, one of those catering to summer visitors who like mountain scenery and the exhilaration that comes from high altitude hiking and biking. It was still early in the year for that. At the gasthaus there were only a few locals having a beer outside, at metal tables under the dense shade of two blooming chestnut trees.

Taking a seat, I showed the proprietor my fish and asked if he would cook it for me.

"Jawohl, mein Herr, mit vergnugen." Then he asked how I would like it prepared.

"Broiled," I said. In Austria at that time it was always wise to specify because, left to their own devices, they would poach it with vegetables - so-called *"blaue forelle"*, a blue trout. Not bad, but this one was too big for that. "And bring me a demi-liter of ein halb liter hauswein, bitte."

Sixty minutes later, the trout and the potato salad served with it were mostly gone. About one glass of the wine remained. Birds chirped in the chestnut trees above, and floating up from the valley the sound of bells announcied the end of church services. It was one of those times when nature and human activity fuse into a moment of such perfection that only poetry can respond. Indelible, as clear and intense to me now as it was that day sixty years ago.

Back in Mondsee, with the lake just in front of the house it was inevitable that my quest for sport would soon lead in that direction. I am not, and never was, a snob fisherman. Although I believe dry fly casting for trout to be the aristocracy of angling, I would happily fish for whatever was there - even switch to bait, if nothing else worked. Also, I must confess to enjoying a meal of whatever the water produced, best sautéed in an iron skillet over an outdoor camp fire. These were the days before "catch and release" became popular. But at that time and in that place, with so few anglers, and a naturally reproducing fish population - no artificial stocking - it was neither necessary, nor even thought of.

Mondsee is a warm water lake, meaning some relatively shallow water with lily pads and mud beds along much of the shoreline. In other words, perfect water for pike, which, with a good food supply of smaller fish, grew to enormous size, up to fifty pounds and even more. A pike is the Tyrannosaurus Rex of the fresh-water fish world, malevolent in its appearance: gaping, teeth-studded jaws and an elongated body built for speed - sudden rushes from out of the weed cover where he lies motionless, waiting for lunch or dinner to swim by.

About half a mile down the road from my house stood the Pichl Auhof Hotel, a small lakeside hostelry, a destination for guests, of whom there were never very many, seeking rest and relaxation. Recreation possibilities were limited, mostly just enjoying the view across the lake where a monumental tor dominated the opposite shoreline and the Scharfling Mountain stood guard at the lower end. There were also a few rowboats tied up at a small dock.

In the course of several visits, sitting at the bar, I had become friendly with the proprietor, the more so as from time to time I donated a bottle of scotch or brandy to his meager back of the bar collection. To show his appreciation, he gave me free use of any of the boats whenever I wanted.

So it was that one morning, in one of his boats, I was meandering along the near shore, enjoying the early summer weather, casting a metal spoon to the edge of the weed beds and cursing when it came back trailing a catch of snagged weeds. But not always, and after almost an hour I had caught and released several small pike. By that time I had worked my way into a small cove with a half circle shoreline ending on a point that projected out into the lake. On this point stood a traditional chalet, good-sized, with a boathouse and a dock by the water.

As I continued my slow progress just offshore, a man came out of the house and stood on the deck watching me. When I got near enough, he asked if I was catching anything. I said I was, but nothing exceptional, a few small pike which was really all I was expecting.

When he heard my reply, he knew that I was American and switched to very good English. "Well, don't be discouraged," he said. "There are much bigger ones in here. If you have a moment, I will show you something interesting."

Intrigued, I said that I would be interested, and maneuvered the boat dockside where he gave me a hand getting out. He was tall, about six-two, perhaps fifty years old, and handsome in his Austrian peasant dress: knee length lederhosen, heavy shirt and stockings.

He introduced himself: "Gottfried Krauthammer," and I did likewise. "Now, please come with me," he said, and led the way into the boathouse.

Inside, there was space for just one boat. The remainder had been floored over, and there stood a work table covered with all sorts of scientific apparatus: a Bunsen burner, scales, a microscope, beakers, retorts, test tubes in racks, and glass tanks, some empty, others filled. It was obviously some sort of laboratory. Then I saw that the inside wall space was lined with shelves, and on these shelves stood literally hundreds of tanks and bottles, all of them neatly labeled, containing specimens of every conceivable creature: snails, slugs, salamanders, snakes, toads, frogs, worms - far, far too many to mention.

I was looking at all this when he said, "Over here is what I wanted to show you," and he took down from a shelf on the wall a large glass tank - maybe two or three gallon capacity.

"Here," he said. "How would you like to catch this one?"

In the jar was just the head of the most enormous pike I had ever seen. It completely filled the jar. Diameter at the cut was a good eight inches so that the overall length of the fish must have been almost five feet.

"Did that come out of here?" I asked.

"Yes," he said. "Two years ago. I did not catch it. One of the men in the village caught it in a net and gave it to me, because he knew I was interested in such things. I save it as a curiosity."

"That thing could eat a small dog," I said.

"Well," he replied, "snakes, even ducks are on his menu."

"This is quite a laboratory you have here," I said. "You must be a biologist - a professor?"

"Yes, I was a professor at the university in Berlin," he replied. "But I was given early retirement, courtesy of you Americans. If you have time, maybe you would have a schnapps with me, or a glass of beer if you prefer, in the house."

I was very much interested in this character and the chance to learn more about him, so I said, "That is very kind of you, but I don't want to impose on your time."

"Not at all," he replied. "I have all the time in the world, and outside visitors are rare, especially those who arrive by boat."

Inside he lifted a shot glass of Steinhaeger. "Prosit," he said. "Zum wohl." The fiery fluid went down nicely.

"Tell me," I said. "How were the Americans involved in your retirement?"

"To oversimplify, my area of specialization in biology was species differentiation as a product of evolutionary processes. Some of this had appeal to the Nazis who picked out of the whole body of my work those parts of it that fitted into their theories of racial superiority. I would never have agreed with the manner in which they used my work, but it was much too dangerous to disagree."

"Didn't this make sense to the Americans?"

"Not a bit. Instead of examining my work as originally written, which they had not the background to really understand, they simply cited as evidence against me the Nazified nonsense. Given the racial implications, it was especially sensitive, also I think they were looking for scapegoats."

I nodded sympathetically. "That is an amazing story." I said.

"Not so amazing," he replied. "In war, the end of the story is always written by the victor."

Back at the Pichl Auhof, I told the proprietor about my visit. "Oh, Krauthammer," he said. "Yes, he was accused of writing the scientific rationale and justification for Hitler's racial theories and persecution of the Jews. They kept him in jail for over a year, but could never really pin anything on him. He had not actually harmed anyone, or incited to violence. His writings were all very scientific, which no one understood anyway. So all they could do was forbid him to teach, which they did. Both in Germany and in Austria."

Chapter Thirty

Problems With Teaching English

As anyone reading this has already concluded, my devotion to the refugee cause had its limits. In and around Salzburg there was simply too much to see and do. Tourists were now beginning to spend thousands of dollars on the diversions that Salzburg had to offer, and here I was, right in the midst of it all, temptation on every side - who could say how long I was to be there? I must admit that my work ethic was no better than that of any other American bureaucrat: nine to five on weekdays, and no work at all on weekends.

Weekends were reserved for fishing, or excursions - to Berchteradan to view the remains of Hitler's *"Berghof,"* to Oberbayern to visit King Ludwig's castles, then all through the Salzkammergut: Gmundun, Bad Ischl, Bas Aussee, and on and on. Given my love of music, it is surprising that I didn't attend more performances. At the *Festspielhaus* they were prohibitively expensive - even for an American. But the *Mozarteum* was just across the river. The chamber music evenings held there more than made up for anything I was missing elsewhere.

With, or without me, the refugee program at Camp Hellbrun went on, now almost routine. A good part of the reason for my light-hearted approach to the work was that it was so easy, so little challenge, so few demands placed on me, and so little opportunity for creativity beyond those demands that were. Julie was right when she said, "I don't know why they sent you here."

The one area not entirely routine, and which did offer some scope for a creative approach, was the English instruction. Because ability to communicate in English was considered a key element in DP orientation, and because the DP Commission was paying my salary, as well as for materials and classroom teachers, responsibility for this part of the program fell into my domain.

Earlier I mentioned some of the conditions that made English instruction in DP camps so difficult:
- A completely heterogeneous learning population: wide variations in age intelligence, national origin, education, etc.
- No common language for translation purposes
- A constantly changing learning group as individuals came and went, meaning that skill development in any organized way was impossible.

From these unchangeable circumstances, I concluded that it was not realistic to attempt to teach English as a skill, with step by step advancement from one level to another. All that was possible was to teach commonly used words and phrases as these would come up in travel, or in day-to-day living: meeting people, asking directions, explaining who you are and where you came from, ordering in a restaurant, finding rest-room facilities, and several others. Also, I felt it would be useful to be able to recognize and understand certain basic documents: driver's license, identification papers, checkbook, calendar, etc.

I'll not try to explain in detail how these abilities were taught. Our basic "text" was a pocket-sized phrase book from which we took situational extracts, as per the list above. These were used with pictorial charts to specify the situation. Given a particular situation, the teacher would model the dialogue, with the class repeating the words, then the same dialogue between the teacher and a class member, with the class repeating the words. Finally, pairs from the class verbalized the dialogue, and then switched roles. Dozens of repetitions and individual critiques followed.

It wasn't much, but with a vocabulary of a few hundred words in about twenty or twenty-five situations, plus the ability to understand half a dozen commonly used documents, it was at least something. And it worked.

Of course, it had very little depth- the conversations were mostly two-line exchanges - but the repetition by everyone hammered the words home with lasting effect, as I could tell because out of class during the day, they would exchange these phrases with much laughter as an ongoing joke.

Julie, with her Oxford English, regarded these puny efforts as a waste of time, but I was quite proud of what we accomplished in a difficult learning environment.

My boss up in Frankfort, as previously noted, was one Gussie Mayerson, Jewish, about fifty, formerly a New York City social worker from the Bronx. Gussie was friendly, conscientious, and concerned to do a good job despite the unfamiliar setting in which she now found herself. She understood bureaucracies and how to operate in them, which meant keeping on good terms with all the relevant power centers, and maintaining an effective public relations front. Since all of this involved constant contact with agencies and people up in Germany, we received very little of her attention, and within mandated guidelines did pretty much as we pleased.

Then one day she called to say that it was high time the various DP orientation centers had a comprehensive view of the total operation, and an opportunity for the various orientation officers to get to know one another personally. To that end, she was scheduling a one-day meeting to be held in Austria, with me designated as host. She would draw up the program, but I was to make reservations for hotel rooms and meals. Also, she wanted our meeting to be held off-site, that is away from the camp. A short tour of the camp was alright, but another location was preferable for the business meeting.

Gussie arrived the night before with three other persons. One was a newly appointed woman, Barbara, also from New York; a young grad student named Mitch; and a girl named Sally from the Lutheran World Federation - altogether only five persons, counting me. I was surprised that there was no one from Camp Grohn.

After the Hellbrun tour we repaired to the Villa Bilroth, overlooking the Wolfgangsee, for our afternoon business meeting and dinner.

The meeting was unremarkable; each representative had to describe his/her particular program. Then Gussie asked if we were experiencing any problems. No, there were very few of these.

What about English instruction? And here, major differences emerged, not surprising, since up to then there had been no attempt to standardize methods.

When I explained what we were doing at Hellbrun, there was very little reaction, rather an unstated sense of disappointment in the group that all we were teaching were a few words and phrases, mostly drawn from a pocket-sized phrase book. As one expressed it, this was a band-aid approach, not really teaching English at all. It did no good to cite the practical obstacles to traditional academic teaching methods, and that any program had to teach to the realities of the learning population and the environment.

Then Mitch got up and announced that he had developed his own unique, revolutionary method - "Thirteen Steps to Better English" he called it, as he took out of his briefcase a thick, typed manuscript bundle. "One Step to Basic English" would be a more appropriate approach, I thought.

"I developed this myself," he declared proudly. "Mainly for US public schools But I think it has great promise for use here in our program. It's one reason I signed up to come over here."

He then spent the next half hour at the chalk board, drawing incomprehensible diagrams, accompanied by an equally incomprehensible commentary. People nodded slowly, with increasing bewilderment, as Mitch, now enrapt in his philosophical message, went on and on. Out of the fog emerged what was, to me, a theoretical skill-development process that ignored reality, and would not work in a public school setting, to say nothing of a DP camp where its chances of success were even smaller.

"Thank you, Mitch, for that brilliant presentation," said Gussie. "You have given us all a great deal to think about. You folks," indicating the rest of us, "Should all check with Mitch individually to see how he can help in your own program." Then, obviously as confused as the rest of us, she rushed into her next agenda item.

I couldn't help but reflect that here we were, responsible for spending a great deal of government money to teach thousands of people how to communicate in English, and not one of us had the slightest expertise, training, or background in how to do this - Mitch included.

Picking Up the Pieces

Other factors were causing me to lose interest, and to question the value of this meeting. One had to do with the newly appointed woman, Barbara. It soon appeared that she had already developed a close relationship with Gussie, and was, in fact, acting like her deputy. Most of Gussie's statements or remarks were made to her: "Barbara, what do you think,....Barbara, how do you feel about,... Barbara, could you summarize what has been said so far."

I did not feel discriminated against, nevertheless, the blatant favoritism going on was an irritant. It was too obvious, but, at the same time, understandable. Barbara was Jewish, and to the unmarried Gussie, the daughter she never had.

As the meeting droned on, my attention wandered out the window to the lake below, and I made myself a promise to get over this way more often. Fishing possibilities looked good.

Carrying on the day-to-day burden of our English classes at Hellbrun, were two teachers, neither of them trained for the job, but both conscientious and speaking English reasonably well. This concern communicated itself to their students, with the result that classroom sessions became a dialogue between friends. Quite often letters came back from pupils who had moved on, some were from the US sending their greetings and saying how much they had enjoyed their language classes at Hellbrun. Both teachers showed me these letters as they arrived, and saved them afterward.

One teacher was Frau Bittner, an Austrian lady, about forty to fifty years old. She was a former schoolteacher and had worked with the occupation since 1945 in various jobs. The other was an elderly gentleman, bearing the title of "Baron." I don't remember his family name because we always called him "Herr Baron." Herr Baron looked the part of a conservative Austrian gentlemani in his high cut gray jacket with bone buttons and green piping. Out of doors he wore a loden coat with a fur collar and an *Astrakhan* hat - all very elegant.

Unfortunately, he suffered from poor health, and some days was so weak that his voice sank to just above a whisper - not ideal for classroom work. We should have let him go, but I couldn't bear to do it since Frau Bittner told me that, despite his prosperous appearance, Herr Baron was actually penniless, and that this job was all that was keeping him alive.

Problems With Teaching English

It was no surprise when one day Herr Baron failed to show up for work. Later that day we received a call from the hospital saying that he had requested we be notified, and how much he regretted the inconvenience of his absence. When we inquired, they could not say when or if he would return. Both Frau Bittner and I agreed that we could not continue with just one teacher. We had to find a replacement as quickly as possible. I asked her if she knew anyone who was qualified and might be available. Yes, she did. There was this young woman - very pleasant and speaking excellent English - who lived in her apartment house. She had gotten to know her from hallway conversation, and as a result they had become friends. That all sounded good. "Bring her over," I said.

The next day Frau Bittner arrived with a most attractive woman; tall, blonde, perhaps in her late twenties, with a dazzling smile, and a great figure revealed as she took off her coat and sat down. As far as I was concerned, it didn't matter whether she spoke English or not, she was hired. But, fortunately, she did speak English, in fact very well, which took care of the problem. Her name was Katarina Mueller. She was unmarried and had come to Salzburg from Vienna where she had worked with the British occupation. She was now employed at the Kreuzberg Hotel as a housekeeper, but the work had no appeal for her and the pay was not enough to live on. She would be willing to start right away. Frau Bittner said she would be happy to help her in the beginning, but that she didn't think much help would be necessary.

After about half an hour of conversation, during which we discussed the job, conditions of employment, pay, and so forth, I said, "Well, Fraulein Mueller, we will be very happy to have you here, starting right away. Here's an application for you to fill out. Normally, we need formal approval from the authorities to go ahead, but we can't wait that long, so I'll OK it for now, which is enough to get started." She thanked me with another of her dazzling smiles and left with Frau Bittner.

We heard two weeks later that Herr Baron had died in the hospital. Frau Bittner went to his funeral service and reported that there were only a handful of mourners. In one respect that solved a potential problem. I don't know what I would have done had Herr

Baron recovered and returned to his old job. Meanwhile, Fraulein Meuller took to the work immediately. Her energy and good looks quickly won over the DP's, especially the men. I myself was giving thought as to how to get to know her better - in a less formal setting.

Chapter Thirty-One

Two Assassinations

Julie, who up to that time had shown little interest in the English program, suddenly decided to make up for lost time. She now sat in during these sessions more than occasionally and offered to help in any way she could. At lunch she almost always joined Frau Bittner and Fraulein Meuller, and often for coffee as well.

I asked Frau Bittner about this - whether this added presence was causing any problems as far as the teaching was concerned.

"No, not really," she replied. "Julie means well even if she doesn't understand what we're trying to do. It's too simple for her. If you really want to know, I think she has - how do you say it in English? - a crush, is that the right word? - on Katarina. In these things it is best not to interfere, so I don't."

"Yes. it seemed to be more then a sudden interest in our English classes, "I replied.

"You don't know this, Mr. Barwick, it was before you arrived, but Julie had a special friend, a Slovenian girl. Just like with this Katarina. Then the girl's embarkation clearance came through, and - poof! - she is gone. Julie was so sad. For weeks she didn't talk to anybody."

Julie dropped by my office one morning, which didn't often happen. "Jack, I really want to congratulate you on your new English teacher, Katarina. She has put a whole new life into the English program. She just naturally relates to people. I've sat in on a few classes, and I can see - people want to learn from her."

"Thanks, Julie," I said. "That's what Frau Bittner tells me also."

Two Assassinations

"Oh, Frau Bittner," Julie went on, "she's all right. She gets the job done. But with her there's no spark, no life, just routine teaching."

So, on that basis, things went on for about another week. Then, I came back from a visit to the DPC office in town to find someone waiting for me in my office - a tall American type dressed in civilian clothes.

"Mr. Barwick?" he said, extending his hand. "Callahan - CID."

"CID?" I asked, very surprised that they could be interested in our little operation..

"Criminal investigation, we work with Army G2. Here's my ID," he replied, flashing a badge in his opened wallet.

"What's this all about?" I asked, now even more surprised.

"You have a girl working here named Meuller - right?" I nodded.

"How long has she been here?"

"Oh, about three weeks."

"And you hired her pending clearance, is that so?"

"Yes," I said. "It's a common procedure for hiring local help."

"Well, you're going to have to get rid of her - let her go."

"What do you mean, let her go? I don't understand."

"Just what I said, Mr. Barwick. Let her go - fire her. You have one week to comply - til next Friday."

"But she's an excellent employee and a key part of our English program. Why do you want us to let her go?"

"We don't give reasons for the actions we take, Mr. Barwick. And there's no appeal from this order. As much as I can tell you at this point is that she didn't pass clearance."

"Well, Mr. Callahan, I don't know. Seems very high-handed to me. What happens if I don't go along?"

"We would have to take steps to remove her from your program, and you will be cited for non-compliance with a federal order. That won't do your own job prospects any good."

"Have you talked to my boss downtown at DP headquarters?"

"He wasn't in earlier, but I'm going back there now."

He stood up. "Nice to have met you, Mr. Barwick. Don't do anything stupid." And with that he left.

Jesus Christ! I was astounded, really shaken by the abruptness

Picking Up the Pieces

and callousness of the order. And by the fact that no reasons were given, that no appeal - not even discussion - was possible.

I sat there for awhile trying to calm down, then asked Frau Bittner to come in before she went home. When she did I told her what had happened.

"Oh, Mr. Barwick, you are quite naïve," she said. "We Austrians lived with such actions for seven years. We are used to it. There is nothing you can do, you cannot fight them. Don't make trouble for yourself."

"Well, even if I can't fight them, I at least want to know more about this mystery. You and Katarina are good friends, right?" She nodded. "Talk to her. Don't say we must let her go, just say you have heard there is a problem - a delay - with her clearance. See if you can find out the reason. Emphasize that we are very happy with her work here."

Then I called our DP office in town. Yes, Callahan had been there and left a copy of the written order, which he had not given to me.

"So where do we stand?" I asked.

"We, meaning you, don't have a choice," was the reply. "Especially on anything relative to security or criminal activity."

"But they won't even give us a reason - tell us what the problem is - which we could perhaps clarify." I protested.

"Tough shit, buddy. We're here at their pleasure. As long as you work for the DP Commission, you do what they say. The last thing in the world we want is a fight with the occupation."

The following morning, Frau Bittner came into my office, looked around conspiratorially, and in a lowered voice said, "It seems we will never be free from our Nazi past. I had a talk with Katarina last night."

"Did you find out anything?" I asked.

"Yes," she said. Katarina says they will probably make you let her go. In Vienna when she applied to work with the Americans, it was the same thing, so she went to work for the British, even though they pay less."

"But why? What do they have against her? I can't believe she's a communist or a war criminal."

"No, not a war criminal," Frau Bittner said. "but she told me her father was. Her father is the man who shot Dolfuss. Assassinated him."

"Dolfuss, Dolfuss - who was Dolfuss?"

"He was our head man - Chancellor - back in 1937, just before the Nazis came in. He was socialist, and he did a lot of good things in Vienna. The Nazis, you know, hated the socialists. Socialists, communists they were all the same to the Nazis. Anyway Katarina's father was one of those fanatical Nazis - I forget his name - not Mueller, that is the name she uses now. Anyway he was the one who assassinated Dolfuss. When the Nazis came in 1938 they made a big hero out of him, but to the Americans he is a war criminal."

"I still can't see that this has anything to do with her," I said. "She didn't assassinate Dolfuss."

"Of course not, but sometimes the innocent must suffer with the guilty, especially if the guilty are their own family."

"What a business! Poor girl! But can she ever find work? If - I mean, when - we let her go, how will she get along?" I asked.

"It could be worse," Frau Bittner replied. "She has a boyfriend, an American sergeant in the army. She says he's crazy about her. In fact, he's paying the rent for her apartment. He wants to marry her and take her back home with him. She says she doesn't really want to leave Austria, but as long as she stays here she'll be known only as the daughter of a murderer - an assassin - the man who killed Dolfuss."

When I called, Gussie Mayerson had already received official notification of the CID order and agreed that we had no alternative but to fire her, and that I was to proceed immediately.

Things were moving so fast I hadn't had time to alert Julie to what was happening. She heard it all from Frau Bittner, including the bit about the American army sergeant. Late that afternoon Julie came charging into my office.

"What is this rumor I hear that you are going to fire Katarina? Have you done it?"

"Not yet," I said. "I had to talk with Frankfurt first to be sure they were informed. That's why I've delayed telling you. I'm sorry."

"But certainly, you're not going to do it, are you?"

Picking Up the Pieces

"What else can I do? It's an official order," I said.

"What else can you do? You can refuse." Julie was walking around the room, very agitated. She turned to face me.

"You can fight this ridiculous order. Make them give you a reason. There must be some sensible person up there who would realize how arbitrary and unjust this is - this thing they want you to do."

"Julie, be reasonable. I'm just a little cog here in the machine. I can't take on the whole occupation."

"That's what they all said at Nuremberg - 'I was ordered to do it' - those who said 'no' are remembered as heroes. You must at least make an effort." She was close to hysteria.

"Well, I don't want to be 'remembered' as a hero. I'm in a lousy situation, but I can't change the rules."

It was no use trying to explain. She sat down and leaned across the desk. There were tears in her eyes. "Jack, please, won't you at least try? This poor girl deserves a chance. She doesn't want to leave her home and marry a man she doesn't love just to get away from here. Can't you see what you are condemning her to?"

I was becoming exasperated. "Julie," I said, "This is not a matter for the YMCA. I understand your feelings, but I work for the DP Commission. That's who pays me. If I don't agree with them, I can always resign, but I'm not ready to do that."

She got up and started to walk out. At the door she turned to face me. "I would have expected more from you, but you're just another bureaucrat - no better than the rest of them." She exited, slamming the door.

Good Lord! What a scene! I was no good at handling confrontations. It was very upsetting, so much so that I put off till the next morning my talk with Katarina.

There were no histrionics at all in that interview. She was resigned to the situation - she understood, and did not hold me responsible. There were times, she said, where she felt the only solution was to leave Austria. "For me, the war didn't end in 1945," she said. We talked for a few minutes. I wished her good luck, we shook hands, and she left. Not very long after that I heard from Frau Bittner that Katarina had married her Army sergeant and was now in the States.

Julie now ignored me completely, speaking only when something came up that required it. This atmosphere of stifled hostility was extremely depressing. I told myself a thousand times, "Don't let it bother you, there's nothing you could have done differently." And even though that was true, it didn't make me feel any better. Otherwise the program at Camp Hellbrun went on as before. We found a new English teacher. This time, I didn't complete the employment process until her application and clearance were approved, which took about a month.

Summer was almost over. I was beginning to feel restless. But the pattern was broken for a week when my two younger brothers arrived on their way to the Middle East to live with my father in Beirut. He had left London and was now part of the UN/Vol Agency relief program for Palestinian refugees, displaced as a result of the 1948 Arab-Israeli war. While I worked during the day, James and Peter explored the local trout stream, and we dined on their catch in the evening They had a wonderful time, and so did I.

About that same time Julie took a vacation to go back to Holland. This surprised me, since vacation from work had been an option that did not exist for her. But, apparently, her father had died, and there was an aged mother needing care arrangements.

Another interruption to the routine came with an unexpected call from Nan Thompson, Julie's boss, who headed up the YMCA program for Austria. We had met at the time of my arrival, but aside from one or two brief visits to the camp, had had no contact. She asked if I could come over to her office the following afternoon for a short meeting.

Her office was in a building on one side of the Mozart Platz which housed the IRO and several vol agencies, including the YMCA. I was a bit surprised when I realized that the meeting was to be for only the two of us.

Nan Thompson was British, about forty, with an air of competence and authority. After an exchange of pleasantries, she said, "I'm sorry we didn't meet sooner, but I was under the impression everything was going so well, it didn't need my attention."

This sounded ominous. She continued, "Jack, how do you feel

about the program? Is it working the way you would like?"

I told her I thought it was, that compared to what I had seen at Camp Grohn, we were doing just about as well here with less support and fewer facilities.

"Do you feel there are any problems where my help might be useful?" she asked.

I couldn't think of any, and said so.

"Well, Jack, the word I'm getting, and I'm sorry to say this, is that the DPC/YMCA working relationship here is not good, and our program is losing the momentum it had before you arrived. This is of great concern to me because that relationship is so important to us, and to the DPC too, I would think. We all had high hopes when you came here, precisely because you came to the DPC after a year with the Y, and because the reports from Camp Grohn and Bad Aibling were all positive. So I decided to talk to you personally, rather than make a formal issue out of what might be only a misunderstanding."

I was astonished. This was so unexpected that I had trouble composing myself enough to give a credible answer.

"Well, Nan, I don't quite know what to say. I really had no idea there was a problem. I've always tried to cooperate. To the extent that there were problems, they came from outside - you may have heard, we had to fire one of our English teachers."

"Yes, I did hear about that. You're sure there was nothing you could have done to prevent it?"

"Absolutely. It was on orders from the occupation CID, cleared with the DPC and my boss in Frankfurt."

"I see. Well, the feeling expressed to me, was that you really didn't take the work here very seriously, that refugees and the YMCA were just stepping stones to a better paying job with the government."

"It is true that I have always wanted to work for the government - to be a career Foreign Service Officer with the State Department. And I believe what I'm doing here is helpful training for that, but that doesn't mean I don't take this job seriously."

"Yes, of course," she said. "That makes sense, but here is something of greater concern to me."

Good heavens, I thought. What could this be?

"Jack, you are said to have told people that in the event of any problem or disagreement with the YMCA here, you could always turn to your father, and he would intervene to set things right. Did you say that - or imply it?"

"Of course not. Never. I never even thought it. That is a complete fabrication. My father has his own job to take care of. It was through his contacts that I went to work with the Y in Germany, but that's the end of it. I wouldn't dream of involving him in anything I do here."

By this time I was beginning to see the origin of all this mischief, but I hesitated to make a direct accusation.

"Jack," Nan said. "I believe you. I'm sorry to have been so direct, but that's how I do things. It my be stressful, but it helps clear the air. So again, I apologize. I don't want you to be offended. Please consider this whole matter closed."

Perhaps for Nan it was ended. But it wasn't ended for me. After our meeting I walked across the Mozart Platz to Tomaselli's Café. I ordered a beer and sat there for awhile, looking at the fountain with the horses and across to the other side where Army G2 was located, and getting madder by the moment.

This was character assassination - never mind that the person at the bottom of it was a deeply neurotic individual. Perhaps evil is just one way that neurosis, or psychosis, expresses itself. It didn't matter - evil is evil. Rage gradually ebbed and was replaced by a feeling of deflation, of depression, of hopelessness. Things were never going to work out here, not after this. Then and there I decided to do all I could to get out.

Chapter Thirty Two

Innsbruck USIS

Events of the past few weeks, plus the routine nature of the work, had left me with a bad taste compounded of boredom and disgust. Early that September I decided to investigate other job possibilities in Austria.

That had to be done in Vienna, which meant traveling through the Russian Zone. So instead of going by car, I decided to take the train. The train that made this run for American personnel was called "The Mozart." It was a sleeper, leaving Salzburg about nine pm, arriving in the Vienna "*bahnhof*" early the next morning - very early for rising, but you could remain on the train until about eight.

Ensconced in my upper berth, lulled by the rhythm of the wheels on the track, I soon fell asleep. Near midnight we reached the Enns River, marking the boundary between the American and Russian Zones. The train stopped, lights were switched on, and two Russian soldiers entered the train, proceeding down the car, checking passenger identification. They were both short, stocky teenagers, pimply, in greenish uniforms, each with a tommy gun over one shoulder.

"Passport," said one to me. I handed it to him. Holding it upside down, he gave it a quick glance, then handed it back. "Okay," he said, and moved on. The rest of the night was uneventful. When I awoke again, the noise of the wheels had stopped, and I realized we were in Vienna. It was too early for business, so I picked up coffee and a croissant in the station restaurant, scanned a newspaper, and waited for things to open up.

At about nine I made my way to the American Embassy,

located in the center of town, and was shown into the Personnel Office. I explained the nature of my visit, and was given an application to fill out. When this was finished, the secretary said that there would be an interview.

The interviewer who sat across the desk from me was a woman in her thirties who would have looked at home in a college admissions office. Reading from the application, she said, "College - Princeton, AB, highest honors - that's great. London School of Economics - also good. Two year's work with displaced persons in Germany and Austria, Presently with USDP Commission - excellent. Languages - German and French. All very good. Excellent qualifications, Mr. Barwick. What is your availability?" I told her I would like to give the DP Commission two weeks notice, but after that I would be ready to start.

"Do you have any openings?" I asked.

"Yes, several where you would fit in - one in particular which we must fill right away."

"Am I allowed to know what that might be?"

"Of course. It's with the USIS - the US Information Service under the Department of State. They operate information centers all over Germany and Austria in the major cities in the Allied Zones. We have one here in Vienna and one in Salzburg. Another is planned for Linz, and one has recently opened up in Innsbruck. That one needs an assistant to the regional public affairs officer who directs the operation. That is the job I have in mind for you. It carries a GS Six rating, and the salary is $4,000 a year, plus a one hundred dollar per month living allowance and occupation privileges. How would you feel about working in Innsbruck?"

"I would love it," I answered, quite carried away by the idea. A job with the State Department, in a city of legendary beauty - there wasn't a single negative. Too good to be true.

"That's fine," she said. "Maybe we can get this settled this morning. Wait here for a few minutes. I want to review your application with my boss, but I can't imagine that he won't like it." And with that she went out leaving me in a state of euphoria.

Half an hour later she returned. "Sorry to have kept you waiting, he had someone with him. But he's on board, as I knew he would be. I have his authorization to complete the hire - that is, if you still want to go ahead."

"Absolutely, I'm so glad I came here personally," I said.

"Yes, it's saving everybody a lot of time. Here are more papers to fill out, plus one for medical, and one for security. The Act of Congress under which USIS was set up requires an FBI clearance for any new hire. That can take forever, so we go ahead on the basis of a pending clearance, to be finalized as they get to it. OK?"

It certainly was. At that point I would have agreed to anything.

"One more item. We would like three references - if possible, one from your present employer, the DP Commission, and two others. Names, titles, and a phone contact so we can call them. Again, it's just to save time."

The rest of the morning was taken up with paperwork. They told me I would receive final reporting instructions in about a week. As long as the references were satisfactory, I could consider myself hired.

I walked out into the midday sunshine with a kind of floating sensation, feet scarcely in contact with the pavement. It all seemed too easy to have been real. Life just didn't work that way. The sense of unreality persisted so that at my desk in Camp Hellbrunn the next morning, I wondered if the whole trip had not been a dream. Dream or not, I immediately got on the phone to Gussie Mayerson and the DPC, informing them that I was leaving the DPC and transferring to the US Information Service, and that I was giving both Gussie and DPC HQ as references. They took this news in stride, and promised favorable endorsements.

For the third reference, I was undecided. In the light of recent events, what could I expect from Nan Thompson? Nothing like finding out, so I picked up the phone and called her. I explained my request

"No, Jack, I have no problem with a reference. Our meeting clarified the situation - I believed what you told me then, and I do now. If working for the State Department is what you want to do, that's fine with me. Congratulations."

I thanked her, saying I would still be around for the next two weeks.

"Good, that will make the transition easier. Who is taking your place?"

I said I didn't know, but would inform her as soon as I did.

"Thank you, Jack. It's going to be a bit of a pinch. I haven't had a chance to tell you, but Julie's not coming back She feels her mother can't spare her right now. So, with you going, that leaves two positions to be filled. Anyway, best of luck to you."

I had a feeling there was more to the story than that. There were no words of regret for Julie's departure. Also, I had the distinct impression that my story had confirmed a problem she had been hearing about from other sources. If that was the end of it, good.

A few days later I dropped into the Information Center - known as the "Amerika Haus" - in Salzburg. My Vienna meeting had been so taken up with personnel details that I knew very little about the actual work involved. This lack of specifics became more apparent the more I thought about it. With an Amerika Haus already here, it seemed like a good idea to have a talk with them.

"Them" was the person in charge, a man named Hopman. "I'm called a regional public affairs officer," he said. "Here in Land Salzburg, you can think of our mission as public relations - presenting the best image we can of the US and its policies as a counter to Soviet communist policies and propaganda. As an influence on public opinion here, in the cold war, we're a key element. But our methods are through information to the press and radio, plus a whole array of cultural activities: libraries, lectures, music, film shows, etcetera - all featuring American talent and creativity. We want people to like us, to trust us and be receptive to our policies."

"Your radio, is it the same as Radio Free Europe?" I asked.

"No," Hoppman replied, "Although we share some of the same objectives. RFE aims its broadcasts internally at countries already under Soviet domination, or where there is danger of a country going communist, not really the case in Austria. We provide information to local newspapers and radio stations, but it appears without US identification."

That was the big picture. A subsequent tour of the facility made it obvious that a lot of money had been invested in it. I was very impressed and wondered if this was what I could expect in Innsbruck.

The Amerika Haus there turned out to be a three-story, substantial building located downtown on the Erler Strasse, one block from the Maria Theresien Strasse, Innsbruck's main thoroughfare. Four display windows at the entrance on the ground floor broke up a dark brick façade. It did not have the flash and glitter of the Salzburg Center, but I was not in a mood to be critical.

Streetcars ran along the Maria Theresien from one end of the city to the other. The northern view ended with the massive wall of the *"Nordketten"* separating Austria from Germany. At the southern end stood the *"Patcherkofel,"* and the ascent to the Brenner Pass leading to Italy. Between these two mountain ranges, from west to east, dividing the city, ran the Inn River, with its bridges. In fact, "Innsbruck" translates as "Inn Bridge." The Inn is a no-nonsense river, usually cloudy from snowmelt and glacier runoff, rushing straight ahead, with few pools or curves to delay its meeting with the Danube.

On entering the Information Center, I saw that the entire ground floor had been converted into a library. My instructions were to report to the director, Henry "Hank" Siemer. His office was on the second floor, overlooking the street. One of the librarians showed me up.

Siemer got up from behind a large desk. He was good-looking, forty or forty-five, with an athletic build and iron gray hair brushed straight back. When he spoke, it was with a faint foreign inflection - German, I inferred from his name.

"Jack," he said, after introductions, "Mind if I all you Jack? I'm not going to start you out with a long lecture. That can come later, I don't have time now. First thing is to get you settled, temporary for now, until we find something permanent. I'm going to turn you over to Frau Binder and Fraulein Tausch - Erica - who keep the office running. I think you'll like it here, I do. We have a good staff, all of whom you'll soon get to know. OK? We'll talk more later"

The women, Binder and Tausch, had already booked a room for me at a hotel just around the corner, which had been taken over by the French occupation, and was reserved for officers. Innsbruck was headquarters for the French Zone of Austria. The hotel had a cozy reception area, dining room, bar, and cocktail lounge. The menu was in French, and there were newspapers from Paris. My room was small, just as at the Villa St. Hubert, but comfortable. It all brought back memories of that summer in France, what seemed to me a lifetime ago.

That evening was my first real introduction to Siemer, by now "Hank," and it left me somewhat perplexed. We had dinner at the Blaue Ganz (Blue Goose) restaurant in the old city. He made an effort to be relaxed and sociable, but the effects of strain on his nerves was apparent. His hands trembled as he held a glass or tried to light a cigarette, and his description of the work was jerky and disjointed. Several times he lost the thread of what he had been saying. After about an hour, he complained of a headache, saying we would continue in the morning. When we did, I observed that he always seemed to be in a rush: short, cryptic instructions, hurried phone conversations - as though there wasn't time to do all that was on his mind. Nevertheless, I did get a sketchy overview of the operation, most of it from the various department heads, who wanted to make a good impression.

In all, there were about twenty employees. One of them, Gerda Gross, functioned as chief administrator, with broad supervisory authority. It was she who acted as my guide as we toured the premises.

On the ground floor were two libraries, one lending, the other reference; with about ten thousand books in all, American authors only. There were also US magazines, including trade and technical publications, as well as three newspapers: two Austrian and the European edition of the Herald Tribune. Even at ten in the morning, the library seemed to be in good use. At the rear of the ground floor was an atelier, where a graphic artist, Walnhoefer, created window displays promoting various themes and events staged by the Center.

On the second floor was an auditorium capable of seating about two hundred people, with a movie projection booth at one end, containing 16mm equipment and a hundred or so titles in cans. In addition, a large closet had been converted into a music room whose shelves contained dozens of record albums, both 78 rpm and LP's, featuring American artists. At the head of the stairs one

Picking Up the Pieces

entered the children's library, which as I looked in was filled with tots and their mothers playing music and games.

I have mentioned that Siemer's office, as well as that of his secretary and bookkeeper, were on the second floor. Mine was in back, overlooking a garage and parking area for three vehicles: a government issue Plymouth station wagon, a large bus-like "Bookmobile" and Siemer's personal car - a sporty Porsche. My office was small, but large enough since I didn't plan to spend much time in it.

The third floor held a maze of offices for individual department heads and the chief administrator, Fraulein Gross. Also up there was Carla Regner, who managed services to press and radio.

That more or less describes our little American outpost, four hundred miles from Vienna in the Tyrolian Alps. The only other American there in an official capacity was a certain Major Ward, charged with maintaining liaison with the French occupation. Both France and Britain supported information services roughly similar to our own, but on a much smaller scale - France through the Institut Francais, and Britain through the British Council.

Given its isolated location, the information center was often mistaken for a consulate. It was hard to convince callers with business interests, or Americans in financial difficulty, that we had no function other than to dispense information. We referred such problems to Vienna.

A more fundamental question was, why were we in Tyrol at all? France didn't need our help with their occupation. The argument that we were there to counter Soviet influence was open to question since the Tyrol was deeply Catholic, and as anti-communist as the US itself. They needed no encouragement from us. Although the strategic rationale was never clear to me, that was completely irrelevant. The fact was that I was there, enjoying every minute of the experience, and looking forward to carrying our message to the Tyroleans, whether they needed it or not.

But first, there was official protocol to be observed. I had to be introduced to the French, who, as one might suspect, were extremely sensitive to any trespass by the Americans onto any speck of French authority. With this in mind, Siemer walked me over the short distance to the French administration building to meet his occupation information counterpart, a certain "Pierre," last name forgotten. Mutual suspicion between the US and France might have been alive and well back in Paris, but there was no sign of it here. From the start, it was "Pierre," "Hank," and "Jack." My French proved to be very useful since Pierre had no English, and Siemer no French. With me as translator, the meeting accomplished no business but rather a convivial exchange of good feelings and promises to keep in close touch.

Shortly after my arrival an opportunity emerged to make myself useful. This was with respect to American students of whom there were perhaps fifty in Innsbruck at that time. Our libraries had become the unofficial gathering spot for them, testimony to that yearning Americans in a foreign country have to seek out and mingle with their own kind. Siemer had called a meeting of a dozen student leaders to discuss ways in which they might become more involved in the center's program. Although Siemer was a talented individual, he didn't have the faintest idea how to run a meeting. Mainly, this was because he did not know, and had not given much thought to what, he wanted to accomplish. So for a time, there was a great deal of aimless discussion, with no apparent direction and no progress.

Thinking back to my days in London, it occurred to me that our Students Association there could be a useful model to build on here. It would be the reverse of the goal Siemer had in mind. Instead, we would use Austrian leaders to educate American students about Austria, of which, despite living there, they knew almost nothing. It was easy to explain, and as in Britain, I was sure that Austrians would be eager to participate. Also, such a program would help to solve one of the occupation's long neglected problems - one that never had been seriously addressed. Most Americans went home after their tour of duty with only a superficial knowledge of where they had been and why.

So I jumped into the meeting with this idea, and when it caught on, the formation of a program committee. Siemer was impressed. The students liked the idea, and we were off and running.

From the start, it was a success. As in Britain, they had no difficulty getting speakers, although most were from the immediate area. We helped by providing meeting facilities, and

Picking Up the Pieces

contacts where needed. Otherwise the students ran the program themselves. Or rather a dedicated cadre of three or four enthusiastic individuals did. Nevertheless, the result was a series of monthly meetings that winter, each featuring a speaker. These included the *burgomeister* or mayor; Tyrol's major newspaper editor; the president of the University; the president of the Austrian Ski Federation; and a spokesperson from the French occupation, among others. Anyone attending those free meetings would have obtained a good picture of Tyrol, its people, and its major institutions.

As that got underway, I began to immerse myself in other projects, always with Siemer's blessing and encouragement. We got along well; I found him easy to work for. This was a surprise, since to everyone else he was a tyrant, moody and unpredictable.. They were afraid of him. His was a fear-driven management style - fear of being fired, a serious matter in that fragile economy. Working for the Americans paid well and carried a cachet of prestige.

But as far as I was concerned, things were going very well, when suddenly - a bombshell. Siemer called me into his office one morning after I had been there about three weeks. "Jack," he said, "I've got surprise for you. As of tomorrow, you're taking over - replacing me."

"What are you talking about?" I managed to get out.

"I've been diagnosed with a severe nervous disorder," he replied. "They're sending me away for treatment, leaving tomorrow. They don't say for how long."

"To where? What will you do? Will I be able to contact you if necessary?" My mind was racing.

"No contact whatsoever," he said. "Its some kind of sanitarium, in Italy, over the border near Merano, I believe."

"My God, this is some news, Hank. I don't know what to say."

"Well, you'll be regional public affairs officer, at least for awhile, 'Acting,' that is, until they find a permanent replacement. No one could say how long that might be. You'll be on your own here, but I have no worries. I'm sure you can handle it."

I sat there stunned, unable to reply.

"Jack, there's one more thing. Since I'm going to be gone

indefinitely, I've cleared out the personal stuff from my apartment; it's really a great place. Since you're still at the hotel, why not just move in? It's the sort of place bachelors fantasize about, believe me. Your girlfriends will love it, mine did."

After Siemer left, I walked over to have a look. He wasn't kidding, and I had a bit of difficulty seeing myself living in such elegant surroundings.

First, the setting: leading into the old city is the Maria Theresien Allee a tree lined boulevard with the *landestheater* on one side and the Maria Theresien Schloss (palace) on the other. (Maria Theresa is an important figure in Austrian history, an 18th century queen, mother of Marie Antoinette.) From the allee one entered the old city through an archway connecting the schloss with an ancient church of the Hapsburg emperors. At the corner of the arch stood a round tower with a wide circular staircase inside leading up to Siemer's apartment, which was actually in the arch, over the street, with a view down the allee, along the façade of the schloss, to the mountains beyond. Four floor to ceiling windows in the parlor framed this perspective. All the furnishings were luxurious with many priceless antiques. For example, a six-foot, carved Baroque wood framed mirror hung on one wall; other walls were covered with landscape paintings and portraits of long gone, unnamed heroes. At the rear was a bedroom, with an enormous king-sized bed; and there was a bath but no kitchen.

The apartment was part of a larger complex known as the *"damenstift,"* in the old days reserved for the widows of high ranking army officers, but now given to the widow of any veteran, regardless of rank. My landlady, Frau Voltin, was such a one. She lived with her two dogs, in separate rooms, and rented out the rest. As a girl, Frau Voltin had been what were known as *"Wiener waeschemaedeln"* - Viennese laundresses, who did soldiers laundry for them, and probably more. Not infrequently, these girls became wives to the soldiers whose underwear, socks and shirts they were washing, a logical next step. When her husband died just before the war, the government assigned the apartment to Frau Voltin.

I simply took over Siemer's lease and moved in, feeling like I had wandered into a stage set, miscast as an Austrian Grand Duke.

Picking Up the Pieces

The only hitch in this whole arrangement was that from time to time the Ministry of Arts and Culture would come in unannounced and remove one of the paintings so that it could be included in a traveling exhibit of Austrian art. But they always replaced it with one of similar size so I scarcely noticed the change.

Siemer's absence did not result in any major disruption. Momentum from the past kept things going, and many activities managed themselves without my intervention. With him gone, employee's concern for job security disappeared and they relaxed since it was obvious that I wasn't about to fire anybody.

Then, a month after his departure, Siemer suddenly reappeared. "Just dropped by for a short visit," he explained. "I'm on my way to take over the new center we're opening in Linz."

"How are you feeling? Are you finished at the sanitarium?" I asked.

"Yes, thank God. I couldn't have stood it any longer."

"Why not?"

"Well, by 'rest,' they mean complete rest. Nothing, absolutely nothing to do - alles verboten. It's total withdrawal from the world. They even restrict personal contacts. It was like 'house arrest,' or being in 'solitary,' like what they do with dangerous criminals back home."

"But, opening up the Linz center, that's a big job. They must consider you're cured."

"As far as I'm concerned, the cure is ten times worse than the illness, whatever that was. It was never made clear to me. But no matter what, I'm never going back there… So long, Jack, come up and see me at the new center. We'll have an opening celebration. You'll get an invitation."

Chapter Thirty Three

Making Friends for the US

Conversations with Siemer and Hopman had given me an overview of the Information Center program, which was not all that difficult to understand. Its simple rationale was to influence public opinion and perceptions via a dual strategy: one, very public and visible, was cultural; the other, out of sight and semi-secret, was political, using the information media of press and radio as well as expense-paid visits to the US for important persons.

This public ffairs side of the program could less charitably be called "propaganda," because that is what it was. However, no apology is necessary. The Soviets were taking full advantage of their military success to follow up with an intensive propaganda barrage aimed at western Europe where the Communist Party was a significant factor in national elections. Czechoslovakia had voted itself communist in 1948, and there was danger that Italy and France might do the same. Communism had lesser appeal in Catholic Austria, but was a factor nevertheless, especially in the Russian controlled provinces.

Beside playing up cmmunism as the wave of he future, Soviet propaganda tried to sow mistrust of the US effort to rebuild the shattered postwar European economy. US aid was depicted as "capitalist imperialism," under which western Europe would wind up controlled by Wall Street, and American "materialism" would permeate European culture, with the destruction of native traditions and national identity.

If this was the message of our cold war adversary, then it was our job in the USIS to do all we could to counter it, thus the need to work through any and all existing national and local communication outlets. In that pre-TV era, the most important were newspapers and radio, especially newspapers where issues could be explained and stories developed in depth; radio was still mostly music and light programming

For our information services - news stories and articles of political significance - we functioned simply as a conduit, usually not even that. Materials were sent directly from USIS in Vienna to the paper, prepackaged for printing, or to the radio station for broadcast. Given the religious-conservative nature of Tyrol, the anti-Soviet, pro-American slant of these articles coincided with both popular and editorial opinion. They were used without attribution as a welcome staple for daily news material.

It didn't take me long to become well acquainted with a central figure in these activities. This was Manfred Neier, editor of the *Tyroler Tageszeitung*, Innsbruck's largest daily paper, and the principal news source for Tyrol. Neier ran the paper with an iron hand and a fierce driving energy. He was a short, balding man of about forty, with an ugly face which could suddenly break out into a crooked smile. Manfred and I became good friends. Also, we were useful to one another: to me, he was a major public opinion resource - one could say, the major resource in the area. He regarded me as a contact with occupation authorities in Vienna, a channel he could turn to for unofficial thinking on important topics.

In that respect, he was constantly after me for a "fuller explanation," for the "real story." Why, really why, was Ambassador Dowling leaving?"... "Who is this new man, Thompson?"... "What was discussed during Foreign Minister Gruber's trip to Washington?"... "What is holding up the peace treaty?" And so on. He didn't want my version - I usually didn't have one anyway. He wanted me immediately to get on the phone to Vienna, as high up as I could get, for an answer, for the unvarnished truth. Yes, he had read the handout, but there were still questions.

Push, push, push - dig, dig, dig - he was never satisfied. Keeping Neier happy was a big part of my job, but I was also intimidated by Vienna, and fearful of becoming as great a gadfly to my higher ups as he was to me. He wore me out. But I now realize, as I did not then, that that is what excellent journalists do. That is how they work.

As long as I was in Innsbruck we remained good friends. He had a lovely wife but no children. I was occasionally invited to their home for dinner

Aside from pure business interests, a good part of Neier's receptive attitude could be explained by the fact that he was an alumnus of one of our programs that provided direct benefits to important people - "opinion molders," as they were called. This was the exchange program by which selected individuals visited the US for six weeks on a prearranged, all expenses paid tour. Candidates were selected by the regional public affairs director from several categories: political, professional, educational, and possibly others, then reviewed and approved by Vienna. Siemer had made a number of such recommendations, of which several recipients had already returned, full of praise and good feeling for the US, its institutions, and its policies.

"Exchange" was one of the most successful programs in the USIS repertoire. Although the visits were unsupervised, it practically guaranteed that these individuals would enjoy their time in the US, and be impressed by what they found there. It also guaranteed that when they got back they would talk about their experiences, and hopefully act on them. All of these returnees were featured speakers in our lecture series.

Another important graduate of the exchange program was *stadt burgermeister*, Greiter, the mayor of Innsbruck. His was one of my first protocol visits. During our hour long session he told me about his US visit, but more interesting to me was the story of his political life. I'm going to give a summary here because of what it tells about life under the Nazis from which the city was still emerging.

Herr Greiter was a grizzled old socialist veteran of the dangerous political period after the Nazis took over in 1938. He made me realize how completely impossible it was to raise any public voice, even the slightest criticism of the Nazi regime, during those years of oppression. As a socialist, Greiter fell under immediate suspicion. Too old for military service, he was left untouched while the Germans completed their overhaul of the Austrian political landscape, first in Vienna, then in the provinces. When they finally did take up his dossier, Greiter was deemed to be a dangerous subversive and sent to Dachau, the concentration camp just outside Munich.

Dachau has been described at great length elsewhere. What I had not realized was that it was, in fact, two camps, one inside the other. The larger, outer camp contained minor offenders and "politicals," not deemed to be a direct threat to the government. Within was a high security enclosure with no connection or communication to the outside. This inner prison was reserved for Jews and persons considered "dangerous." No one left there alive - worked to death, starved to death, or both.

After two years Greiter's case was reviewed by the authorities. He was released and allowed to return to Innsbruck, but at the time of his departure was warned by Gestapo officers not to resume political activity, and, above all, not ever, under any circumstances, reveal what went on in Dachau. "If you do," they said, "We will know about it. You will be returned to Dachau, to our inner camp, and you will never come out of there alive."

Naturally, Greiter took that warning seriously. With the end of the war, his Dachau experience gave him automatic political clearance by the Allies, and his political career resumed, even flourished. The risks run by anti-Nazi political figures, and members of the resistance underground, more than justified the heroic place accorded to them in Austria's postwar society.

I also had occasion to meet figures from the other side. One in particular stands out. This little story shows the complexities involved in making dogmatic judgments.

On the cultural front, our libraries were the heart of the program, open every day except Sunday, with lectures, films and music in a supporting role. The lending library attracted a general but English-speaking audience, since all of the books were in English. It filled a real need in the community, not so much to prevent the area from going communist - there was never any danger of that - but rather to deepen the cultural roots and understanding between the US and this part of Austria.

Reaching the more intellectual circles at the university was more difficult, but our reference library with its many resource publications provided accessibility to recent information not available there for more than a decade. It made a useful supplement to the university's own library.

We even harbored ambitions to penetrate the mountainous interior, to carry our message to the smaller towns - there was only one real city in Tyrol - and even to remote valleys and villages. The means to do this was a "bookmobile" about the size of a Greyhound bus. Inside, were shelves for a supply of books and films, as well as 16mm projection equipment. Crew consisted of a lecturer/librarian and a film projectionist. They traded those jobs as well as the driving. The bookmobile made two circuits, one east, and one west, stopping at each location about once a month. Schools were the target at each stop, with a film/lecture, followed by book distribution and returns. Its arrival was always a big day for these isolated hamlets.

The bookmobile was an example of our library extension services. There were others. For example, one summer afternoon instructions arrived from Vienna directing us to assist a conference scheduled to take place in about a month in the tiny village of Alpbach, high above the Zillertal, about fifty miles from Innsbruck. This conference was the brain child of Otto Molden, one of two brothers, both important figures in postwar Vienna - especially Fritz, editor of *Die Presse*, Austria's largest daily paper. Fritz's fame derived from his role in the *Wiederstands Bewegung*, Austria's underground resistance movement against the Nazis. It was he who secretly met with OSS Chief, Alan Dulles, in Switzerland to negotiate Austria's surrender and withdrawal from the war. He was a real man of action and much admired by the American occupation.

The other brother, Otto, was a more cerebral type, an idealist who dreamed of a Europe unfettered by frontiers, where intellectual ideas and friendships could blossom in the absence of war and national rivalries. This conference was to be a first step in that direction. I forget the exact title, but it was something like "The New European Intellectual Forum."

The site he had picked for his conference metaphorically matched the dream itself, isolated in an Alpine village of surpassing charm, high above the clouds. No nasty thoughts from the world below were to be permitted here. Neither I nor the information center had any direct role in the conference itself so, unfortunately, I cannot report on its meetings and discussions. Our role was strictly a supporting one, to supply books from our reference library, on the theory, I suppose, that no self-respecting intellectual can exist for even a short time without a book within easy reach.

Just in case more than books were needed, I had Freineck, the head of our reference library, on site; I also checked in by phone to get a report on how things were going. The second day he suggested that I come and have a look for myself. It was a beautiful summer day, with nothing special going on at the center, so why not?

I found him at the registration desk where he got me signed in. It was mid-afternoon, and various groups were still in session. We poked our heads inside to listen for a few moments. In one, an Oxford don was lecturing on "Religion in Colonial America," In another a discussion was in progress on "African Art." Clearly, the intellectuals participating were drawn from many different areas of study.

We adjourned to a room where they had set up a refreshment center. It was empty except for a woman who was taking a cup of coffee to one of the tables. Freineck greeted her, then introduced me.

"Miss Riefenstahl, this is Mr. Barwick, the head of our information center. Jack, Miss Riefenstahl is a famous filmmaker and photographer."

"Please sit with me, if you have the time," she said, taking a seat herself. Her English was German accented.

Film, that was interesting. "Are you making a film now?" I asked.

She laughed. "No, I think my filmmaking days are over. Besides, the amount of money it takes to make a film these days is impossible. Photography is much cheaper, so I do that."

I looked at her closely - about fifty, tall, with an athletic build, dark hair with a reddish tinge. Riefenstahl. ..Riefenstahl...The name was in some way familiar, but I couldn't place it. She and

Picking Up the Pieces

Freineck were talking.

"Have you talked to Molden?" Freineck asked.

"No, he is avoiding me. I am quite upset. I would never have come here just to be ignored, or shunned like a leper," she said.

"What a pity," he replied. "Who in the world of film has better qualifications to participate?"

"I wouldn't say that, but this whole conference was to be for the free expression of art, intellect and ideas. Whatever else, I am an artist. They study my films to learn how to do it. When I first inquired, Molden said he would be delighted to have me. Why does it now make sense to exclude someone like myself? Oh, I am so sick of politics...Excuse me, Mr. Barwick, but I fear it is you Americans who have banished me. They are financing this conference, and Mr. Molden probably had no choice where Leni Riefenstahl is concerned."

Now all was clear. This was Leni Riefenstahl - THE Leni Riefenstahl - Hitler's favorite filmmaker; the girl genius who produced the greatest propaganda films ever made - *"The Triumph of the Will,"* on the 1935 Nuremberg Nazi party rally - and who went on from there to do *"Olympia"* on the Berlin Olympic games of 1936.

Politically speaking, at this time, given her past services to Goebbels' propaganda machine, she was pure poison to any kind of official recognition, regardless of how brilliant or artistic her films may have been. Their sponsor and powerful content made artistry irrelevant. I had seen *"Triumph of the Will."* It is called a documentary, but the word "documentary" does not begin to describe the film. The Nazi party rally itself was a masterpiece of outdoor theatrics - the huge stadium at night encircled by vertical columns of light out of which Hitler miraculously appeared by plane, like a god from Valhalla, to address the massed ranks of soldiers assembled below, with close-ups of the frenzied, ecstatic faces of civilians caught up by the drama of the spectacle. We know all this because Leni Riefenstahl's camera caught the panorama in every detail, and then proceeded to amplify it through dramatically lighted images in black and white. Even the most dedicated anti-Nazi could not but be impressed by the power of her presentation.

Although I hated Nazism and everything about it, at that moment there was nothing I would rather have done than to sit there over coffee with her for an informal chat. At the same time I didn't want to get our information center into political hot water. If word of our meeting had gotten out, the Soviets would have exploited it to the last degree - "American Officials Meet Secretly With Nazi Propagandist." However she saved me from my dilemma.

"Mr. Barwick, it was a pleasure to meet you. But I think they are about to recess between sessions. Since you are here as a government official, it would not be helpful for your career to be reported having had a nice talk with Leni Riefenstahl."

And on that note we parted. Afterward, I warned Freineck also to be careful, and not to be seen as her sponsor or protector.

It was a fact that in my position one had to be careful. Soviet propaganda directed its thrust about equally between singing the praises of the communist workers' paradise and attacking American policy in Europe as capitalist aggression taking place under the cover of economic assistance and cultural distractions. Along with this went a counterpoint theme: that US declarations for peaceful solutions to the world's problems were false and hypocritical, and that the US was actually a nation governed by big business war mongers. In many places, they said, American arms were supporting colonialism and suppressing the legitimate aspirations of downtrodden masses: in Korea, China, French Indochina, and the Philippines. And, of course, it was the US who had used atomic bombs against the Japanese.

To many persons this argument had a certain appeal. It was endlessly hammered by the Soviets with a reflexive echo from intellectuals, commentators, and the left wing press. I was very much aware of this sector of public opinion but did not take it too seriously, given that the Tyrol was so resolutely anti-communist and pro-American. But that kind of complacency can get an official into trouble. It led to an incident in which I momentarily lost my sense of what was appropriate to be included in our program, and more to the point, what was not.

The incident in question occurred as part of our regular film program: showings scheduled on a monthly basis, featuring documentaries on American regions and institutions as well as a few productions on our national parks and wildlife - positive, wholesome fare for all ages.

Somehow, into this mix the powers in Washington had included a wartime production by the armed forces entitled "*The Fighting Lady*"- about one of our aircraft carriers, "the Big E"- the Enterprise, which had played a key part in early naval battles in the Pacific. . I had screened the film myself in advance of the showing. Just as the descriptive material stated, it was an excellent film, very well made, exciting and perfect as a wartime morale builder. Having served in the Pacific myself in the Navy during World War II , the action carried me right along with it.

But it was quite another matter when shown in our auditorium that evening to an audience of about a hundred people. In fact, it was a terrible mistake. Non-stop explosions, flying fragments of ships, flaming aircraft plunging into the sea - where in all this was the message we were in Austria to deliver? People sat there and watched without visible reaction. No one actually got up and walked out, but at the end the usual applause was missing, and when the audience left they were shaking their heads

Later we got letters and phone calls, almost all from friends of the Amerika Haus, regular attendees at our events. They voiced bewilderment and sadness at such a departure from our usual themes of friendship and cultural interests. More than one said that the film closely resembled those they had been forced to watch during the war celebrating violent Nazi triumphs. Our own staff were much harsher in their verdicts: "a disaster"…"how to lose the propaganda war"…"incredibly stupid"…and similar opinions. However, they spared me despite my part in the fiasco, and put the blame on Vienna for sending it out, and on Washington for including it in an overseas PR program.

Thankfully, except for one local leftist publication, the episode got no attention, and there were no lasting ill effects. This was a relief to me, since in a hands of a hostile journalist, difficult issues could have been raised demanding answers.

The entire episode was an object lesson: in the future be careful, very careful.

Chapter Thirty-Four

Cultural Experiments

Carrying out our USIS program appealed to my political interests and the knowledge that we were actually doing something good for US interests as well as for world peace and stability. Also, being fully in charge was a lot of fun: twenty-seven years old, my own boss, in a big job with lots of local prestige thrown in - I was on top of the world.

Our lending and reference libraries were usually at least half full; people appreciated this new access to American writers. That their books had been considered degenerate and banned by the Nazis only increased their interest and popularity. The reference library was used regularly by scholars from the university seeking data on the US from reliable sources. These and our bookmobile program to communities in the outlying areas were completely non-controversial.

But I wanted to push out beyond traditional approaches. There was a lot going on back in the US that couldn't necessarily be found on our library shelves, and I wanted to bring these developments to public awareness, at least to that part of the public capable of appreciating them. This did not always please the very traditional conservative - especially intellectual - circles in Innsbruck. They were too polite to make any overt criticism, but expressions of condescension and disdain occasionally reached my ears: "Typically American,",…"What a country does when it has too much money," and so on. No matter, I soon gave this clique more reason to feel superior.

Of all our cultural programs, music was the least popular. Anyone would have to concede a certain difficulty in convincing

Austrians - in the land of Beethoven, Mozart, Schubert, and Brahms - to accept American composers as belonging in the top ranks of the world's musicians. Compared with those giants of the past, even the recent past, who were Harris, Ives or Diamond? Our musical lectures featuring these composers were sparsely attended and aroused little interest or enthusiasm - in some cases undeservedly, I thought. Nevertheless, it was clearly an exercise in futility.

Then I had an idea. In our music room were shelves full of American folk music. Resting there, almost totally untouched, was an entire set of recordings made in the mountains of Appalachia by John and Alan Lomax. And many others: sea chanteys, country and western, Cajun - a treasure trove. I spent hours listening to them. At the same time, nights in the gasthaeuser and taverns I was hearing Tyrolean folk music and songs with guitar, harmonicas or zither accompaniment.

I thought, since American symphonies aren't going over too well here, why not try American folk music? So we did.

The program format had two parts: first, a lecture, illustrated with snippets from our library, with me reading bits of explanation from notes in the albums. Then we had the group sing two or three easy folk songs from sheets we had printed up and distributed to the audience - usually, about thirty to fifty people. One of our staff did a piano accompaniment,, and another led the singing. For comprehension, we translated the words into German, not perfectly, but surprisingly good. At any rate, it was highly entertaining to hear them singing "On Top of Old Smoky," "Down in the Valley," "The Streets of Laredo," and "Camptown Races," all in German. Compared to the symphonic sessions, these *"Amerikanische volkslied abende* (folksong evenings) were highly successful and much talked about. This was before TV when you could still do such things.

And then I had an even better idea. If American folk music could generate lively interest, what about jazz, or its direct descendent, swing? Back home, jazz had moved out of the bars and clubs of Memphis, New Orleans, and Kansas City into more upscale environments. People were taking it seriously as an American art form. And in addition to its energy and totally

American character, some of the musicianship in swing was of the highest order, nothing to apologize for.

In the midst of these thoughts, Frau Binder came into my office one morning to announce that a certain Herr George wanted to see me. Herr George turned out to be "Fatty George," the leader of a German jazz band, specializing in American styles - jazz, Dixieland, blues, swing, whatever. He was in Innsbruck for the day, and dropped by to see if the Information Center would be interested in holding an American jazz concert.

That was exactly what I had in mind. But a German band? Could they really make American jazz sound like the real thing?

I told Herr George - I didn't want to call him "Fatty," although he was quite fat - that we would come up to Munich - that was his home base - to hear him play, and give him an answer then. Unable to get away myself, I asked two American grad students to make the trip and report back. Upon returning, they said the band was first rate - unbelievable that these were German players. So, with that endorsement I decided to proceed.

As arrangements for the concert progressed, word leaked out. It developed that we had seriously underestimated the interest in our experiment. Originally, we had planned to use the lounge at one of the hotels. This turned out to be too small; then a larger auditorium, also too small. Finally, we wound up booking the Musikvereinsalle, capable of holding over a thousand. We had issued tickets, but the night of the performance there was a mad rush at the door as dozens of people without tickets tried to get in. But every seat was taken, and the performance had to be delayed by fifteen minutes while we tried to create some sort of order. Those without tickets were allowed to stand in back and along the sides.

When things had quieted down, Fatty George with his saxophone and the band all dressed in powder blue suits, appeared on stage and immediately launched into Benny Goodman's arrangement of "One O'Clock Jump," followed by Charlie Barnet's "Skyliner." I thought the place would go mad. This was long before the era of rock concerts, and the drug-fueled mob scenes to come in the 60's and 70's. The audience of mostly young people could hardly stay in their seats, while the band gave them what they had come there to hear - and feel. More Benny Goodman, Count Basie and Artie Shaw followed, with an occasional blues number and dixieland thrown in. There were no vocal numbers, it was all instrumental with solo riffs and some extemporaneous jamming. It could have gone on all night; the audience wouldn't let them stop. Only after multiple encores was the weary band permitted to escape.

I had to admit that the musicianship was superb. It brought back a real pang of nostalgia in me for the good old USA. Dammit, there were things America could contribute to world culture, and no better proof of that than here we were, listening to one of them through the talent and artistry of a group of young Germans. All of us from the center scored the concert a great success.

But not everyone did. The next morning the music critic of the *Tiroler Tageszeitung*, Herr Tepfer, weighed in with a ponderous opinion. Quite clearly, he had not the slightest idea what jazz was all about. His ear was tuned to an entirely different frequency. He confessed to being mystified by the music - in fact, he questioned whether it was really music at all. To him it was more a "spectacle," everything on the surface, with none of the deep emotions and truths that serious music can convey. And so on, for a full column.

We would never convince him, there was no use trying. As a matter of fact, I'm not sure we could have convinced our superiors in Vienna had we decided to get their permission. But it was one of those events we did entirely on our own, for reporting purposes entitled "An Evening of American Folk Music." It made the attendance numbers look very good for that month - almost too good, but there were no questions or repercussions. Privately, I resolved that from then on, jazz was to be part of our program, even if it was expensive. Fatty George cost four hundred dollars, and the Musikvereinsalle another two hundred - almost our entire music budget for the year. Oh well, we would find a way.

In addition to lectures, libraries, films and music, we also did readings from American plays - not full scale, staged versions, but no-set, no-costume adaptations, with our staff members reading the parts. Even though there was no admission charge, we had to get permission from the publisher, usually granted.

One of these readings was from Thornton Wilder's *"Our Town"* - very good for our purposes since it required almost no scenery or complicated stage sets. Its action develops entirely through the voices of the inhabitants of a small turn-of-the-century New England town. The play is a classic, a work of genius, that even in our stripped down version left the audience sniffling and wiping their eyes.

Our amazement knew no bounds when, about a month after the performance, who should walk in the door but Thornton Wilder himself, a somewhat short, stocky gentleman, about fifty, his sparse hair graying, wearing horn-rim glasses and a gray suit. He introduced himself, and as soon as I recovered from my astonishment, I asked what brought him to Innsbruck in the dead of winter.

"I've always liked Austria," he said, "And I wanted to get away from the US for awhile. I'm still writing these days, and there are too many interruptions back there. Innsbruck seemed to be a good place to escape to."

I asked where he was staying, and if we could be of any help.

"Quite the contrary," he said. "I would like to help you - to offer my services, whatever I might do to assist in your work here. I'm at the Hotel Europa. I write during the day, but from late afternoon on, I'm available."

His manner was so friendly and unpretentious that in no time I lost my initial awe, and found myself speaking to him as to a college professor interested in helping one of his students. Unlike many academics of distinction, Thornton Wilder genuinely liked people and to be around them. His gregariousness quickly communicated itself to our staff, all of whom became adoring subjects.

Given his offer to help, we lost no time in scheduling two lectures, organized thematically. The first was called "America as Places"- literature that created a sense of "place," or regional distinctiveness. I can only summarize the presentation in which he discussed a few out of many writers whose works conveyed an understanding of a particular region, its people and the lives that were lived there. He commented at length on Sherwood

Anderson's Midwest (*"Winesburg, Ohio"*), Mark Twain's Mississippi (*"Life on the Mississippi"*), Willa Cather's western prairie (*"O Pioneers"*), and William Faulkner's deep south (*"Light in August"* etc.) To conclude, he spoke of New England and its small towns, and how he had tried to show without caricature or sentiment how environment of place shapes character, as it does in *"Our Town."*.

Although delivered in English, the lecture was well attended and received a rapturous review in the *Tiroler Tageszeitung*, so enthusiastic that his second lecture filled our hall. This one had for its subject, "How American Literature Changed American History. Taking only large events, he started with the Civil War, and how *"Uncle Tom's Cabin"* inflamed northern public opinion against slavery and the south. He went on to the reformist period, citing *"The Jungle"* by Upton Sinclair which led to the imposition of safety measures in the food industry, and *"How The Other Half Lives"* by Jacob Riis, which helped bring about fifty years of social legislation. It ended with him speaking of the Dust Bowl in the 1930's with John Steinbeck and *"The Grapes of Wrath."*

Someone asked about Thomas Wolfe, did his novels influence American history?

"No, he did not influence events as these others did," Wilder replied, "But he was part of a huge movement all across the country as young men left the farms for life in the cities, or to work in the factories. This movement changed the face of the country.

Another asked about Ernest Hemingway. Wilder laughed. "No, I would not say that 'Ernest' has influenced American history. What he has done is to change to how writers write. He created a whole new way of using words and syntax to express a preoccupation with violence and manly virtues. Many have been influenced by him, I am not one of them." The audience laughed with him.

There were more questions but our emcee eventually called a close to the evening. While there were still people in the room, Wilder said that after the lecture, for relaxation, he felt the need for a nightcap, and invited anyone who wanted to to come along. As a result, some five or six of us from the center and a few from

Picking Up the Pieces

the audience walked around the corner to the café lounge in the French hotel which was still open The lounge was deserted; we took seats and ordered drinks with Wilder in the center as the focus of attention..

The questions continued. One of the group asked him, "Mr. Wilder, are you here as part of a government sponsored program? Will you be visiting other cities in Europe?"

He replied, "No, I'm here in Innsbruck as a private individual, at my own expense, trying to find a little peace and quiet so I can get some writing done. But I also feel the Amerika Haus here is performing an important service in reestablishing contact between the United States and Europe - trying to make up for those lost years, 1939 to 1945, and rebuilding the cultural bridges between us. In my own small way, I want to be part of that effort, and have volunteered my services."

"In that effort, do you feel that Hollywood is working for you or against you?" another asked. "Should we restrict the type of films coming over here?"

"Well, if you did that, you would also have to restrict books, magazines, newspapers; there would be no end to it," Wilder replied. "Look, there's plenty of garbage out there, but there are good things too - some controversial, that's inevitable. I believe in free expression, and that criticism and discussion - like we're doing here - will separate out what is worth retaining, and we'll all be better for it."

Suddenly there was an interruption. A man whom I had not noticed, sitting in a far corner stood up and came to the edge of our group.

"Mr. Whatever your name is, that is all balderdash." His accent was British, and his demeanor suggested too much drink. "What are you, some kind of writer? A paid hack to come over here to wave the flag for America? We don't need you, and we don't want you. Go back home, there are too many Americans here already."

"Shut up. Throw him out," came from various members of the group.

"No, no," said Wilder. Then, to the drunken Englishman, "Why don't you sit down and talk it over with us?"

"I have no intention of sitting down to talk rubbish with a

gaggle of simpletons and a paid agent of the American government. As a matter of fact, I've heard about as much of this twaddle as I can take. I'm going to lodge a complaint with the French authorities for allowing the use of their premises for American propaganda sessions." And with that, he stumbled out.

Wilder brushed off my apology for allowing such a situation to develop. "Please, it's of no consequence. I've met quite a few Englishmen who can't adjust, or reconcile themselves, to the loss of England's position in the world - that their empire is gone, and England today only a second or third class power, just above Belgium or the Netherlands. To those who were raised to 'Rule Britannia,' this is intolerable, and they blame it on the USA."

Over the course of the next two weeks, I spent considerable time with Mr. Wilder. I was able to arrange a few dinners with Austrian friends - he seemed to have no connections in town, and was glad to get out of the hotel. For my part, I was grossly ignorant of American drama and the stage, incapable of any meaningful conversation on that topic- what a shame. He, on the other hand, expressed an interest in my years at Princeton, and in my opinion of the English department faculty. He reminisced about his undergraduate days at Yale, and counted himself extremely fortunate to have been there at that time because of the brilliant collection of talent among his classmates, although I can't recall who they were.

Mr. Wilder showed up in the Center from time to time to use the reference library, and to chat. When I described our *volkkslied abende* he was more than enthusiastic, exclaiming how it fitted into his "America as Places" theme. When I complained about the poor quality of our phonograph, he nodded sympathetically.

About a month after he left Innsbruck, a huge crate arrived containing an equally large cardboard box. Whatever could it be? No such shipment was expected. We set about immediately to find out. What a surprise! Inside was an enormous phonograph, - a state of the art instrument, with multiple speakers capable of delivering concert hall sound. There was also a note from Thornton Wilder, with his best wishes and thanks for making his time in Innsbruck so agreeable. I wish I had saved it.

When I included this item on our quarterly inventory report,

Vienna admin advised me that it was not permitted to accept gifts from private individuals, and that I should return it immediately. Of course, I never did, just omitted it from the next report.

Chapter Thirty Five

In The Russian Zone

My relations with USIS headquarters in Vienna were always at arms length, determined by distance as much as by anything else. The breakup of the Austro-Hungarian Empire after the first world war had left Vienna, one of the largest capitals in Europe, surrounded by very little of the original country. Of the fragment that remained, the provinces of Tyrol and Vorarlberg in the west were the most remote. The result was that, for American officials, Vienna was Austria. To anyone operating in that politically charged city, still under four power occupation, the provinces were of only vague and intermittent concern. As long as things were quiet, don't disturb them - which was all right with me. Tyroleans themselves had acquired this same attitude toward the central government. In local conversation, one point of certain agreement was that "Vienna" could not possibly understand local problems.

Since things were going smoothly, I saw little of my superiors. Days would go by without even a telephone call. To keep it that way, I made sure that all my "RFP's" (Request for Purchase) were justified, that we stayed within our operating budget, and that any visiting lecturer dispatched by Vienna left Innsbruck in a happy frame of mind.

Plans for the new Linz information center's grand opening were now ready for implementation, and, as promised, I received an invitation to attend. This was an opportunity to get out of Innsbruck for a few days, en route revisit Salzburg, and take part in the festivities in Linz. Also, I decided, since I would be already more than halfway there, to go on to Vienna for a little face to face time with the people that counted. During this trip I wanted freedom of mobility, so this time I decided to drive.

All went according to plan. I got to know the new center director in Salzburg, a gentleman named Ptak who had replaced Hopman, and dropped by Camp Hellbrunn, where not much seemed to have changed, except that Julie was no longer there.

The new center in Linz was all that American money could buy: a fancy downtown location, sidewalk entry, plate glass display windows revealing a brilliantly lighted interior space of bookshelves and people seated comfortably in up-to-the-minute designer furniture by Herman Miller. Hors d'oeuvres and drinks matched the high class décor. As the host, Siemer was too busy to talk, but in the short time I had with him he seemed to have recovered from his breakdown.

The next day I set out for Vienna. The Russian Occupation Zone took up most of the eastern half of the country, with Vienna approximately in the center. To the west, the boundary between the Russian and American zones was located at the Enns River, close to Linz, and the crossing point was at the bridge. Drivers traveling between Vienna and Linz were restricted to a single highway patrolled by the Russian military. It was forbidden to stop for any reason. In case of a breakdown, all you could do was to wait to be picked up by the Russian patrol, hopefully get the car repaired and be allowed to continue. As a check on travelers using the route, two stations were set up, one at the Enns bridge, the other on the outskirts of Vienna. A reasonable time was allowed for drivers to make the trip. If it went beyond that, the American checkpoint would notify the Russians who would take over from there. Needless to say, no one wanted to find themselves in that situation. Remember, this was the depths of the cold war, and anything could happen.

My stay in Vienna was pro forma - to meet with the USIS directorate and let them know that I was still alive. The big boss, whom I had not met before, was one William Harlan Hale - another Yale graduate - tall, with a "born to command" demeanor, but otherwise friendly. His official life was entirely taken up with Austrian politics, and with running the *Wiener Kurier*, the US-owned German language daily paper. I don't think he could have found Innsbruck on the map. Since things were so quiet in our

Picking Up the Pieces

sector, there wasn't much to discuss. My second meeting was with the cultural affairs director, name unfortunately forgotten. He was relatively well informed about our operation, and listened attentively to learn more. We had a good talk. I liked him. Next was with the business office director, with whom we had most of our day to day dealings. This was "Sandy" Marlowe, an accountant type, balding, with thick glasses. He had come of age some fifteen years earlier in the depths of the Depression. He spent most of our time together telling me how lucky I was to have a job, especially one that paid so well and required so little. We got along well.

Two days were enough to keep communications healthy, so at the end of the second day I decided to get on the road for home. It was seven in the evening by the time I left the Vienna checkpoint. An overcast sky had turned to snow, light at first, then heavier as I traveled west. To someone like me, accustomed to winter driving in the Alps, the flat road to Linz was no problem. There were no other cars on the road. Despite the snow, there wasn't much accumulation, and I was able to make decent time.

Then, about two hours out of Vienna, the car's engine suddenly died. I steered the vehicle to a stop at the side of the road. It was an abrupt malfunction, nothing intermittent, no coughing or other warning signs, just a sudden stop.

In such a situation, it made no sense for me to investigate the source of the trouble. Even if, in the unlikely event I did find it, what then? There was no way I could have made a roadside repair and got going again. But I got out anyway, opened the hood, and with the aid of a flashlight inspected the engine. I really didn't expect to see anything, the trouble was likely buried deep inside. But, lo and behold! - a wire coming out of the distributor cap was broken. Even a mechanical ignoramus like myself could see that this was not right.

Very good, but what to do about it? - stranded in the middle of the Russian Zone at night, with snow falling all around, waiting to be picked up by the Russian patrol, and disappear forever into the Gulag. A bit exaggerated, but not entirely. In cases like this, a happy resolution depended very much on the current state of diplomatic/military relations between the US and the USSR. If all was normal, there was no problem. But in a time of crisis, as was sometimes the case, the Russians could feel the need for one or two "bargaining chips." Any stranded motorist, accused of departing from the prescribed route, or even spying, provided an easy and convenient hostage. It had happened.

I did not fancy myself as a bargaining chip. Then I remembered having just passed a small village, not far back, within easy walking distance. Maybe there was help to be had there. But that could involve even more risk since instructions in case of a breakdown were explicitly clear - remain in the vehicle, and wait for the Russian patrol.

I decided to chance it. Ten minutes on foot brought me back to the village, a row of buildings built right up to the road, all of them shuttered and dark, no sign of life anywhere. One, however, advertised itself as a *"tankstelle"* (gas station), with one pump outside. Its garage door was tightly closed, but inside I could hear sounds of music and laughter as though a party was going on. I knocked on the door. Instantly all sounds of merriment ceased. I knocked again. Still no response.

On the third knock, a side door opened, just a crack and a voice said, "Was wollen sie?" (What do you want?) I explained the situation. He opened the door and indicated that I should come in. Two other men joined us in what appeared to be an office. I repeated my tale of distress, and asked if they could help. Much shaking of heads. "unmoeglich...strengstens verboten," (impossible, strictly forbidden), I heard them say.

. With my limited German it was difficult to describe the probable cause of the malfunction, but I emphasized that it would be an easy repair. Still no agreement. As a last resort, I got out my wallet and extracted several hundred shilling notes. "Here," I said, holding them out. Dubious looks all around. Then the matter was settled by the oldest one, presumably the father, taking the money and putting it in his pocket. "Okay, aber mach's schnell. (ok, but make it quick)" he said.

They grabbed some tools and we all piled into an ancient Steyr car. The repair, as I thought, was completed in a matter of minutes with the aid of a roll of electricians tape. An hour later I was at the American checkpoint at the Enns bridge.

"What took you so long?" asked the American sergeant, holding a clipboard as he marked off my name. "We expected you half an hour ago."

"Bad weather," I replied. "I don't try to make time in a snowstorm."

"Another fifteen minutes, and we would have had to notify our buddies on the other side to start looking for you."

"Well, thanks for holding off," I said, meaning every word of it.

Chapter Thirty-Six

An Alpine Mystery

Austrians are natural intriguers, with conspiratorial tendencies which developed almost into a way of life during the political conflicts of the thirties, and then the war that followed. Since free expression was forbidden, no one was sure what might be considered subversive. Fear replaced spontaneity, secrecy replaced openness. Any American in an official position during the occupation became a magnet for attention from all sorts of individuals, some for motives of business and profit, some simply because they wanted to be friendly, or were interested in the work and wanted to help. But there were still others with obscure motives; it was never quite clear what was driving the relationship, or where it was going. This habit of adding a cloak of mystery flourished during the cold war and the occupation with us innocent Americans at the focal point.

In Salzburg, the wife of the regional public affairs officer, Marcia Hopman, was lured into the machinations of a shadowy group by a woman named San Michele, who at the same time made a sustained effort to get to know me better. Typically, who, and what she represented, was never revealed. There was just this persistent effort to be my "friend," to get me to meet her friends whom I would "adore," just as Marcia Hopman had in Salzburg. Her manner was so filled with flattery, so oily but at the same time pushy, that I couldn't stand the sight of her, and always managed to find an excuse for declining her overtures - which, by the way had no romantic intent. Of this I am certain. Something else was behind it; I was being recruited. But for what I never knew because San Michele abruptly dropped out of sight, and Marcia's husband was at the same time transferred to another post, outside of Austria, rumor had it because of his wife's compromising involvement in San Michele's activities. Exactly what they concealed, I never learned.

However, I must confess to not being entirely immune to this sort of appeal. Judgment may depend on the person involved. At any rate I became friendly with a more than somewhat unstable individual, but brilliant, amusing, and completely irreverent and unintimidated by any kind of authority. Not the kind of person my superiors in Vienna would have approved of. But that was just what I liked about him: his fearlessness and ability to tease me, mock the occupation, and America generally in ways that would make anyone laugh.

An amusing character, but also a mysterious one - no one knew for certain what he actually did for a living. Officially, he was a "journalist," and from time to time articles appeared in the lcal press under his byline. Also, he was a talented photographer and produced a few glossy books on art and architecture. But none of these could explain the curious position he held in Innsbruck at that time. His name was Wolfgang Pfaundler III, his physical appearance less than impressive: small - below medium height - with wizened features that made him look prematurely aged, although he would not have been more than thirty or thirty-five. However, these features were usually wrinkled into an expression of amusement, with a gleam in his eye at the thought of some outrageous joke on the government he was about to tell you, very confidentially, of course.

Before I get too far into my story, I should point out that Pfaundler was also a great womanizer. With his short stature, wizened face and careless dress, no one could account for his well known success. His current flame was Brigitte Stollwitzer, one of our reference librarians. She was tall, almost six feet. With Pfaundler at about five and a half, they made an amusing couple.

Ridiculous, perhaps, but "Wolfie" was actually a great back channel into the affairs of government at all levels: local, national, international. The mayor, the governor, and in Vienna, the Molden brothers, they were all his friends. I think they found his inexhaustible store of gossip useful, and his outspoken personality refreshing. But the real reason for Pfaundler's acceptance was the part he had played in the *Wiederstands Bewegung*, the anti-Nazi resistance movement. During part of the war he had fought in the Caucasus ("Jack, you have never seen such beautiful women!"). Returning home, he joined the resistance, in a cell that operated out of the Oetztal - the Oetz valley. Just what they accomplished, I don't know, he never talked about it in detail. But that kind of conspiratorial activity, especially in a good cause, suited Pfaundler's personality. The men and boys who carried out those high risk operations were bound by blood as brothers for life.

With this background, not unsurprisingly, Pfaundler detested the Germans, and even more the Italians. (Americans generally are unaware of this distaste Austrians had for Germany, regarding Germans as cold-blooded, who, on the other hand, viewed Austrians as "unreliable"). But now the war was over; there was no longer any reason to hate Germany. With Italy, however, grievances remained, the memory of a raw injustice that still lingered. That was the "South Tyrol Question." Discussion of it will create a detour in our narrative, but it helps us to understand Pfaundler, and what I meant by calling him "unstable."

In several places I have mentioned how, in a cynical gesture of big power politics, South Tyrol was handed over to Italy at Versailles in 1919 as its reward for late entry into World War I on the side of the Allies. Both South and North Tyrol had been parts of the old Austro-Hungarian Empire, virtually similar in language, customs and culture. The dismemberment was brutal surgery, performed without anesthetic. All of Austria, but especially the Tyrol, was left seething in impotent outrage. "Irredentism" - loss of a homeland - is one of the most powerful forces complicating international relationships, and one of the hardest wounds to heal. Although more than thirty years had passed, and Italian efforts had done a great deal to reconcile Austria and Tyrol to the situation, there were still diehards who would never accept it, and were determined too keep memory of the loss alive.

Pfaundler was a leader in their councils and a participant in their escapades. For him, it was a sacred cause, much like the

An Alpine Mystery

IRA's in Ireland. Their program consisted of organized protests, lectures, a newsletter, formation of student groups, and so on. But there were also those who wanted to go further. While I was there, it never spilled over into actual violence. The authorities never seriously tried to curb them, because the issue was politically popular, and an outlet for widespread indignation, still simmering in 1951. For Pfaundler, aside from it being a holy cause, the semi-secret nature of the planning, the underground meetings and inflammatory articles were a continuation of his past role in the Resistance. With that now gone, he needed something to replace it. Knowing that the authorities had him under close observation only made it more exciting.

To complete this character sketch, I must skip ahead of my story by a few years. What was brewing in 1951 turned out to be more than just ideological posturing. In the early 1960's I traveled back to Innsbruck and had lunch with Pfaundler. He looked and was just the same; the intervening years had provided material for a whole new store of satirical jokes. I urged him to visit us in the States.

"I'm afraid I can't," he said.

"Why not? What do you mean, you can't?" I asked.

"It's a long story, but the end result is that the Italian government has succeeded in getting me listed as an international terrorist. In fact, I'm under sentence of life imprisonment in Italy. I have to be careful, even here," he explained.

I was shocked. "How can they do that? Lectures and writing aren't terrorism."

"You're right, they aren't. But a few years ago things kind of got out of control. People were starting to forget. We wanted to create a major incident, one that would put the story back on the front pages where it hadn't been for a long time. The plan was to blow up the railroad station on the Italian side of the Brenner. I knew about the plan but had no direct part in carrying it out. The idea was to do it at night when there was no one there and no trains passing through. Well, something went wrong. There were a few people there we weren't aware of. They were killed in the explosion. Unfortunately."

"That made it murder. We were all indicted. Italian agents had been collecting material on us for years. By selecting those parts that suited them, they could make a clear case against everybody, including me. We were tried in absentia and all found guilty But the Austrian government refused to extradite us, Gott sei dank (thank God)."

"Good Lord, Wolfie," I said. "How has this affected your life?"

"Like I said, I have to be careful. I'm afraid to go outside the country - cross a border, especially not to Italy. But even France or Germany, you never know."

"But at least you're not being punished here."

"Far from it. To many people, I'm a hero. Unfortunately, not to the government. They're trying now to satisfy the Italians that they're not harboring a terrorist organization. So they're making it harder for us to operate - with permits, for example."

That conversation took place in the early 60's. Back in 1951 Pfaundler never made any attempt to enter my official life, or to enlist me in his South Tyrolean crusade. He didn't have to, I was totally in sympathy with the Austrian grievance.

Once or twice he did request a favor of me. The first seemed insignificant at the time, but which in the light of subsequent events made me wonder. It concerned a "friend," introduced to me as Otto von Bolschwing, who was leaving Austria hurriedly to the US for reasons not explained. The American government was paying his way, and had issued a work permit visa. Over dinner with Pfaundler and me, he said he was a chemical engineer, and that he would be seeking employment when he got to the US and would appreciate any contacts I might have that he could use. This von Bolschwing was a very impressive looking man - tall, handsome, well dressed, with excellent English. Unfortunately, I didn't have much to offer, but didn't think he was going to have much trouble finding something. He gave me a telephone number and asked me to get in touch with him if and when I returned to the States. I did, a few years later. We had drinks in the King Cole bar in New York. He was living in New Jersey and working for Warner Lambert Pharmaceuticals, with the title of Vice President for European Operations. Only in retrospect during my stay in Austria did this story raise questions.- but ultimately many more

The second time Pfaundler came to me for help was

considerably more dramatic.

It started with a "heads up" telephone call from Vienna, one of Bill Hale's underlings informing me of the impending visit of a certain Mr. Espy - Bill Espy, I believe. He would be driving down to Innsbruck as a private individual to renew some old friendships in town. Evidently he held an important position in the State Department. We were to do all we could to help in case he needed anything during the two days he was expected to be in Innsbruck.

"No problem," I assured Mr. Espy when he appeared in my office to "touch base," as he said. No, he had no requests, he already had a room here, and his friends were expecting him for a dinner get-together. He particularly wanted to renew his friendship with "Manfred" - meaning Manfred Neier of the *Tiroler Tageszeitung*. We shook hands, and he left.

About three in the morning my phone rang. "Jack, its Wolfie. We need your help. It's an emergency."

"Good heavens, Wolfie, what's going on?"

"I can't explain now. Meet me with your car in front of the Amerika Haus in twenty minutes. Will you do that?" As soon as I said I would, he hung up.

When I got to the center, a car was already there with Pfaundler, Neier and a third person in it. When this stranger got out, with difficulty and with the other two helping him, I could see that he was injured. They transferred him into my car. He was an Austrian country mountain type, maybe forty years old, and obviously in a good deal of pain. He had with him a backpack of the sort carried by mountaineers, and an alpenstock - one of those tools used in mountain climbing, with a long, sharp spike at one end of the head.

"What happened?" I asked.

"Just a little accident," said Neier. "Schnapps and wine are a bad mix. Our friend here has sustained a wound in his upper leg, in the thigh, no damage to the artery though. We need you to take him home right away."

"But shouldn't he be in the hospital?" I said.

"We can't do that. If we did, the hospital would have to report it to the police and there would be an investigation. We've had a doctor we know dress the wound and bandage him up so he can be moved."

"Was that the weapon?" I asked, pointing to the alpenstock.

"Yes, it's his," said Pfaundler.

"Where's Espy?" I asked Neier. "I thought you were supposed to have dinner with him. Was he with you when this happened?"

"Yes, but he has already left Innsbruck. He's one very important reason that this accident has to go unreported, and why we need you to help us."

It was all coming at me too fast. "Good God," I said. "What a business! Now what is it you want me to do?"

Neier answered, "We want you to drive our friend - no names, please - back to his home, or rather to a place where some people will pick him up. Perhaps an hour and a half to the west.. We've already made arrangements for someone to be there at the pickup point. Once you drop him off, come back to Innsbruck and forget all about it."

What the hell was I getting myself into? But because Espy - an "important State Department official" - was involved, it never occurred to me to say no.

With Mr. "X" beside me in the front seat, I drove out of town along the Inn river. From time to time, he shifted position and groaned, but otherwise said nothing, and did not respond to my questions. It was midsummer. Dawn was breaking, and a heavy fog lay over the river and the valley. I drove slowly with the lights on.

After about two hours, Mr. "X" said, "Langsam" (slow), then "Hier, links ab" (Here, off to the left). We turned into a small dirt road leading toward the Oetztal and almost immediately crossed a wooden bridge.

"Hier, stop," he said. Then, "Helf mich, bitte, aussteigen." (Help me get out.) Getting out was painful for him, he could scarcely bend the wounded leg. Eventually he stood, leaning against the car. Cupping both hands to his mouth, he gave one of those Alpine "halloo's," a musical call that echoed up and down the sides of the mountains. A moment later came an answering call, and a moment after that two figures emerged out of the forest. Like him, they wore typical Tyrolean mountain dress.

"Servus" (hello), one of them said to me, and then "Danke viel mals" (many thanks). With an arm over the shoulders of a friend on either side, and with a foot dragging, Mr. "X" disappeared into the trees.

I had plenty to think about on the way back to town as I pondered this incredibly weird experience. What exactly had happened? Who was Mr."X"? And, most intriguing, who was Bill Espy? What was the nature of Pfaundler's and Neier's involvement? Why the extraordinary secrecy? And why had they picked me to help?

When I asked Neier and Pfaundler, both took the fifth. "Thank you Jack, you did us all a great service. Now, just assume it never happened." And that is all I ever got out of them. Vienna was no better. I didn't want to cause an uproar by revealing details of the story, but I told them Espy had unexpectedly left a day early. "Yes," they said. "He finished his business in Innsbruck and had to move on." They had obviously been informed of the sudden change of plan. I asked what Espy's position was. The reply: "A State Department Officer visiting Innsbruck as a private citizen." No more than I knew before. A conspiracy of silence on all sides.

At the time I was totally mystified, but with longer reflection an explanation emerged. I'm surprised that it took me so long to see it. Here is my theory:

The story had its beginnings in the Tyrolean resistance movement during the Nazi era, operating out of a cell in the Oetztal, a remote mountain valley where the Gestapo would have been very conspicuous, had they ventured there to investigate, and where underground fighters could easily hide if they did. My theory is that this underground group was coordinated and supported by the American OSS (Office of Strategic Services, precursor to the CIA, which was not established until 1947), and that Bill Espy was an important figure in the liaison, if not the actual handler. It included Pfaundler and Neier, as well as others.

At any rate, the unit was later folded into the CIA, with Pfaundler and Neier as paid agents, both of them ideal recruits - persons with either position, or contacts or both. This arrangement continued on into the early 50's. How else to account for Pfaundler's prosperous lifestyle in the absence of any visible means of support? And, come to think of it, who really was Otto

Picking Up the Pieces

von Bolschwing, and why did he have to leave suddenly with all expenses paid? Who were these other characters? I can only guess, but they were likely supporting members of the Oetztal resistance group.

Nor do I know what actually happened that night. A reasonable guess is that the dinner was planned as an "alumni reunion" of the old Resistance soldiers and their OSS/CIA handler to celebrate those days of high risk and danger, and the success that crowned their efforts. But somehow, something went terribly wrong. Who can tell what long festering tensions lay beneath the surface, suddenly unleashed late at night by too much alcohol?

One last question: Why did they ask me to come to the rescue when things turned bloody? Weren't there other Resistance alumni who could have been called on? Maybe, maybe not. But my guess is that since American security issues were involved, Espy wanted an American official, someone who could be controlled and sworn to secrecy, even recalled to the States, quickly if need be, with no questions asked. Also, both Pfaundler and Neier knew me well, and knew that I could be trusted. They had to make a decision quickly, and I was a logical choice.

So many questions and so few answers. No one will ever know the whole story. All of the other participants are dead. I am the only witness left to this incomplete mystery. It was my second immersion in the deep waters of international intrigue, first at Bad Aibling, and now in Innsbruck, both affairs with high drama, completely outside my own experience, the kind of thing I had only read about in books - in the light of day more like a dream, or something that had happened to someone else

.

Notes

For an updated explanation of this mystery, see the notes section, Chapter 36, at the back of the book.

Chapter Thirty-Seven

Love's Labors Lost

Taken as a whole, working in Innsbruck was as ideal as life ever gets. But one drawback kept it just short of perfection; that was a phenomenon known as the *"foehn"* - pronounced "fern." The *foehn* was a special wind, most common in late winter or early spring, rather like the chinook in the northwestern US - soft, balmy, seductive, with hints of springtime to come. One would have thought it to be a welcome messenger among the still prevailing snow and ice, and for some people it was, but not for me. Instead of rousing my spirits out of the winter doldrums, this insidious wind had the effect of casting me into a state of indecisive depression, a loss of energy as well as any will to act. There was no escape, it followed me everywhere; food lost its taste, wine its lift.

The only comfort in all this - if you can call it that - is that many Innsbruckers suffered the same psychological malaise with the advent of this mysterious wind. However, it did not seem to affect everyone equally, some not at all. But for those who were affected, I never heard of a cure or an effective antidote.

On especially bad days I would take refuge in the public baths. This was a wonderful institution, and only a few steps from the Information Center. Its ordinary outside gave no hint of the marbled magnificence inside. There were changing rooms, one for men and one for women, and the baths themselves of several different kinds. For example, high and low pressure showers, with water jets like needles, and small pools: boiling hot, warm or ice cold. Then, at the center was a large relaxing pool, built in a fifteen foot circle with curved wall seats around the circumference

- a whole mosaic of black, green and white marble chips.

On Men's days, mid-afternoon when I usually had the place to myself, I would sit there in water up to my chin trying to fight off the *foehn*. Occasionally, there were a few others: businessmen, government officials, the men who made up Innsbruck's "establishment." There was also a steam room for those so inclined, but not for me - the combination of baths was just the right cure, for at least a few days until the *foehn* blew itself out.

While I'm on the subjects of "negatives," one other comes to mind: this was the American student group registered at the university. As a newly arrived assistant regional public affairs officer, one of my first projects had been to set up a lecture series for their benefit, by which they could become better informed about the country and the region through meetings with influential local figures. This was a success, perhaps too much of a success. It had the unintended effect of confirming the Information Center as a gathering place for these students - a regular American "clubhouse," far from its intended purpose. There were times when the number of Americans in the library exceeded the number of Austrians. More and more these students developed a proprietary attitude toward the Center, and with that went a feeling that the Center was "ours," or rather, "theirs" - that they owned it.

As with students everywhere, there were a few malcontents whose interest in their studies, if it existed at all, was distinctly secondary to their desire for power and group leadership in some cause, if they could find one. Meanwhile, the Information Center would do until a better one came along. After discussion among themselves, a committee of activists was formed to meet with me to air their grievances. What these amounted to was that I was not always there at nine o'clock in the morning; that they as taxpayers were paying my salary, and entitled to a full day's work from me.

I found this extremely annoying, As far as I was concerned, it was unauthorized meddling by a bunch of irresponsible drifters masquerading as students, interfering with a government official in the performance of his duties. (A few years later, this same youthful hunger for power erupted as the student protest movement - but with a better cause. Nevertheless, I would have made a terrible college dean if willingness to capitulate to their demands was what was required.) In this case, I was angry, not just because my position, which I did take seriously, was being questioned by an irresponsible, ragtag group, but also because of our past effort to bring them into the program: how we had welcomed their presence into a facility specifically not intended for them, and this was how they showed their appreciation. It ended by my telling them that they had no role in this operation, that they were making my job harder, and that they were acting contrary to American interests here. If it continued, I would complain to the embassy in Vienna with a copy to the Veterans Administration, which administered GI Bill benefits and sent them their monthly checks. That had a silencing effect on the complaints.

A short time later, they provided me with a good laugh. As non-resident aliens, American students lived on the Austrian economy; they were in no way part of the US occupation. If they wanted to exchange their monthly benefits checks, issued in dollars, for Austrian schillings, they had to do it at the official, controlled rate. On the other hand, a few hours train ride west to Liechtenstein, and they could make the exchange at a more favorable free market rate, thereby saving a significant sum. To avail themselves of this opportunity, a group of students would collect their checks each month and entrust the collection to one of their number who would go to Liechtenstein, make the exchange, and reenter Austria with the proceeds concealed and undisclosed - all, of course, illegal.

It happened that there was one student in Innsbruck, there more to ski than to study, who was usually available to make the one-day trip. He had done it twice before, and was considered to be reliable. As per standard procedure, checks were gathered, endorsed and handed over to the amount of thousands of dollars. The trusted courier left, never to be seen again. Anguish was universal. What made it all the more amusing was that the victims could not report it to the authorities. They had been eager participants in a money smuggling venture. That it had gone sour, too bad - just live with it.

With all that was going on, my life in Innsbruck was never routine. Something interesting happened almost every day, creating a pleasant rhythm; an agreeable blend of stimulating work and relaxation in a magnificent setting. Then suddenly into this orderly pattern there came a major distraction. I fell in love, natural enough at my age, but I wasn't ready for it. So unready, in fact, that when love appeared I didn't recognize it, until it was too late.

The girl in the story was Ilse Lasser - her full name was Ilse von Zollheimb-Lasser. She was one of two young women working in our children's library, managing a program of songs, stories, games, art - the usual activities to keep preschool tots amused and out of mischief. The children's library was far down my list of priorities; in fact, I didn't see why we should have it at all. What part of our mission did its activities fulfill? But, there it was, and a success so far as popularity was concerned.

I dropped in from time to time, just to see what was gong on, and was impressed by the way the women handled noisy and obstreperous four-year olds, and managed to keep a roomful of them focused on a single organized activity. This was one part of the USIS program beyond my ken, and to which I could not make the slightest contribution. Then I began to be aware that one of the two young women was uncommonly attractive, quite tall, with high cheekbones and vaguely Slavic features. After that, my interest in the program perked up, and I found reasons to drop by more often.

Longer conversations led to a dinner invitation at which Ilse - it was now "Jack" and "Ilse" - told me that her forebears were minor Austrian nobility from the family seat in the town of Budweis, now in Czechoslovakia. Before and during the war her family had lived in Vienna, but the mother and father were now living in Klessheim, near Salzburg. She had two sisters, one in Innsbruck and one in Vienna. All this was communicated in English so fluent that we almost never had to rely on my German.

From that point on, things took a course driven by mutual attraction. One dinner led to more dinners, then to intimate suppers in my apartment, prepared by Frau Voltin - who totally approved of such romantic trysts - and then on to breakfasts, prepared by Frau Voltin and served in bed. Ilse and I got along beautifully, never a disagreement, never an argument; whatever I wanted to do, Ilse wanted to do, and vice versa. That included weekend tours in summer and skiing in winter, interrupted only once when she broke her ankle skiing and had to stay in her own bed for two weeks. During that time, completely oblivious to me, bonds were being wrapped around my heart that I no longer had the power to break - had I even been aware of it, or wanted to.

Her father represented the old school aristocratic army officer-gentleman type. At the university he had belonged to one of those "dueling" fraternities, where members sealed their undying friendship in blood, by carving each other up in supervised mock combat, using razor sharp sabers. No one, as far as I know, was ever killed; but he lost the tip of his nose - quickly reattached - and ever after, carried several scars on one cheek. These distinguishing marks of heroism, however, only added to his handsome good looks, and made him irresistible, not only to his wife, but to dozens of other Viennese ladies with whom he carried on endless affairs in the best Viennese tradition, but to his wife's despair. As a wartime colonel in 1945 he was directing a Waffen SS intelligence unit in Yugoslavia - a chapter best not examined too closely, although he always regarded himself as an old fashioned soldier with nothing but contempt for the Nazis.

April 1945 saw the final disintegration of the Wehrmacht, with Russian troops just a few miles outside of Vienna. Horrifying tales of rape and pillage from fallen cities to the east had created panic in the city. For the colonel still in Yugoslavia it was a desperate situation: a wife and three teenage daughters at home, unprotected, and the Red Army coming closer every day. The city was virtually sealed: no trains, no air flights and only a few roads open to the west.

At this hopeless juncture, at the last possible moment, a member of the colonel's old dueling fraternity came to the rescue with a car, a tank full of benzine, and a chauffeur. With six people in the car the family headed west, as far west as possible. In addition to the driver, there were Frau Lasser, Ilse and her twin sister Inge, her older sister, Waltraut, and Walraut's husband, still recuperating from wartime wounds. They ended their journey in Tyrol, in the village of Udenz, exhausted, and with no visible means of support. Nevertheless, this part of Austria seemed safe, well beyond the reach of Soviet arms. General Patton's Third Army had already arrived in Vorarlberg, and would likely penetrate along the Inn River valley during the coming weeks. So it was decided to remain where they were, in a beautiful village, nestled in the Zillertal with Alpine peaks on three sides.

But scenery would not feed a family. The colonel, now a civilian, joined them, but employment possibilities did not exist. They kept alive only by Frau Lasser's selling off piece by piece items of heirloom jewelry. Then, once again a miracle. Another fraternity brother, owner of a large insurance company, appointed Ilse's father manager of its Tyrolean district at a small but livable salary. It was a foothold, enough for the girls to finish their education at the University of Innsbruck over the next four years.

Up to this point, the past five years had been mostly dislocation and danger, driven by war from upper class comfort and luxury in Vienna to a new place and life as a refugee among strangers. Ilse recounted this narrative to me in a very matter of fact way, with no dramatics or appeals for sympathy, almost as though it had happened to someone else. None of this seemed to have left scars, only willingness to accept hardship, but along with it a desire for new experiences - for adventure.

Our affair continued for several months, each of us apparently living for the pleasure of the moment; I, at least, was completely unaware of the feelings building up under the surface. In the midst of this unconscious bliss, I took two weeks to fly to the Middle East to visit my father, now dividing his time between Beirut and Jerusalem by way of Damascus. When I got back, Ilse and I had dinner. She seemed in a somber mood - unaccountably, I thought. Suddenly she pushed her untouched plate aside and said, "Jack, there is something I must tell you."

"Is anything wrong?" I asked. "You don't seem to be yourself this evening."

"Not wrong, really. It's just that I will be leaving Innsbruck," she replied.

"Leaving Innsbruck! Where to? What will you do?" I was astounded.

"I am going to South Africa to live," she said.

"South Africa, my God! What will you do down there? Do you

have friends there?"

"Yes. I am going down there to be married."

Good God in heaven, this was too much! "Ilse, give me a moment to understand this. You say you are getting married down there, who to? Do I know him?"

"I don't think you do," she said. "We dated before you came along, but he had left, just about the time you arrived - to go to South Africa. He wanted me to go with him, but at the time I wasn't ready."

"Well, why are you ready now?"

"Because I don't think you want me, or that I have a real place in your life." There were tears in her eyes. "You are here having a good time in Austria, but you will soon be gone, and my life will go back to what it was before you came. Here I have a chance to be with someone who does want me, and to be in a place I've dreamed of visiting."

"But do you love him?"

"I don't know. I think love is what you make it."

I sat there stunned. Finally I said, "I had no idea you were feeling this way. You never said anything."

"No, I suppose not. I was waiting for you to say something, but you never did. And then, when you went away for two weeks, there was not a word, not a telephone call - nothing. That gave me a chance to make up my mind. So I did."

I may have been an egotistical, young fool, but not so far deluded that I couldn't see the reasonableness of her decision. At the same time, I was still unable to listen to my deepest feelings and make a determined effort to win her back. My precious freedom was still too dear to me to be willing to share it with anyone.

The remaining days at the Center until Ilse's departure were a sad time. She was popular and all the staff were sorry to see her leave. They gave her a big going away party. The emcee made many double-entendre jokes about our affair, which elicited laughter from everyone but me. I couldn't get used to the reality that in a few days she would be gone.

The ship sailed from Venice. We rode down on the train. That night in Venice was eerie. The city was deserted. An inch of snow covered the Piazza San Marco, and a few flakes drifted down on the canals illuminated by solitary street lights. Her ship was moored in the very center of town, looming over the wharf like a ghostly presence. One last embrace at the foot of the gangway, and she was gone.

On the way back to Innsbruck, the actuality of what had occurred, of what I had lost through selfishness and unfeeling, finally cracked my protective armor. It took the fact of irretrievable loss for this to finally happen. There was a lump in my throat and tears in my eyes, but the deed was done and could not be undone. There came to me the words of the poet Whittier's lines:

> Of all the words of tongue and pen,
> The saddest are these,
> It might have been.

Notes

Fortunately, the story does not end here. For the sequel, see Notes - Chapter 37 at the end of the book.

Chapter Thirty-Eight

If at First You Don't Succeed

As anyone can tell you, if you do not already know, the best way to get over a failed love affair is to start a new one. In my case, the object was not far distant. In fact, the Center was staffed with tempting possibilities; two thirds of our employees were young ladies. A twenty-seven year old bachelor in charge of this seraglio was, as the saying goes, to "put the fox in charge of the hen house." And in the words of the Broadway musical, "If I can't be near the one I love, I love the one I'm near."

Her name was Carla Regner, in charge of our public information services to radio and the press. Her job was to keep information flowing in two directions: first, to make sure that local outlets were kept supplied with publicity materials from Vienna; and then to report back to Vienna on how these were being used, reactions to them and needs expressed, plus anything of more than routine interest. Carla was good in her job, intelligent, well educated and fluent in three languages, with a doctorate from the University of Innsbruck. She was also ambitious.

To these professional qualities, I should add that she was extremely good looking - a beauty with looks reflecting her dual origin, part Austrian, part Italian. She came from the vicinity of Merano in South Tyrol, but had taken Austrian citizenship.

Under her management, public information activities ran with noiseless efficiency, so much so that there was little for me to do to improve it. In any case, I had my own relationship with the press through Manfred Neier, and with Pfaundler for any back-channel contacts. The result was that Carla and I had only intermittent contact during business hours, and none at all afterward.

That changed after Ilse's departure. My free evenings when there was nothing scheduled at the Center were going to waste. I had trouble adjusting to solitary dinners and whatever might follow. A romantic setting was incomplete without romantic company. So just as I had acquired an uncharacteristic interest in the children's library, I now experienced a desire to become more involved in the public information program.

This was not hard to do. As I mentioned, Carla was ambitious and wanted to be near the center of authority. Gerda Gross was my de facto deputy and good in that position, but I often felt that Carla would have been happy to take it over. However, she never schemed or criticized to that end.

The fact that Carla was intelligent and well educated meant that we could have real conversations, beginning with work related subjects, then branching out to include European and world affairs. She read several daily newspapers: local, Austrian and international, and always knew what she was talking about, even on abstruse subjects.

For example, Heidegger, the famous philosopher, but a Nazi party member, had been a professor at the University of Innsbruck. Carla's doctorate was in philosophy, so she was able to explain his rationale, without agreeing with it. She also introduced me to an interesting visiting lecturer at the university, Erich von Kuhnelt-Leddihn, famous for his political and philosophical defense of monarchy - at that time still a live political issue in Austria. I needed this type of intellectual stimulation and good-natured sparring with someone who was at least my equal, if not superior.

However, things did not remain long on this lofty intellectual plane. Carla was a complex person. It was possible to get to know her via any one of several approaches: intellectual, professional, or even emotional - romantic love, which may seem at odds with ambition and career advancement, but that vulnerability was still there. However, there was yet another side to her personality, a sensual side, a love of luxury, of good food and wine, the best restaurants and exclusive resorts. She had grown up missing all these things, except as they were featured in the pages of travel and fashion magazines. That was the life she wanted to live, and would take the nearest opportunity and the quickest road to get herself there

Barely a month into our new found friendship, still platonic at that point, I had to drive up into Germany, to Garmisch Partenkirchen, an Oberbayern four season resort, largely taken over by the Army as a recreation and administrative center for southern Germany. I had to make this trip once a month to cash my paycheck, get gas coupons, shop at the PX , the commissary, and otherwise enjoy a beautiful trip up over the Nordketten Alps, through Seefeld and Mittenwald to Garmisch. nestled under the Zugspitze, Germany's highest mountain.

Carla and I had been chatting late that afternoon, and without giving the matter much thought, I asked if she wouldn't like to drive up with me. Fifteen minutes later we were in the Citroen headed north. Garmisch, although overrun by American servicemen, was still beautiful - quaintly Alpine without being cheapened by trashy tourist enterprises. Business concluded, we made a quick trip through the PX, commissary and the liquor store for toiletries, brandy - and a box of nylons for Carla. Then we had to make a decision: back to Innsbruck as originally planned? or have dinner in Garmisch? Well, here we were, why not make an evening of it?

The Army had taken over several of the largest hotels at different price ranges, all of them absurdly inexpensive, but payment could only be in US scrip currency. Not to worry. I had a month's wages in my wallet aching to be let loose. Along with the hotels, the Army had commandeered the services of Germany's most prestigious chefs, many of whom had been in the private service of bigwig Nazi party officials, Goering, von Ribbentrop, et al., now with their talents on display for a new set of masters.

Half a century later, that dinner is still memorable: soft individual table lamps, waiters in dinner jackets carrying silver serving dishes, then a menu of appetizers, entrees and desserts to boggle the mind. I asked Carla to order for both of us, anything, whatever she fancied - it all cost so little. She chose shrimp cocktail and crab-meat stuffed lobster, having only heard about, but never having had, either. I ordered a bottle of champagne, and for theatrical effect a "Baked Alaska" dessert. It arrived looking like the Zugspitze itself, a mountain of ice cream under a cover of toasted meringue. Plus - why not- two brandies.

Cynics, I suppose, would call it a seduction. At the same time, it was all so much fun, so spontaneous, that any suspicion of cold-blooded planning never crept in to spoil a perfect evening - up to and including what followed.

What followed over the next few months simply enlarged the scope of operations, including one trip down into Italy as the winter ended, leaving Innsbruck behind, still locked in snow and ice. Once over the Brenner, spring was already well underway, warm sun, and lemon trees blooming beside the road. We feasted on smoked Garda trout at a lakeshore inn on a small peninsula called Punta San Vigilio. In the library hung a photograph, taken from the rear, of a stocky figure under a broad brimmed sun hat, at work with paints and a brush to capture the view on canvas. I knew immediately who it was.

"Yes," said the proprietor, an Irishman named Leonardo Walsh. "Mr. Churchill came here twice after the war for relaxation and to paint. Arrangements were made secretly under an assumed name. As far as we were concerned, he was Mr. "X," although once he got here, everyone knew who he was. But back in England he had simply gone missing."

In this manner an idyllic summer passed into fall. One evening we had planned a dinner date, nothing very ambitious, just here in town. It was after normal business hours when I dropped into Carla's office to ask when she wanted to leave. To my surprise, I found her crying.

"What's the matter? Are you OK?" I asked. "Why the tears?"

She nodded dumbly, and indicated a letter on her desk, beside a leaf tinged with autumn colors.

Nonplussed, I said, "What is it, some kind of trouble?"

"It's from Chris - Christopher - you know, I've told you about him."

Yes, I did know. Chris was an impoverished graduate student at the university where they had met. He was doing post-doctoral work, and keeping himself alive - barely - by teaching a few courses. He was also madly in love with Carla and could not be deterred, although I suspected that she was secretly flattered by his persistent, lovelorn declarations. It was all so romantic, so operatic, with me cast as the evil capitalist seducer.

"I've explained to him a dozen times that it's hopeless, that I'm not in love with him or with anyone else, but he will simply not take no for an answer."

"Can't you just ignore him?"

"I try to. I wish I could, but there are times when he makes me feel heartless and awful, like this - this letter."

"What does it say, if I may ask?"

"Well, first of all, it's to wish me a happy birthday - to day, he remembered." (I had not.) "It's beautifully written - a poem. He says how painful it is for him to offer me so little, that words alone are inadequate to express what he feels. So he will make me a present of this leaf. Its colors tell his story better than he can himself."

She picked up the leaf. "The green is the joy of being together, and the hope that it gives him. The gold is the happiness that we could have. The red is the wounds that are caused by my indifference. And the brown is the despair that he feels."

Here she began to cry again. "I can't help it. I'm just not strong enough."

"Carla," I said, "Don't make it a test of strength. Why? You have your life to lead without interference or harassment from anyone. Your friend Christopher is obsessed with his infatuation to the point where you are just an object. He wants you to allow him to adore you, to own you. Never mind reality. He needs to get along with his life, and let you get along with yours. Best for you is to take that letter, and the leaf, and throw them in the wastebasket. A drink and dinner - a change of scene - are what you need right now. So let's go. We had a date, remember?"

She paused for a moment, then smiled weakly. "All right. I must run to the loo. See you downstairs."

Waiting for her in the car, I reflected on Chris's letter. It was pure "Winterreise," a missing song from music's greatest song cycle. How Schubert would have loved it! What he would have done with those few words - and that leaf! I could almost hear the music.

At the restaurant two glasses of wine failed to dispel the

gloomy mood. Suddenly she looked up and, "Chris is right. I don't deserve a pure love."

"Oh, for heaven's sake, Carla," I said, "Will you please stop blaming yourself."

"Who am I to blame? I just can't seem to be able to resist temptation." she answered.

"What do you mean by temptation?"

"All he nice things we do - this restaurant, dinners, trips - things I could never do on my own."

"But why the guilt trip? Why do you feel you have to resist? I don't get it."

"Of course, you wouldn't. You have nothing to feel guilty about."

"Well, neither do you, Carla."

"No? Sometimes I think I'm like one of your stupid fish flopping around on the end of the line because I couldn't say no to all of the nice things you offer me."

I let this sink in before trying to answer, then I said, "To me, that's taking a really nice relationship and making it sound cheap and ugly. Is it bad that I'm attracted to you, or that you enjoy being with me? And don't tell me it's because you've been bribed, because I don't believe it."

'No - no, not at all." And then a sigh. "Yes." she said, "you're right. I'm sorry to be so unreasonable. I don't know what I want."

"Well I know what I want. I want you to stop hurting yourself. You're a good person, and I'm not a bad one."

"Yes, it's just that --- I don't know. I'm by nature independent. I want to be myself. I don't want to owe anything to anybody. Maybe I can't have it all."

"I don't see why not. Just accept the nice things that come along without feeling bad, or guilty for enjoying them. And don't let other people be your conscience."

"No, I suppose not."

Our dinner date never really recovered. Too many deep issues and feelings had come to the surface for which there were no easy answers.

During the next few weeks we continued pretty much as before without coming to any clear cut resolution. Then one morning

Carla came into my office and said, "Jack, I want you to write me a letter of recommendation."

"Of course I will," I said. "You can write it yourself, and I'll sign it, but what's this all about?" Nothing had ever been said that she might be thinking of leaving. Good jobs weren't all that easy to find. "I hope this isn't a sudden impulse, and you know what you're doing. Have you thought it out?"

"Not entirely," she said. "But, you know, I was just up in Munich, and while I was there I met a lot of people, including representatives from a big American bank - the Chase Bank, I think it's called. They want to expand their operation in Germany and are hiring people to help them get started. One position they want to fill is information to press and radio. I told them that is exactly what I do, and that I would be interested. He gave me an application form and asked for three references. So that's the story. Actually, I'm very excited."

"Well, no problem with the letter. I might even be able to help with the application although I know nothing about banks."

"Don't worry, just get something nice on paper. I'll be down later to pick it up for typing, and for you to sign. Isn't this wonderful?"

I wasn't too sure about that. This was going to take getting used to.

Actually, it didn't, because not long after that conversation, it was I who left Innsbruck, having been reassigned to Vienna for duties to be specified. Our parting was friendly, affectionate but without tears. I felt there was definitely something missing, but, as Carla said, "Maybe you can't have it all."

Chapter Thirty-Nine

Auf Wiedersehen Innsbruck

Despite these diversions, business at the Center was running smoothly, as indicated by the statistical reports sent monthly to Vienna, which is what they really cared about. Like a successful retail store, the Amerika Haus had found, I felt, a useful place in the Innsbruck community, with the general public as well as with local institutions and officials and the French occupation authorities. How much of this could be attributed to my efforts, I'm not sure - it was running well when I got there, but the year I was in charge had seen numerous innovations as well as growth in the existing programs.

At any rate, confidence in myself was at an all time high. That my appointment was classified as "acting" made little difference to me. Irrespective of title, I was running the whole show, and had been ever since Siemer's departure. That it would not go on forever did not really occur to me. Therefore, it came as a complete surprise when a phone call from Vienna informed me that a "regular" regional public affairs officer would be arriving in two weeks to take over, with me as his assistant. Having once tasted freedom and power, it went totally against the grain to give that up. For me, it carried the bad taste of an implied demotion. Actually, I think it was just Vienna bureaucracy filling a vacant slot in the organization chart.

The new man was named Earl Titus. He was being reassigned by the State Department from Spain where he had been attaché for agricultural affairs in the American embassy. He was about sixty years old, a small man - only about five and a half feet tall, and friendly, not someone who would be difficult to work with.

Kitzbuehel

Accompanying him was Mrs. Titus, about ten years older and a different person altogether.

Anne Titus was a holdover from another generation; autocratic, imperious, from a monied aristocracy accustomed to making the rules to suit themselves. She was extremely unhappy at the Innsbruck appointment, regarding the location as a backwater, and the position as one of no importance. These opinions were delivered in a most forceful manner, completely tactless, consequences be damned. Shortly after their arrival, Bill Hale, head of the USIS operation in Austria, made a first time ever trip to Innsbruck for the sole purpose of extending a welcome and soothing Mrs. Titus's ruffled feathers, but with complete lack of success. Her opening greeting to him was "Mr. Hale, I would like an explanation as to why my husband has been exiled to this godforsaken place." Hale did his best, but Mrs. Titus snorted and cut him off: "You can be sure that we will be taking this matter up at the embassy with the ambassador."

In her self-appointed role as manager of her husband's diplomatic career, Anne Titus practically guaranteed that it would go nowhere. Even if he had been extremely talented - which was not the case - nothing could have mitigated the effect of her haughty, abrasive, outspoken style. Utterly fearless, she would direct her tirades against anyone, even those in highest authority. I heard later that their transfer to Innsbruck had been just to get them out of Spain, where Mrs. Titus had become a disruptive force, and had incurred the personal displeasure of the Queen.

It was comical. The two of them arrived in a style dictated by Mrs. Titus's sense of importance, that is to say, in an enormous Packard limousine, by far the largest car in Innsbruck, the kind that does not look right without a motorcycle escort. On their excursions, Mrs. Titus sat like the queen mother in back, little Mr. Titus scarcely visible. On the few occasions when I saw him drive, I felt concern because even on a cushion he could scarcely see over the hood; the Packard looked like it was driving itself. But our two drivers loved the car, and were quickly commandeered to be personal chauffeurs. For this new status both drivers purchased visored caps of the type worn by professionals, and spent half their time waxing and polishing that mighty vehicle to keep it in showroom condition.

Surprisingly, I got along very well with them, even with the old dragon herself. "Exile" to Innsbruck was bad enough, but self-imposed isolation - because there was no society worthy of their participation - left them lonely and in need of a dinner companion from time to time. Despite her dismissive manner, Mrs. Titus enjoyed a good argument much like Mae Ballou back in Bremen. When she felt she was losing ground, she would end the discussion by saying, "Jack, you're a nice boy, but you have no principles."

One reason for the good relationship was that, despite the change in titles, things went on very much as they had before. Mr. Titus had not the slightest idea what an information program was all about, and was perfectly content to let me manage without comment, suggestions, or interference; an arrangement which suited me. To maintain an appearance of authority, he would scrutinize our expense statements minutely, once commenting in a serious manner that he thought we were spending too much on toilet paper. But that was far as his involvement ever got.

At that time the State Department was under heavy criticism for being out of touch with cold war realities, and of being an old boy network of "striped pants cookie pushers," loaded with "dead wood" in need of vigorous clearing. The Titus case gave some support to that charge. It certainly showed how far the department would go to take care of its own "dead wood," assigning them to positions of low visibility where they could do the least harm. I'm sure many of them were gentlemen like Mr. Titus, decent people, but completely unfitted for the tasks assigned.

Somewhere in the upper reaches of the bureaucracy, someone must have become aware of the situation in Innsbruck. Perhaps Mrs. Titus's complaints had reached a sympathetic ear. At any rate, after a short time on the job, Mr. Titus received a directive transferring him back to Washington pending further reassignment. He left as quietly as he had come; I never learned to what further destination. The most merciful outcome would have been early retirement to enjoy his wife's fortune.

The same directive that announced this transfer also included the news that his place would be taken by a certain Mr. Roberts, whose first name I've forgotten, and that I was being reassigned to Vienna, to be in charge of the country-wide film program.

It was hard to know what to feel about this change. I had been in Innsbruck long enough to make many friends and put down roots in the community, and had come to feel myself to be almost a resident. I had learned to love the Tyrol, its people and the work itself. In terms of government operations and US foreign policy interests, this kind of over- identification with local personalities and culture was regarded as dangerous - too much of a good thing. The point is well taken, but at that time it did not seem as though it applied to me. I thought I was simply doing the job I was sent there to do.

This feeling of loss was on both sides; those I worked with seemed genuinely sorry to see me go. The two weeks remainng before my actual departure were devoted to numerous farewell parties. One in particular, organized by my friend Pfaundler, saw the presence of several local notables: Greiter, the mayor; Neier of the *Tiroler Tageszeitung*; Freddy Achammer of the International Ski Federation, and a dozen or so others. The food was good, wine flowed freely, spirits were convivial. At the end there were toasts and speeches, to which I contributed my own appreciation for the opportunity to live in Tyrol, and my heartfelt regret at now having to leave it. Wine had put everybody in a sentimental mood, and my speech, although a bit maudlin, elicited cheers and applause.

Roberts and his wife arrived with only a few days left for introductions and briefing before I was scheduled to report for duty in Vienna. Time was short, but the Center was operating in routine fashion. About all he had to do was hang up his hat and unpack his briefcase.

Roberts was about forty years old, of medium height, dressed in a double breasted blue business suit, white shirt, carefully knotted tie and a white handkerchief in his breast pocket, looking as though he had just stepped out of a JC Penney window display. An otherwise unremarkable face was attenuated by an overlong, pointed nose, giving him a kind of rat- like appearance. His manner was all business, emphasized by an incisive voice, each word precisely articulated as he ran through several pages of notes and questions. This was definitely not my type of guy.

From the start, he made a big point of the difference in status between us: that mine had been only an "acting" appointment, whereas his was "regular," and that he was in no sense replacing me, but was there to replace Titus. It was pretty obvious that status meant a lot to Roberts, He wanted everybody to be clear about his position, the authority that went with it, and the deference due to him, and by extension to Mrs. Roberts, who was no more appealing than her husband.

Much of this became clear only later after I got to Vienna. At the time I did all I could to make his takeover go smoothly, which it did, except for the staff who were intimidated by his manner of brisk housecleaning efficiency.

I was still inexperienced and unused to the ways of the world, naively expecting some appreciation for the effort and time I took to help him get settled, both professionally, and personally with living accommodations. Roberts was that type of individual, of whom I met several later on in the business world, whose method of scoring points to secure their advancement is to run down, deprecate and trash everything that had been done prior to their arrival. "I inherited a disaster. The place was a mess, but I managed to straighten things out." And so on. With variations, that is the usual refrain

I would never have been aware of all this had it not been for a friend in USIS who sat in on meetings where Roberts had given a preliminary report after taking over in Innsbruck.

"Boy, did he do a job on you," said my friend. "According to him, he found the place in chaos, poorly run due to years of neglect, partly because you were too young and didn't have professional background or training. Personally, I think that was a pretty stupid line to take, because after more than a year, if things were that bad, why didn't we know about it?"

For a moment I was stunned at these revelations, then perplexed as to what I should, or could, do about it. My thoughts went back to a routine State Department inspection made months earlier but independently of Vienna, to assess the efficiency of field installations, and to see how well each was meeting mission objectives. To this end the inspector spent two days in Innsbruck, only a small part of it with me. Needless to say, I was anxious to get a favorable report. At the end of the second day, he came to my office and said, "Mr. Barwick, I'm not permitted to share with you any details of my investigation, but I am allowed to tell you that I am rating this operation as 'excellent.' I think you are doing a fine job here."

As to whether or not to pursue the matter, eventually I thought, why bother? If any, the damage is already done; if not, it will only create a nasty situation. Except for my friend, no one had said anything. So I decided to let it drop. I had a new job to get on with.

Chapter Forty

Kitzbuehel

My transfer to Vienna is getting too far ahead of actual developments. I don't want to say goodbye to Innsbruck without finding space in this memoir for a place where I spent weekends, holidays, and weather bound shut-ins, so that it became almost a secondary residence. This was Kitzbuehel, an alpine ski resort about an hour and a half between Innsbruck and Salzburg.

I had actually started going to Kitzbuehel in the winter of 1950 as a neophyte skier, then returning winter and summer weekends whenever I could. At first I stayed in small hotels and pensions. The European Recovery Program in Austria was devoting a large part of its budget to reviving the tourist industry, so these hostelries were springing up everywhere, with a plaque prominently advertising the source of their funding - US dollars. After that, I rented the second floor of a chalet above the village and next to the "idiot hill," directly under the zeilbahn (cable car) swinging up to the Hahnekamm mountaintop station.

Gradually I became part of a community of mostly expatriates, forming friendships still alive and well after more than sixty years. At that time Kitzbuehel exuded an excitement of pent up energy released after the war years that affected, and infected, anyone who spent time there. It was one of the first winter resorts to regain its prewar style and prestige - fashion, sport, and glamour - set in a tiny old world village surrounded by some of the finest snow terrain in Europe. Into this mixing bowl were gathered an intoxicating cocktail of aristocrats, millionaires, adventurers, ski champions and ski bums, plus eccentrics of every type and calling. Sitting at a bar any evening you might find yourself next to an

Arab prince, an African safari guide, a world class mountaineer, or a movie star. A normal pace of life didn't exist except for the *einheimisch*e (natives) who managed this circus. For the rest of us excitement seekers, it was a diurnal pattern of sun and snow by day, with evenings of unplanned adventure, never knowing when or where the night would end.

It wasn't for everybody. Several of my more serious-minded friends, after one weekend became disgusted with the whole business. "Superficial," "empty," "self-destructive," they called it. And I willingly concede this to be true - but only partly true. The elegance of the spectacle, the brilliant talents on display, were fascinating, and to me made such complaints seem small minded and irrelevant. At any rate, I ate it up.

However, under the quaint image of Tyrolean peasant culture, which was Kitzbuehel's stock in trade, lay a darker layer of recent history that everyone wanted to forget. The very picturesqueness which made the village so appealing to postwar tourism had made it just as attractive to high ranking Nazi officialdom for whom during their years in power Kitzbuehel became a refuge, far from Berlin and from the battlefield. Several, including von Ribbentrop (the Nazi foreign minister), made it their official residence with plans for retirement there. Near the end of hostilities, fleeing from Allied justice, Goering was cornered and arrested in Kitzbuehel. But, as time passed, the same people who prospered under the Nazis prospered again under the so called "liberation." Among them was one Guido Reisch, owner and operator of the biggest nightclub in town, the "Casino" - where Goering was found hiding and taken prisoner. But by then the Nazi *zeit* (period) had become a disagreeable memory, the cries of its victims lost in the beat of dance music and the popping of champagne corks.

Day and night I plunged right into the "Kitz" lifestyle. It was all part of the European experience, and I didn't want to miss any of it, not even the athletic part, which had never been one of my more conspicuous enthusiasms. But skiing as a sport was different from sports in their American version. Although it had its competitive aspect - there were teams and races - you could ignore all that to be alone with nature in a winter paradise. Skiing took you outside, to places where you would otherwise never go, where you often stood still to look at the trackless powder, the soaring mountains, and the tiny village far, far below. A fresh wind from above blew away any cobwebs left over from the night before.

Despite private instruction and many hours on the slopes, I never advanced beyond the intermediate level. I could ski about anywhere, and go down almost anything, but it wasn't always a pretty sight compared to those "Kannones" and "Vedettes" skinning past me, out of sight in a few seconds. Oh well, I thought, comparisons are irrelevant.

Many of the instructors were army veterans, and several were cripples - victims for the most part of mine explosions which left them with foot and leg injuries. One, with whom I skied frequently, had lost both feet, to no discernible effect. Even those who had lost a leg were in no way deterred; they skied on their remaining leg, using poles fitted at the end with a small ski for use in turns. Innsbruck had a team composed entirely of one-legged veterans who competed against similar groups over Europe.

At that time and for many years thereafter, Austrians dominated Alpine racing. One reason, I believe, is that as children and adolescents they couldn't afford the lifts, and had to climb up the mountains on foot in order to ski down. Years of that kind of non-prescribed training developed powerful leg muscles. To make this kind of ascent possible, they used seal skins. These long strips with fur on one side were attached to the tip and tail of each ski. The back-slanted fur provided almost 100% traction, making even the steepest slopes climbable. In fact, I saw one race in Zurs where the race started at the bottom of the mountain, demanding a most difficult exercise in judgment, in order to arrive at the top with enough muscle power and endurance left to manage the stresses and strains of the downhill course. When not on the skis, these sealskins were worn around the waist, like a belt.

A lasting benefit of those years in Kitzbuehel was a love and enjoyment of winter. Having grown up in south-central Pennsylvania and gone to college in New Jersey, winter, to me, was something to be endured - slushy and dirty when not encrusted in ice, dangerous both on foot and in a car. Alpine winters were different. Perhaps it was the altitude; Kitzbuehel was at one thousand meters, and the top of the Steinbergkogel about

2,400 meters - say 8,000 feet. During my years there, the snow stayed remarkably consistent from early December to the middle of March - deep, fluffy powder, comforting in its way. It capped the huts and chalets with a three foot blanket of white, and stood high on either side of the cleared paths and roadways. Most of all, it was incredibly clean, at times looking more artificial than real. On the ancient village buildings it enhanced the architecture to give them a "Hansel and Gretel" appearance - "kitchig" (tasteless) to some, but altogether authentic and seductive if you were in it. Everything conspired to please the senses, including winter temperatures that always seemed to be congenial - no frostbitten noses and ears; no numbed, desensitized feet. People relaxed on sundecks, discarding parkas and snow jackets to soak up the high altitude sun rays. All in all, unlike my previous take on those in the US, Alpine winters were your friend, and wanted you to have a good time.

It could also be your enemy, not often, but often enough to ruin any plans you might have made - a trivial consideration compared to the destruction that fell on the remote hamlets and villages built into the sides of the mountains. I'm talking about avalanches. After a thousand years Austrians were still building in places where not only had avalanches occurred, but where it was practically guaranteed they would occur again. Passing through the village of Heiligenblut in summer, I saw crews clearing away the remains of destroyed houses from a slide site, and putting up replacements.

An avalanche occurs when heavy, wet snow piles up on a layer of dry unstable snow until its accumulated weight breaks the whole mass loose, to slide down the mountain with frightening velocity, carrying all before it - trees, rocks, huts, and houses. This is called a *"rutsch lawine"* (slide avalanche}. Its destructive power is enormous. I visited the site of one not long after it happened. Three or four houses had been carried away -"obliterated" would have a more accurate description. Nothing of any size remained, as if a gigantic hand had smashed the houses down against the frozen earth and then smeared the pieces downhill for a quarter of a mile.

I'll never forget a Sunday night in January 1951. Skiing had been ruined by a persistent rain all afternoon. The frozen roads were dangerous, and I was wondering whether I would be able to get back to Innsbruck by Monday. Several of us were at a table in Praxmaier's Café listening to a portable radio as bulletins began to come in, gradually describing a major disaster. It was eerie. First one village, then another, all with fatalities and missing persons, adding up to over fifty deaths by morning.

That is the more familiar avalanche. But there is another type, somewhat related, called a *"staub lawine"*, or powder avalanche. In this version, the snow mass falls almost as a cloud of powdery flakes, but with enormous velocity, generating a wave of compressed air pushing out ahead of it. People caught in a *"staub lawine"* are not crushed but rather killed when the compressed air ruptures their lungs. Manfred Neier told me of being trapped in one of these while driving in the area of St. Anton. "Suddenly the car was shaking and enveloped in a cloud of snow," he said. "And I couldn't breathe. I was blown up like a football."

No matter how beautiful the weather, up in the mountains danger is never far away. I was skiing Kitzbuehel's most popular run, the Steinbergkogel, along with hundreds of others dotting the slope. Having completed one run, I was in the chairlift going up for a repeat when, just below me, I saw men probing the snow with long poles, and several dogs who appeared to be searching that area. The snow slide they were probing had suddenly spilled off a higher elevation. There was not a lot of it, maybe six or eight feet deep, but enough to sweep a skier off his feet and bury him until next spring. It didn't look dangerous, more like a few acres of freshly made whipped cream. However, the immediate problem was that the area, only minutes before, had been full of skiers; no one knew how many, where they were, or whether they were accounted for. With only limited time to work before suffocation or hypothermia set in, it looked like a hopeless task to me. Meanwhile people continued to ski down the mountain as though nothing had happened. Later reports said that there had been no casualties.

Chapter Forty-One

An Englishman Abroad

As a byproduct of their imperial history, the English have always been very good at finding places on the earth of unmatched beauty - for rest, relaxation, retirement, or simply to escape from the cold and fog of their own little island. Corfu, the French Riviera, Florence, Goa, and others less well known. Eventually, English colonies grew up in these enclaves, including Austria, especially in the Tyrol and in Upper Austria around Bad Aussee. Kitzbuehel became one such sanctuary. Then, beginning with a visit from the Duke and Duchess of Windsor in 1938, the village morphed from an expatriate colony of primarily English into an international winter resort, following a pattern set by St. Moritz in Switzerland. Except for a six year hiatus, 1939-1945, these developments coexisted happily, holiday visitors mixing in with English retirees and long term residents.

I suppose it was natural for me to merge into and become a junior member of this expatriate community. Outdoor sport makes quick friends, but it takes more than one season for these quickie friendships to become permanent and real. I had three years. In just a paragraph or two I will try to give some idea of why they were so stimulating and varied in their opinions and backgrounds - outspoken, obnoxious at times, but always thoroughly civilized.

To begin with, our group contained two admirals, but I knew only one of them well. This was Admiral "Dick" Ruck-Keene, formerly captain of a British aircraft carrier that had seen action in the Mediterranean and the Pacific. Ruck-Keene had not adjusted to civilian life; he thought he was still in command - rude, overbearing, demanding, impatient as only a certain caste of the

British military can he. He had his friends but the rest of us were fit only to be ordered about. An impossible man, but also colorful and impressive.

Ruck-Keene's redeeming feature was that he brought with him several fliers from his carrier who had been with him all through the war - young men only a little older than myself. We skied together by day and drank together at night. They were wonderful chaps, great fun to be with, and a loss when their holidays were up and they went back to their regular jobs at home.

Then there was the Schlee family: Mr., Mrs. ("Ma"), and four boys. They were tea importers based in Hong Kong, and arranged their schedule to be in Kitzbuehel three months in winter and three months in summer, the rest of the time in Hong Kong, with stopovers in London and New York. This impressed me as the perfect way to live, the best of all worlds. At their chalet after dinner, Mr. Schlee would bring out his violin and play light or classical selections.

The further from home, the more they had that sense of being "English," a race apart, and all the stronger for having just fought and won a war in which their very existence as a free people had hung in the balance. I felt this sense of "Englishness" strongly one Christmas day when traditionally the King broadcasts a Christmas message to his subjects in the farthest corners of the Empire. In this case, I believe King George VI was ill, so his queen read the message for him. In the room there was rapt attention to every word, and at the end a toast, "To the King, God bless him."

On one evening during my first season in Kitzbuehel in the group there was this young Englishman whom everyone seemed to know, about my age, professorial in appearance, tortoise shell rimmed glasses and a distinctly upper crust accent. But from time to time when addressing locals he switched to German - not just German, but pure Tyrolean dialect - he was obviously bilingual. His manner was typically British, reserved but not unfriendly. I was just another out-of-towner there for the weekend, so it took several visits before we got to know one another, and to form a friendship that has lasted a lifetime.

This was George Cochrane, a Cambridge graduate in Engineering, with army service during the war and, at the moment, unmarried. He was a full time Kitzbueheler, living just outside of town on a large estate, where he had fitted out part of the basement as a laboratory cum machine shop. In this space he tinkered with various projects during the day, and passed evenings with friends in town.

One of the appealing things about George at age twenty-seven was that he had in him all of the old English spirit of romantic adventure. This took the form of a small plane - soon to be abandoned after a crash - too dangerous for Alpine flying; as well as a much modified army surplus Land Rover he was repairing for a Cairo to Capetown journey. Other adventuresome types were always around. A frequent house guest was a middle aged woman whose wartime job had been ferrying B-24 bombers from the US to their bases in Britain. And it was George who introduced me to Heinrich Harrer, world famous for his escape from British wartime captivity in India to Tibet, and his subsequent friendship with the Dalai Lama. Many others of this type made the evenings memorable.

As we came to be better acquainted, I learned bit of George's family history which read like a tale from Somerset Maugham, realized on the screen by Darryl F. Zanuck. His father had been an officer in the British Indian Army - young and dashing, but unfortunately poor, at a time when a private fortune was the usual key to advancement. This was especially unfortunate in his case since he was a superb polo player. To compete in this most patrician of sports demanded that he maintain a string of polo ponies. So the elder Cochrane was forced to find a solution where so many officers in similar circumstances had found it before him - a wealthy wife; in his case, a blonde beauty, friendly but flighty, who brought to the altar an intelligence far inferior to her bank account. Not to worry. Polo in the peacetime Indian Army opened many doors, and the elder Cochrane had been able to retire to Kitzbuehel as a gentleman of distinction, joining the English colony already established there. The family moved into an imposing Tyrolean *"landhaus"* - house and barn merged into one large chalet structure - overlooking rolling meadows, and in the distance the "Wilde Kaisers" range. The estate was called "Hoerlen." In this setting young George grew up among the hired hands who worked the farm and their children, speaking dialect like a Tyrolean peasant, unmodified by three years later at Cambridge.

With the outbreak of hostilities in 1939, the British contingent was forced to flee back to England, their property confiscated as the Nazis moved in. Hoerlen was taken over by von Ribbentrop, then restored at the end of the war when von Ribbentrop, along with most of the other ruling Nazis, was tried for war crimes, found guilty and hanged.

By the time of my arrival, Cochrane senior had separated from Vera, his wife, and was living in luxury somewhere on the French Riviera. Hoerlen had resumed its role as a family residence with Vera presiding. She had, in the meantime, grown quite fat, but was still as flighty and feather-headed as ever, talking constantly, and without waiting for an answer rushing on to a new topic, whatever entered her head. After awhile, you just settled back and let her ramble on, nodding and smiling from time to time to feign understanding.

On the two or three weekends I spent at Hoerlen there were other houseguests, in the grand English houseparty tradition. One such guest comes to mind. George had a sister some ten years older than he, a perfect blonde beauty. She had married an Italian prince quite a bit older than herself. They lived in Italy and had driven up to visit Hoerlen on this particular weekend. George and I were having a pre-dinner drink when the prince appeared in a state of nervous agitation.

"Georgie, old boy. Be a good sport. I was wanting to have a bath before dinner, but I can't seem to get the confounded thing to work properly. At home I don't have to bother. Gino, my man, gets it all ready. So sorry to disturb you, but there was nobody up there to ask."

The two of them disappeared upstairs leaving me to wonder, is this really the twentieth century when a grown man doesn't have enough commonsense to fill a bathtub, and all his life must depend on servants to do it for him? Incredible.

As the years passed, the expense of maintaining an establishment the size of Hoerlen had become greater than the income from the farm. It may have been too expensive to begin

Picking Up the Pieces

with. An experiment raising chickens for additional income had just come to grief one wet September when most of them died of pneumonia. Masterminding this venture was a friend of Vera's, an ineffectual type named Cyril, who had become a more or less permanent house guest.

At Sunday morning breakfast it was raining outside, and gloomy inside. An autopsy into the failed venture was underway at the table. Cyril was distraught.

"I'm devastated, simply devastated, Vera," he said, his voice breaking.

"Try to cheer up, Cyril," she replied. "It's only birds, not horses or cows."

"Yes, I know, but they're still living things, and to see them all lying around back there, and the sick ones…." He pulled out a handkerchief and dabbed at his eyes.

"Let me say it again, Cyril, this is not your fault. Maybe we got a bad batch, I don't know. I always thought chickens raised themselves. Perhaps we should have turned them all loose outside, like they do in India, instead of keeping them in that drafty barn. Anyway, Austria is not really the place for chickens. Other birds maybe. There's a man in the town market who sells rebhuhns - partridges - cute little things, simply delicious with preiselbeeren…Now, where was I? Oh yes, Cyril, dear boy, please don't blame yourself. You did all you could. Now, have some breakfast."

" I don't think I can. It's all too depressing."

Tragic for the birds, but I felt like laughing all the same. However, the economic situation really was anything but funny, as long term prospects rapidly became short term bills. Eventually the property was sold to a member of the Swarowski family, heiress to an industrial empire of glass manufacturing. At least money would be there to care properly for that magnificent estate.

With the sale of Hoerlen, Vera and Cyril migrated to the south of France, and George moved into a large house more or less in the center of town, with a ground floor area large enough to accommodate his laboratory. During this time, we exchanged visits and advice on our ongoing love affairs.

Mine, of course, came to nothing. It would have been better

had his suffered a similar fate. Unfortunately, he fell under the spell of a dangerously attractive green-eyed girl, half Polish, half English, and altogether wild. Despite uneasy doubts about the match, I kept them to myself. He would probably not have listened to me anyway, at that time being completely in thrall to this seductress

The resulting marriage was a disaster. She quickly tired of George, and amused herself by openly sleeping with various men and teenage boys around town. It was an open scandal, but soon burned itself out. Kitzbuehel was an exciting place, but this driven woman needed even more. Risk, danger, scandal were the oxygen she breathed to keep going, and she later found two of them in high altitude mountain climbing. She became an expert mountaineer, scaled all of the highest peaks in Europe and eventually retired back to London, a burned out alcoholic wreck at fifty.

During the early part of this drama, I visited George in his new digs. It was late and we had put away the best part of a bottle of Scotch when he said, "Come into the lab. There's something I want to show you."

Sitting on the table was an odd looking contraption about the size of a home laundry appliance without the metal outside cover. Where the agitator would have been was a round base with three phallic stainless steel prongs at one third intervals, angled upward. Off to one side reared a hinged arm. I couldn't imagine what this thing was.

"What is it?" I asked.

"It's a tester that I've been working on," he said.

"A tester," I said. "What does it test?"

"Well, actually it tests condoms - 'French Letters' we call them back home," he explained.

I burst out laughing. "Condoms, for God's sake, you can't be serious, George."

"Don't laugh, my friend. Of course I'm serious. It's the answer to a big problem in Europe right now. Condoms are about fifty percent defective, shockingly poorly made, with no provision for guaranteed integrity or reliability. The consequences for family planning and disease control are obvious."

Yes, put that way I could see this queer-looking thing as a solution to social problems instead of just a bawdy joke. "Well, how does it work,?" I asked.

"The key is that the latex has to be thin enough for sexual stimulation, but without even the smallest loss of surface integrity - no holes, not even microscopic ones. That's the trouble now, mass production methods with no testing. I've talked to public health officials here in Austria and in Czechoslovakia. They're very interested in a device that will guarantee a safe product."

For a demonstration, he turned the machine on by pressing a button switch; then he rolled a condom onto one of the three metal prongs. "Ready to go," he said, and pressed another button. The circular base made a one third turn bringing the dressed prong directly under the hinged arm, which had a kind of rubber pad at the end. The arm then descended to make contact with the prong for just an instant, then lifted as the base made another one third turn. A device rolled up the condom and flipped it into a marked box.

"That was a good one," George said. "If it had been defective, it would have gone another turn and been sent into the reject box."

"But how does it know whether it was good or bad?" I asked.

"You saw that pad at the end of the arm? That's the positive pole of an electric circuit. When it's closed - that is when the current gets through - that means there's a leak in the latex and the condom is no good. But if the circuit stays open, the current has not got through, and the condom is OK. Of course, there's a lot more to it, but you get the general idea."

I suppose I did, but it all seemed like some kind of a crazy movie, this ridiculous machine zipping up the condoms and flipping them into one box or another. Somehow the social benefits got lost in the craziness, with Professor George, the mad scientist, in his demented laboratory.

As the effects of the Scotch wore off, I began to wonder if the entire evening had not been an alcoholic dream.

One would have thought this was enough for one night, but not quite. Dawn was now breaking. I felt the urgent need for a cup of strong, black coffee. And maybe breakfast even though it was only four-thirty or five o'clock.

As if reading my thoughts, George said, "I know a place not far from town where early farmers stop by for a bite on their way to the fields. We can give it a try?"

Moments later we were in my car on a two lane road heading out of town at a brisk but not excessive rate of speed. Low clouds hung over the mountains. In the half light I had my high beams up. Fields and fences flashed by, when suddenly a whole herd of cattle burst out of an open gate in a barnyard wall onto the road directly in front of us. Smoking brakes couldn't quite stop the car in time. We hit several cows glancing blows. An angry farmer appeared.

"Stay in the car and don't say a word. Let me handle this," George directed. "If he sees that you're American there'll be hell to pay. He'll go for all he can get."

With that he jumped out, and in the purest Tyrolean idiom began to berate the man before the latter had a chance to open his mouth. Apparently there was a law to the effect that, before releasing livestock onto a thoroughfare, it was necessary to make sure the road was clear, which the farmer had not done. To this oversight George added threats for repairing possible damage to the car, etc., etc., until the farmer was only too happy to forget the whole business, especially since the cattle seemed to be none the worse for their experience.

The incident had left me slightly shaken as we sat in the small gasthaus among a group of "*bauern*" (farmers), eating slab bacon, greasy potatoes, and eggs, and drinking black coffee.

"Good thing you were along, Georgie," I said.

"Yes," he replied. "It could have cost you. They've learned to love Americans."

Chapter Forty-Two

Vienna

I began my new assignment in Vienna in the late fall of 1952, thoroughly spoiled and not well conditioned or prepared to function inside a bureaucratic organization. Consider my background up to this point: two years in charge of my own LCT during the war; and almost two more years as sole director, running the US Information Center in Innsbruck, both relatively isolated, away from the centers of power and authority, doing pretty much as I thought right and proper. In each, I had a fair degree of success - in jobs that would normally have been given to a much older person. Dropping from that level of personal power and prestige to become an anonymous cog in the machinery of the Occupation did little to satisfy my idealism or offer a new sense of challenge.

The US Information Service for Austria was administered out of a large, four-story building in the Schmidgasse, just off the Ringstrasse. As in Innsbruck, operations were divided into two areas: public affairs and cultural, of which public affairs received by far the largest share of attention and support - rightly so, I suppose, because it most directly impacted cold war policies. And Vienna at that time was the very center of the conflict. Political divisions there were intense, control of the city a major cold war objective, and by extension, to the country itself, since in a sense, Vienna was Austria. The provinces counted, but less so.

The Austrian government at that time was a coalition, a small group of socialist and conservative politicians who had managed to steer an independent course between the conflicting demands of the Allies on one hand and the Soviets on the other. The city itself was divided into two zones: Allied and Russian. This division of authority was symbolized by Jeep security patrols, each vehicle manned by soldiers from the four occupying powers: England, France, the US and Russia. National elections were held while I was there. Principal issues were the peace treaty: how soon? and the age old differences between secular socialists and conservative Catholics. Their differences, however, tended to disappear under pressure from the communists and fear that Austria could disappear behind the Iron Curtain, as had happened with Czechoslovakia. There was also a debate whether the Hapsburg pretender, Otto, should be allowed to return from exile in Liechtenstein.

Preventing a communist takeover by popular vote was the major objective of US foreign policy in Austria, necessitating a constant struggle to influence public opinion. Each side had its weapons. As in Innsbruck, the US Public Affairs Program made heavy use of press and radio. However, in Vienna we actually owned one of the two principal daily newspapers, the *Wiener Kurier*. The other paper was *Die Presse* under the friendly leadership of Fritz Molden. A similar situation existed with radio. In addition to direct control of major stations, there were services to independents as has previously been described. None of this should be confused with Radio Free Europe, based in Munich, Germany, with a different mission. RFE's programs were beamed directly to countries already behind the Iron Curtain, aimed at weakening Soviet rule by encouraging resistance and fomenting discontent and discord.

Maintaining the kettle at full boil in Vienna, as well as keeping the four information centers supplied with press and radio handouts, required a staff of several dozen people on two floors of the Schmidgasse building. Operating anonymously behind such outlets as the *Wiener Kurier*, the public affairs part of the USIS program remained completely invisible to the Austrian public. The visible part was the cultural aspect. There, our modus operandi was exactly the opposite - to be as visible as resources and creativity permitted, mainly through a very large Information Center in Vienna, plus the provincial Centers in Linz, Salzburg, and Innsbruck, operating as semi-independent satellites.

Left to pursue its less political mission, the Cultural Affairs Department somewhat resembled an institution of higher learning, but one largely confined to administrative functions; that is to say, there were no persons of real cultural or artistic distinction among its staff members. Perhaps there were back in Washington but not in Austria. On the other hand, these people were knowledgeable, well educated, and believed in what they were doing. It was not essential that they be famous artists, writers or musicians, only that they could manage talent recruited and brought over from the States, as well as that obtained locally.

It was not surprising, therefore, that the Director of Cultural Affairs was an elderly, pipe-smoking gentleman, whose name I have unfortunately forgotten. His background was in academia, where he would have been - probably had been - president of a small liberal arts college. Under him were two principal assistants: Angelo Egan, who dealt with cultural issues, and "Sandy" Marlowe who had finance and administration. I had met both of them previously when, as a team, they came down to Innsbruck on check-up visits. Below them were operational types, such as myself. Of these, the most important was a bright, energetic lady, Theresa ("Tessie") Druml, who directed the Vienna Information Center as well as the entire library operation for Austria.

Why I had been elected to head up the film program, I cannot say. Perhaps they simply needed somewhere to put me, having made a judgment that two managers were not needed in Innsbruck. Anyway, here I was. No training was necessary; I already knew the entire film library, which really didn't amount to much. The job would be mainly presiding over hundreds of film reels, cans and 16mm projectors, distributing them to the Centers, and maintaining everything in operating condition. For films, this meant inspection, occasional splicing and lots of shipping and receiving; for the projectors it meant mechanical repair or replacement.

Before my arrival this had been the domain of a middle aged Viennese woman, Frau Stolzmeier, a person of iron will and fearsome reputation who guarded her territory like a lioness. No one wanted to tell her that she was being replaced, that is, moved to another position. Eventually they did, but she was still indignant, convinced that she was being shuffled out of her beloved film library.

On my first day there Frau Stolzmeier complained, "Mr. Barwick, will you be so good to tell me why they are not satisfied with my work here?"

"Well, Frau Stolzmeier, I've only just got here. This is my first day, so there's not much I can say."

"Yes, Mr. Barwick. To me they say very little, only that I will now go to the Amerika Haus. I have worked very hard to keep everything just as they want. Look around you - alles in besten ordnung. There is nothing more for you to do," she said.

"I believe there is a better explanation, Frau Stolzmeier," I said soothingly. "You have done such an excellent job here with the films that they feel they can now turn it over to an inexperienced person like myself, and move you on to where your special skills are really needed."

Frau Stolzmeier visibly relaxed at this unexpected line of thought. "Do you really think so, Mr. Barwick?" she asked dubiously.

"I'm sure of it, and that they need you over at the Amerika Haus. You will like Miss Druml who is in charge, I said.

"Well, hoffentlich, you are right. I always try to do my best, but -- we will see... Now, let me explain to you our inventory system, and you will meet Josef who does repairs and the shipping."

So we went through the minutiae of managing the film program which was really just another kind of library, in those days based on a paper system of endless record keeping - totally uninteresting. It would have been different if we had been making films instead of just warehousing and distributing them. To me, this was mindless work, isolated in my storage area of shelves containing the reels, cans, shipping containers, screens and projection equipment, completely removed from the point of contact with our live audience. That was what I missed. For the past four years, first with DP's, and then in Innsbruck, I had been on the front line of a people-directed program - live action and a real audience with whom I could interact, as opposed to this sterile, suffocating "supply sergeant" detail.

If the months in Vienna had been only this, it would not have been worth writing about, and I would have ended the story upon leaving Innsbruck. But two elements combined to make continuing the story possible - even desirable: first, Vienna itself, and the experience of living in one of the world's great cities; and second, the intense turmoil and trauma as the USIS overseas program came under political attack from the United States - from the US Senate in Washington.

A few pages here cannot begin to describe all that Vienna had to offer a historically minded, culture hungry neophyte such as myself. If my new job was somewhat less than inspiring, the city and surrounding area more than filled the void. The current cold war conflict seemed only an added chapter in two millennia of struggle. Five hundred years of Hapsburg rule had left massive monuments scattered all over the city: palaces, churches, museums, and equestrian statues of dead heroes. Styles went from medieval, to baroque, to classical, to 19th century Teutonic, and a burst of creativity in early 20th century *Jugendstihl* - more than I could ever hope to take in. But I would try.

Upon cessation of hostilities, the first act of any occupying power is to seize the best living accommodations for its personnel: villas, mansions and, of course, hotels. For Americans in Vienna, it was the Bristol, an elegant edifice on the Ringstrasse, just a few steps from the opera house and the Graben, Vienna's central square. Not to be outdone, the Russians commandeered the Imperial, another luxury relic of prewar life, only a few steps further along the Ringstrasse.

As in Innsbruck and now at the Bristol, I experienced delusions of grandeur with this scale of living. My room for example: a large parlor/living space, French windows with heavy drapes looking out onto the street, ornate furniture on thick carpeting, silk lined walls hung with giltframed oil paintings, and on and on. Also on the wall was a panel with five buttons; these five buttons would get you anything; dinner? drinks? a girl? or all three? I never tried the third option, but made occasional use of the first two. But I couldn't help asking myself, what was there in my nondescript job that justified this scale of luxury?

Surrounded as it was by the Russian Zone, like Berlin, Vienna was an isolated city, hard to get out of for weekend excursions. So, in contrast to my days in Salzburg and Innsbruck when I was out exploring the surrounding countryside, almost every weekend in Vienna I stayed put.

It would be hard to imagine a more wonderful prison; many would never want to leave. But I must be careful. With one of the grandest cityscapes on all sides, it would be all too easy for this little account to degenerate into one of those boring travelogues in which the narrator rushes breathlessly from one overwhelming travel experience to another until their accumulated weight stifles all interest. In this instance less is more; a taste will have to do.

Every great city has, over time, created its own spirit, its own identifying mystique, its own blend of life and physical presence into an accepted image. As Henry Van Dyke wrote years ago:

> London is a man's town,
> There's power in the air,
> And Paris is a woman's town,
> With flowers in her hair.

In the same sense, Vienna has been the world's concert hall for classical music for four centuries, from the days of Haydn, Mozart, Beethoven, and Brahms to Mahler, Bruckner, Strauss, and Lehar - Vienna and music are inseparably linked.

I promptly proceeded to dive right in. The newly renovated opera house was next door, the Burg theater was staging opera, and there were numerous small halls for instrumental and chamber music. One of my favorite Sunday morning rituals was to walk over to the Hofkapelle, a small chapel attached to the Hofburg - the Hapsburg Palace - where the Vienna boys choir sang at Sunday morning services. Their pure, bell like tones, without organ or other instrumental accompaniment, came as close to the angels as human sound ever gets. In those moments, in that place, I could almost have become a believer.

On anther plane entirely were the Mozart operas. Up to that time I had been under the spell of Beethoven's genius, especially the heroics of his middle period. Back in Biarritz, Professor Desrosier and I had friendly arguments - who was the greater composer? - in which I took the Beethoven side. My familiarity with Mozart rested entirely on half a dozen late symphonies, plus a few concertos and chamber works. Of the operas, I knew nothing. Vienna introduced me to Mozart the entertainer - Mozart the showman. In Da Ponte, his librettist, he found a kindred spirit who could contrive ridiculous plots, but which were then raised by Mozart's music to the highest form of art. Of those I saw, no two were alike; each exhibited its own display of human personality: comic satire (*"The Marriage of Figaro"*), immature foolishness (*"Cosi fan Tutti"*}, mysticism {" and moral judgment (*"Don Giovanni"*}. They were all wonderful. After all is said, my argument with Professor Desrosier has no answer - both composers are beyond human comparison, neither between themselves, nor with any other.

It is probably a mistake to begin writing about cultural opportunities in describing my brief life in Vienna, because one does not know where to stop - the *Stefansdom* (the cathedral), the churches, the palaces and architecture were all part of the experience of living there. But as I said a moment ago, I don't want to turn this into a guidebook. Having said that, I am still unable to move on without mentioning the *Kunsthistorisches* Museum. In its enormous galleries are to be found half a millennium of art masterpieces accumulated by Hapsburg emperors who ruled the Holy Roman Empire from Vienna. Titian, Breughel, Rubens, and dozens of others - way too many for a single visit. I used to walk out of there feeling overstuffed, suffering from cultural indigestion.

Evenings up in Grinzing were a good antidote for over-intellectualizing. Grinzing was, and I hope still is, a charming area of old time houses and taverns, once a village, now connected to the city proper, but still ancient in appearance and spirit. Beethoven toward the end of his life lived and worked in one of its houses. The village is strung out along a main street. On either side vine covered hills hem the houses in and are the source of Vienna's locally produced wine. This is the famous *"Heurigen"*, or "new" wine, its arrival eagerly awaited and cause for an annual celebration. When word of its arrival is passed down, each tavern ties a small pine branch above the entrance, and gets ready for the crowd. In they come, and before long the place is rocking with music, songs, whoops and laughter in a general hubbub. And not just in one tavern, but in all of them, of which there are a great many. It is lovely to watch, so many people having such a good time, so civilized - no boorish drunks, no loud arguments, no fights, just doing what wine was meant to do - bring joy to ordinary lives.

That is, for the evening. Next morning can be another story. *Heurigen* is "new" wine, by no means a great wine, but plentiful and cheap, one that lends itself to serving in unlabeled bottles or carafes, and to losing track of their number in the general merriment. But, oh, the morning after - a head never to be forgotten. That is, until the next time.

It all started with the Romans, and evidence of their presence two thousand years ago can still be found, sometimes far below Vienna's city streets. My favorite cafe, the Urbani Keller, was reached through a virtually unmarked streetside doorway, and then down a long descent of narrow stone steps into virtual darkness, fitfully illuminated by flickering torches mounted in wall brackets. Gradually, as your eyes became accustomed the gloom, the outlines of a vaulted cavelike subterranean chamber began to reveal themselves, the walls lined with those flat bricks typical of so much Roman architecture. "*uhr alt*" (ancient), mysterious, another world, one of the imagination - so much so that I had a problem deciding what to drink. Barroom cocktails? Definitely not. Even beer didn't seem quite right. That was for barbarians - the Gauls the Romans were there to fight. But, as they say, "when in Rome, do as the Romans do." So I settled for a bottle of Tuscan red from an area not far from Rome.

For more conventional tastes, or when I was entertaining female company, there was a restaurant called Die Drei Hussaren, softly lighted, but you could read the menu. The maitre'd, with many bows and flourishes, tucked us away in a cozy corner with candles on the table. The cuisine was Hungarian, with menu listings in that language. My date's father was Hungarian so she translated for me. But no translation was necessary for the cart of appetizers our waiter wheeled to the table. Among the array of options was a display of small trout, five or six inches long, their colors shining through a sheet of clear aspic - totally illegal in the US on several counts. Dinner was delicious and very eastern European; after all, Budapest is only a few hours downriver. There was lots of sour cream, with wild boar, chicken, and pork dishes, paprika for color, and sauerkraut for crunch. Nothing light about it, but nothing a good appetite couldn't handle. However, the dessert tray with heavily decorated cakes and tortes was simply too much. Instead, we had a demi-bouteille of Tokai - sweet enough to be a good substitute.

The evening had unfolded at a leisurely pace - low light, muted voices from other tables, our waiter looking discreetly in to see if anything was needed, and as quickly vanishing. Then, as though someone had decided the moment was right, a gypsy violinist appeared at our table, and with his body movements arcing and bending to the music, poured out an emotional recital of the Hungarian spirit. Corny? Overdone? Too much? Maybe so, but as far as I was concerned, it was just right, the perfect end to a perfect dinner. Wine, women, and song, each a force in itself, but put them all together - irresistible.

My life at this time was an odd mixture of disparate elements: boredom in the film library, an active social calendar outside, with occasional glimpses of diplomatic high life thrown in. Despite my lowly official position, the embassy from time to time required an American representative to "show the flag" at state sponsored functions, and I would be elected to attend. These affairs could be a cocktail party, or more often than not a long drawn out meeting, sometimes with high ranking politicians or ministers in attendance. There were times when I actually found myself seated next to the Chancellor - Julius Raab - himself, or to his predecessor, Figl. Half the time I didn't know what they were talking about, but since all I had to do was keep awake and look intelligent, it didn't matter.

However, I did want to regularize my status with the State Department, if possible as a foreign service officer. To that end I made out an application, and was subsequently scheduled to be interviewed by a panel of senior embassy officials. Whether this was all there was to it or just preliminary, I never did find out. At any rate it seemed to be a crucial step, and I was more than a little

Vienna

nervous in anticipation. As it turned out, I need not have been. The interview was more like a small social gathering - very friendly, only a few background questions. They seemed to be more concerned that I was still a genuine American, and had not become over-Europeanized by years outside the US. There were a lot of questions about Princeton's recent football season and its all-American running back, Kazmaier. I had followed the season closely and was able to speak with convincing authority. So I emerged from the session feeling confident about the future.

Had I then realized the significance of events transpiring in Washington, and the impact this was to have on US foreign policy, the State Department, and me personally, I would have been seriously concerned.

Chapter Forty-Three

McCarthyism Up Close

Once again, time for some history. To understand better this chapter and what follows requires a brief review of the events of that era - a tumultuous time in American politics, and one of the least attractive. I will try to tell it here entirely from memory in an effort to convey the principal events, but more importantly, the mood at that time which made these events possible, and the despicable characters who helped carry them out.

Roosevelt's sudden death in April 1945 catapulted Harry Truman into the presidency. Unknown and woefully uninformed, Truman was regarded by many as a hack politician, totally unequal to the leadership role that had been thrust upon him. However, with the aid of a first class Cabinet and participation by Republican moderates, he succeeded in bringing World War II to a successful conclusion and reshaping the postwar world through a series of major accomplishments. Despite these gains, to the American public it often seemed that we were losing ground.

On the negative side, there was the Korean war which lingered on in a stalemate that neither side seemed able to break. After ten years, the American people were sick of conflict, the more so as we weren't winning. And in China the communists were making steady advances against the weak, corrupt, US backed government of Chiang Kai Shek.

Worse yet were failures in national security. Soviet intelligence had succeeded in stealing our most closely guarded secrets: first, with the Rosenberg spy ring and loss of the US atomic weapons monopoly; then the Klaus Fuchs betrayal by which our H-bomb monopoly passed to the Russians. Also damaging was the trial and conviction of Alger Hiss, a senior State Department official, for lying about his prewar communist connections.

As a result, the entire country experienced a massive wave of insecurity and anxiety which quickly metastasized into hysteria - hysterical anti-communism. Neither individuals nor our institutions of law and justice were safe against what had become a true witch hunt. Right-wing Republicans who had never reconciled themselves to a bipartisan foreign policy now attacked the administration as being "soft on communism." That it had succeeded in halting the spread of communism everywhere except in China had no effect on the virulence of their attacks. Secretary of State George Marshall, who had done as much as anyone to bring about our victory in WWII, was vilified as a "front man for traitors." The House Un-American Activities Committee, in hearings using false and sometimes perjured testimony, ruined the careers of many liberal or left wing Hollywood actors and writers, some of whom left the country to avoid testifying. To anyone who believed in the values on which our country rested, it was a sad, sorry spectacle. But worse was yet to come.

Out of this morass of fear driven hysteria, there now emerged a master manipulator, a demagogue whose name would become a label for the whole sick era. His name was Joseph R. McCarthy. With the election of General Dwight D. Eisenhower as president in 1952, McCarthy became chairman of the Senate Committee on Government Operations, He was a man in whom principles did not exist. To help himself get elected, McCarthy had fabricated a false war record. He was a gambler, an alcoholic, and a womanizer, a crude opportunist going nowhere until fear of communism began to sweep the country. The nation's mood demanded scapegoats, communist sympathizers if not actual traitors. They needed to be identified and rooted out from their hiding places in the government and our national institutions.

McCarthy was a street fighter and proud of it. His dirty tricks he claimed to have learned from a backwoods roughneck, "Indian Charlie", in the wilds of Wisconsin. If these low blow tactics worked back there, they proved to be even more effective in Washington and with the US public. A "show no mercy, give no quarter" street fighter was exactly what an insecure public wanted.

As chairman of the senate committee, with virtually unlimited power to investigate, McCarthy was in an ideal position to fill this role. He proceeded to do so with devastating effect. Government officials suspected of leftist leanings were hauled without legal counsel before his committee to be grilled based on rumor, innuendo and the testimony of questionable witnesses. Smear tactics were the rule by which McCarthy's committee operated. Since these were only committee hearings, and not a court of law, judicial protection did not apply. If the careers of innocent persons were ruined, that was too bad.

In this miserable travesty, McCarthy had the assistance of a young man who was, if possible, of lower moral and ethical standards than the Senator himself. This was Roy Cohn, and his position was that of chief counsel to the committee. This can be an important position at any time, but given McCarthy's prestige and political power in the country, acting as his proxy elevated the twenty-five-year old Cohn to an unprecedented point where highly placed persons of long and distinguished service - agency heads, ambassadors, even generals - quaked in his presence, or faltered under his hostile cross examinations. McCarthy, the master, had found the perfect understudy - brash, aggressive, and with no ethical inhibitions. Cohn never found it necessary to upstage his boss; instead he proceeded to carve out his own niche, becoming quite indispensable in the committee hearings, always at McCarthy's side, from time to time leaning over to whisper a tactical suggestion.

After 1952, with a Republican administration in power, McCarthy could no longer attack the government indiscriminately; that would be attacking his own party. Therefore, a strategy was developed to concentrate fire on individuals who had "fostered the worldwide spread of communism," or at the very least had not done enough to stop it. Both, according to the committee, were to be found in the US Department of State. The first group were those foreign service officers who had, in the phrase of the day, "lost China." They were recalled and paraded before the American public as self-evidently "guilty." The other group within the State Department considered lacking in anticommunist zeal were those responsible for projecting America's image abroad - the USIS, now renamed the US Information Agency. From this charge the Voice of America and Radio Free Europe, both heavily propagandistic, were exempted. It was the information libraries and public affairs programs that became the focus of McCarthy's attacks.

To a demagogue, the information program offered a tempting target. To begin with, the American public knew next to nothing about it. How could they? It operated only overseas with no domestic counterpart, unless one wanted to count public libraries, which no one had ever suggested were a subversive influence.

As we have already seen, the information program had as its original mission the projection of America's image of freedom and western cultural values, in contrast to the Soviet tyranny and its eastern European mentality. Under the new administration, this goal now underwent drastic reinterpretation and implementation. The original concept rested on a spirit of confidence that US policies could be defended objectively, that our history and literature were strong enough to stand on their own without alteration. Now, information was to be tailored to fit a message; literature and history were to be censored and rewritten as propaganda. Ironically, what seemed to escape these zealots entirely was that their spirit and methods were directly antithetical to a free society, and were in fact those that the information program had been designed to counteract.

To generate publicity and public discontent with our overseas information services, in the spring of 1953 it was decided to send Roy Cohn on an "information" gathering tour of the major western European countries, to highlight the subversive slant of the libraries, whose shelves were supposedly laden with the works of leftist authors. Preparations for the trip provide a good example of its un-American nature. What happened in Austria was probably typical of practices followed elsewhere. In Vienna, paid Austrian "spies" were sent to the Amerika Haus to pinpoint the location of books by specific authors, so that the inspecting party when it arrived could immediately locate them. This undercover tactic was executed with extreme clumsiness. The "spies" were ignorant persons, speaking broken English, who had to ask where the books were, reading from a list of names they could not pronounce. That

Picking Up the Pieces

list gave away the whole show, although there was no secret as to which books the McCarthy committee found objectionable. I can't remember all of them, but included were such writers as Upton Sinclair, John Dos Passos, Erskine Caldwell, John Steinbeck, and Ernest Hemingway. In any case, American employees were disgusted that the McCarthy Committee found it perfectly legitimate to pay foreign nationals of unknown loyalty to spy on Americans.

In this questionable journey, Roy Cohn was accompanied by his special "friend," G. David Schine. Schine, tall, blond, about the same age as Cohn, was the son of the owner of a chain of movie theaters. With no previous experience or expertise in foreign affairs, what Schine could possibly contribute to the enterprise is a question that answers itself.

However, that was not the reason for his presence on the trip. Cohn was a practicing homosexual all his life; in fact he died of an AIDS-related illness. It is to his eternal discredit that throughout his career he kept his own orientation secret, while at the same time using his position to punish and discriminate against gays. Hypocrisy was just another piece in Roy Cohn's moral makeup. Given the widespread homophobia in the US at that time, the fact that Cohn felt completely free to travel with his "friend" Schine on a highly publicized official mission shows how immune he felt himself to be from popular disapproval or political risk. Such a display of indifference at that time would have been inconceivable for any other government employee.

The plan was for them to visit each country in turn during a period of about three or four weeks. I forget the exact sequence, but to the best of my memory, they had already been to London and Munich before arriving in Vienna. Waiting for them to arrive, USIS staff had reached a pitch of acute anxiety. We talked of nothing else. Cohn, Schine and McCarthy dominated every dinner and cocktail party conversation. Planning and preparation at the embassy were on a scale befitting a visiting monarch or head of state. Hysteria reigned, so in thrall was our diplomatic corps to the power of McCarthy and his henchmen.

The much feared visit began with a protocol call and meeting at the embassy, attended by the Ambassador, Llewellyn Thompson, and higher ups in the information program. I never got an account of what transpired there; I think it was mostly an exchange of formalities. The real evidence Cohn was looking for was not there but at the Amerika Haus in the center of town. My presence was pretty much an afterthought in case questions arose regarding the film program, but that was considered unlikely. Intelligence received from Munich indicated that their real interest was books.

Theresa Druml ("Tessie"), the director, a small, pert woman, acted as hostess when they arrived. Cohn was dressed in a dark blue suit, his hair slicked down; Schine, looking like a golden god in tan gabardine. After a tour of the premises, they adjourned to Tessie's office where extra chairs had been brought in. Visibly relaxed, Cohn settled into a chair and, without asking permission, proceeded to light a cigar, puffing and blowing smoke. Despite a youthful appearance, he exuded an air of aggressive authority, reinforced by a sinister aspect, probably due to his eyes which looked out from under partially drooping lids.

There then ensued a kind of debate - or more properly, an exchange of views. Cohn was on his best behavior that day, but went immediately on the offensive. I can't remember the exact words, but it proceeded more or less as follows.

Cohn: "Miss Druml, I want to compliment you and your staff on this beautiful center. David and I agree that it's a great place for people to come to find out about our country and its message of freedom for the world. However, there is an important exception, but one that can easily be remedied. We believe the information program, and particularly the libraries, are not operating in a manner consistent with the goals of the program as it was set up by Congress in 1948."

Druml: "Could you explain that, Mr. Cohn."

Cohn: "Certainly. We were in a cold war then with the Russians, and we're still in it. It's a war necessitating the full use of every weapon we've got - militarily, as well as information - to counter the attacks the Soviets constantly make against us. We're in this to persuade the people of Europe to reject communism and cast their lot with us, but in many quarters they're undecided. They want to be on the winning side, or at least one they can put their trust in and feel safe with."

Druml: "Of course. That's why we're here."

Cohn: "I believe you mean that. Unfortunately, many of the books now available on your shelves, not only do not carry out that intent, but actively work to undermine it."

Druml: "In what way, Mr. Cohn?"

Cohn: "They do it in several ways, all of which echo and reinforce the themes the Soviets use in their propaganda against us. One, of course, is the evils of our capitalist system and free enterprise. *"The Jungle"*, by Upton Sinclair, right now on your shelves, is nothing but an attack on the meat packing industry as it existed fifty years ago, not today. *"God's Little Acre"*, by this man, Erskine Caldwell, describes poverty and racial divisions in the south with no redeeming features whatever. If you include degenerate behavior, you can include William Faulkner. I'll give you one more: persecution of migrant workers in the fields of California, as described in John Steinbeck's books. I could go on, but it's not necessary to make my point. All of these are about America - unfortunately, the underside of America, the side the Soviets like to talk about. I ask you in all honesty, Miss Druml, who, in his right mind, would have positive thoughts about a country as described in these books?"

Druml: "Well, first of all, these books are only a tiny, tiny part of our library, just as the conditions they describe are only a small part of life in America That is the real point- that our library tries to provide a total picture of our country - its history and achievements - and where they exist, its problems as well. Any good public library is a broadly educational institution, ours included."

Cohn: "Yes, Miss Druml, but yours is not just any library, and these are not just normal times, even though your superiors act as though they are. That's why David and I are here, why Senator McCarthy is trying to wake up the bureaucracy to the fact that comfortable peacetime attitudes won't do when we are engaged in a life and death struggle with an adversary who will not rest until they have defeated us, starting with the battle for men's minds."

Druml: "We certainly have no difference there. It is a war for men's minds, in our case right here in Vienna. Sometimes I think it's difficult for anyone back in Washington to fully appreciate the reality of the environment in which we operate. This is a university town; the Viennese are an educated, sophisticated people. After almost a decade under the Nazis, they are hungry for knowledge about America, and to reestablish ties to the writers and artists they have heard about but were forbidden to read. These people are our audience, the ones we are trying to reach, not only in Vienna but all over Austria. And we are succeeding; our surveys and opinion polls confirm this beyond any shadow of a doubt."

Cohn: "All right, but why should we do the Soviets work for them? Get rid of these negative distortions of the USA, and the whole program will be better for it."

Druml: "With all due respect, Mr. Cohn, I must beg to disagree. Under Hitler the Austrians were force-fed a diet of canned, official news, information and literature, all designed to promote government policies. The Austrian public is very much aware that the Soviets do exactly the same today, and they don't like it. They don't trust it. They much prefer an honest picture to being told what to read or what to believe. The fact that our publications include some of the bad along with the good builds trust in what we say. It is by no means a sign of weakness. On the contrary, it is a mark of confidence and strength."

Cohn: "Well, Miss Druml, the United States is a democracy. It is the Congress who makes the laws and votes the budgets. I think you are going to have a very hard time persuading our elected representatives to vote for using American tax dollars to support the same goals and tactics as Soviet propaganda. It simply goes against reason and common sense. As an idealistic theory, it might be something for intellectual academic debate, but as a strategy for the cold war, it is unacceptable, so I think for the moment we'll have to leave it at that, and get on with our visit. On behalf of David and myself, thank you for your time."

They left. The room smelled of cigar smoke. The remains of Cohn's cigar lay in an ashtray. It had a plastic holder. After everyone had gone, I picked up the holder and put it in my pocket as a souvenir of the meeting.

Chapter Forty-Four

Terminated

Results of the visit were not immediately forthcoming; those would be issued in the form of directives from Washington at a later date after the entire tour had been completed . Having generated an enormous amount of publicity, Cohn and Schine were off to Rome and Paris. Sad to say, their tour appeared to have achieved an important objective: far from arousing opposition to the methods employed, its effect on the American public appeared to be one of encouraging doubt and suspicion that things were not right in our overseas information program. "Where there's smoke, there's fire. Maybe a thorough housecleaning of the State Department from top to bottom was really needed to get rid of all those woolly headed liberals and communist sympathizers. Whether as a result of formal instructions or simply acting on its own, that is what the public affairs department of the USIA in Vienna decided to do. In my case, it was a three-stage separation.

The day after the confrontation, I was called into the office of the deputy cultural affairs officer, Angelo Egan, with whom my relationship went back to my first days in Innsbruck.

"Jack," he said, "We've got a problem."

"What's that?" I said. He sounded serious.

"You'll recall that back in 1951 you were hired locally to fill that vacant slot in Innsbruck?"

"Right."

"Well, that was done provisionally pending an FBI investigation and clearance. You're probably not aware that legislation creating the USIS in 1948 stipulated that all employees had to have an FBI clearance."

"So what's the problem?" I asked.

"The problem is that your investigation was never completed, and your clearance is still pending."

"You mean that in the two years since then they still haven't finalized it?" I was astonished. Without any reason to think otherwise, it was one of those bureaucratic procedures that I had simply taken for granted as accomplished.

"I'm afraid not, and I really don't know why. In any case, now, with these investigations looking for whatever they can turn up to smear us with, lax on security, for instance, your case is a risk that we can't afford to take," Egan said.

"What does that mean?" I was in a kind of shock. The whole thing seemed unreal.

"For now, it means we have to move you out of USIA because we inherited all the old USIS regulations. We're going to place you over in "Psywar" - Psychological Warfare - for the time being, until things settle down. Fortunately, psywar was set up before 1948 so this same restriction doesn't apply."

"Golly, this is big news. I'm not sure how to take it," I said.

"Well, we must act right away. They may have internal spies reporting on us right now. Move your things up to the fourth floor, where they have a desk for you. I don't have to tell you how sorry I am about all this."

As I sat there at my desk at the end of the first day on the new job, I couldn't help but reflect that this was the irony of ironies. Twenty-four hours before I was presiding over an activity - a film library of innocuous titles of no security significance whatever, but because of a missing FBI clearance, I became a "security risk" and forbidden to handle them. Worse yet, my new assignment to psywar was to one of the most sensitive areas in the entire US program for Austria. In this new capacity I was authorized to handle material truly critical to cold war operations.

I now spent more time going through files of background material, including a mission statement for psywar activities. Everything in it carried a "top secret" security classification. During my whole time in Vienna I had scarcely ever seen a top secret document; here, that label was almost routine. However, top secret classification meant what it said and was treated

Picking Up the Pieces

accordingly. I'm sure that level of concern was justified, since psywar operated much more aggressively than other parts of the information program, mostly aimed at creating dissension and unhappiness in the Soviet Zone - both in and outside of Vienna.

Quite a bit of reading was required to bring me up to speed before I could be assigned to any specific project. To cover it all, I used to take some materials back to the hotel for after dinner reading. Perhaps I was beginning subconsciously to disconnect, to not take the whole thing as seriously as I once did - and to get careless.

Leaving the office late one afternoon, I had the usual bundle of documents with me, most if not all of them bearing the top secret stamp. To free my hands, I placed the pile on the roof of the car while I got my keys out and unlocked the door. Without thinking I got in, closed the door, started the engine and drove down the Schmidgasse preparing to enter the Ringstrasse. I had not gone far when, looking in the rear view mirror I saw papers flying in all directions in the street behind the car. It was a moment of pure horror but lasted only a split second. Thank God, traffic had not yet built up to the evening rush. I braked to a halt, jumped out, and dodging cars and people tried to retrieve the scattered sheets. Several passers by joined in the chase. In a few minutes I had all that I could see. Then I sat back in the car and, with trembling fingers, went over each document, page by page, to make sure they were all there. They were. The relief I felt cannot be expressed. This was the kind of lapse people were sent to jail for in that inflamed security conscious era.

Nothing seemed real anymore. I couldn't focus on the new job. After a little more than a week the second shoe dropped. The interview took place in the personnel office with someone I did not know.

"Mr. Barwick, I hope you understand that this action is something that is been forced upon us. I apologize for the suddenness with which we have to move, but I think you understand the circumstances. The upshot is we have been instructed to terminate any employee whose file is not entirely in order - in your case, the missing FBI clearance. I can't explain why it's still pending - who knows? But that doesn't change anything. We can act only on the basis of the information we have - or don't have."

"So what's the result?" I asked.

"Since your situation falls within the instructions we have received, you are to be terminated as of today, with two weeks of accumulated leave and return transportation to the United States."

"How will the termination read? I mean, what grounds will be given? " I asked.

"Nothing negative," he said. "It will be a simple 'reduction In force', an administrative catch-all, with no fault implied. Again, I'm sorry."

At the Schmidgasse I had a crying session with four or five other victims of the purge. Most of them were young, about my age, people I had gotten to know well enough to hold discussions and trade opinions with. I couldn't help noticing that as a group they were predominately liberal. It made me wonder if some kind of political or ideological test had been factored into this "reduction in force." It seemed suspicious.

Outside, in the spring sunshine, Vienna never looked lovelier. Cafes had moved tables outside, and people were walking their dogs along the avenues. Up in the Wachau, and along the Danube, apple trees were blossoming. After so many years I had trouble realizing that I was saying goodbye to Europe.

Or would I? That was a question turning over in my mind as I sat there contemplating a suddenly uncertain future. Uncertain either way: to stay in Europe? Or go home? At that moment, Europe was for me more familiar territory. Attitudes, language, friends had all combined to make me feel thoroughly at home there. Quite the opposite for the US. With the exception of that senior year at Princeton, I had been away from home since 1944 - nine years. With each year the memory had receded bit by bit, and was now overlaid by the news coming out of Washington and by my being fired. If this was the new US, would I fit in?

I had grown up under Franklin D. Roosevelt and the New Deal, a government that believed in freedom, opposed tyranny, and was a friend to its people. Now that entire philosophy was under attack, both at the policy and the personal level; and the bad people seemed to be winning. Did I want to hold onto my original career aspirations of working for the State Department? Was there a future for me in this new regime? Even if there was, could I compromise my own basic principles enough to stay with it? Did I want to?

But if not government service, what then? Not only did I have little knowledge of the private sector, but what little I did have was colored by a deep seated, anti-business attitude. In my youthful, immature opinion, most businessmen were ruthless predators. If government was an unacceptable option, was the world of business any better?

In this dubious mix of alternatives, one undeniable fact was clear, even to me. That was that I had been thoroughly spoiled by years of subsidized living: first with my family in London, then on the GI Bill in Biarritz, and finally by the lifestyle and privileges conferred on occupation personnel in Germany and Austria. I had acquired fancy tastes: vintage wines, an apartment in Kitzbuehel, weekends on Lake Garda. Would it be possible for me to return to a commonplace, hardworking life in America - probably to a starting level job, with neither position nor special privileges?

Wherever I looked there were problems with no clear answers. What finally made up my mind for me was the feeling at the root of all others that, when all was said and done, I was an American, perhaps one with a superficial Europeanized overlay, but at heart still an American. I decided that I would go back home.

Chapter Forty-Five

A Stranger In My Own Country

> Breathes there a man with soul so dead
> Who never to himself hath said
> "This is my own, my native land."
> Whose heart hath ne'er within him burned
> As home his footsteps he hath turned
> From wandering on a foreign strand?
>
> Sir Walter Scott

Scott goes on to castigate "This wretch, concentered all in self," and to warn that "For him, no minstrel raptures swell."

I was not expecting a chorus of "minstrel rapture," nor was my heart burning with anticipated homecoming. Instead, my mood was one of resignation to the role in the ongoing play that fate had written for me. Acts I and II had been comedy: so full of adventure and romance that deep down in my bones I knew it couldn't go on. But what turn of plot the master dramatist had in store for me was unknown.

What a contrast to that arrival on the *Queen Elizabeth* in Southampton, almost exactly six years earlier, full of undiluted enthusiasm and untested optimism. I felt that those six years and then my abrupt termination had left me prematurely aged in spirit, world weary, and only half responsive to what might come next.

This made me poor company for those returning from their European tours aboard the *Excambion*, which sailed from Genoa with a stopover in Barcelona. There were the usual manufactured shipboard festivities into which I was dragged, unresisting because there was no escape. And I contributed little to conversation at mealtimes where everyone had excited tales to tell of where they had been and what they had seen. In this manner the one-week voyage stretched out to a tedious passage.

The ship docked in Boston on July 6th, and from that moment my interest in life began to pick up. We stayed there overnight before sailing on to our final destination, New York. As I walked around Boston that evening, the full force of American life and energy hit me in a multimedia explosion of flashing neon signs, lighted store windows, honking horns, and an unceasing stream of cars, trucks - and bright yellow taxicabs. Entering one of the stores I was immediately enveloped in a blast of frigid air. Surging crowds of women packed the aisles and pushed up to the counters in a frenzy of bargain hunting. Outside on the sidewalk a gang of laughing teenage girls passed by, dressed in blue jeans and white shirts open at the collar with the tails hanging out. They all wore big round buttons which read "I Hate Everybody." A movie theater further down the block was playing *"The Beast From 20,000 Fathoms."* On its advertising billboard a hyper-developed blonde struggled in the grip of a scaly claw. On the grass of the Common sailors lay about with their girlfriends. Beside a bush an old derelict unfolded a newspaper, sat on it, and pulled a bottle out from somewhere for a long swig.

It was all so different from Europe, and the transition so sudden - the lights, the noise, the traffic, throngs of people in the streets at night, romance on the grass - even the air conditioning. I couldn't imagine that any of this had ever been familiar to me.

New York deepened the discontinuity. Boston at least had been pulsing with energy and life. In New York the crowds and the energy were probably all there, but less visible, overwhelmed and pushed down by the scale of the buildings. As a midshipman and Navy ensign, I had never felt this oppression; my life had a real direction and purpose then. Now, as I looked up at those shiny concrete, steel, and glass towers, I felt like one of the most insignificant of God's creatures - an insect, an ant, dropped into this hostile environment by mistake. The prospect of attempting to scale those walls was totally intimidating, but it was here I had to begin the job hunt, now that my quest for a career in government service had been aborted.

This was a poor state of mind in which to undertake a job search. To begin with, there was the loss of confidence, of drive and positive thinking, leading to a diminished self-appraisal of what I really had to offer. Looked at objectively, my resume was impressive - unformed and unmatched to the American scene but still impressive. But there was also the fact that I didn't know what I wanted to do, or what I could do, or where and how my background fitted into the American marketplace. At that moment, I was not thinking in terms of a career, just a job, preferably something creative.

But it was midsummer. Everyone said that July was a poor time to be seeking employment, better take a few weeks to readapt and get your thoughts together. That is what I decided to do. So for the rest of the summer it was back to Lititz, Pennsylvania, a small town of about four or five thousand Pennsylvania Dutch inhabitants, drowsing amidst the neatly laid out fields of corn and tobacco in Lancaster County.

For me, Lititz was a second home, as in fact it had often been as our family came and went from one foreign tour of duty to another. I had almost grown up there in a large house where my grandmother, Lizzie Hershey, provided an anchor of much needed stability. The intervening years had done nothing to change things; Lititz remained a quintessentially small town, almost a parody of itself.

There on the side porch in the shade of canvas awnings, afternoon sounds only emphasized the stillness: a banging screen door, a push lawnmower coming and going around a neighbor's house, cicadas rattling away in the trees. I was a stranger here. My friends were long gone - to graduate studies, to married life somewhere else, or to careers far from home. Walking into town, I would get a passing nod from strangers and along with it a questioning stare - who is this guy? It was not often that they couldn't place someone. Some newcomers to town were Puerto Rican migrants out of New York in search of work, but I obviously didn't fit that category.

Faces from the past appeared at church on Sundays. My presence there is explained by the fact that Grandma Hershey was a devout churchgoer, had been all her life, and expected everyone else to be, especially family members. To please her, I went along and listened to oldtimers denounce such worldly ideas as plans for a choir, or defend the practice of washing one another's feet on Good Friday.

After church the men walked around to the parking lot in back to get the car, leaving the ladies to their weekly social: the latest on Mary's new deep freezer, and Gloria's letter from Slippery Rock State Teachers College where she was taking courses in education.

As a long lost son, I enjoyed reestablishing contact with those I used to know, and. the best place to do that is at church - or more precisely, after church.

"Well, Jack - I never - Jack Barwick, I would almost not know you - you so much favor your father. Don't he, Dorothy? I would have almost swore it was John Barwick."

"Ye-e-s, he has changed a bit - some heavier, ain't he? Well, he's a man now. Ha, ha, ha. Went away a boy, and comes back a man. How long you been away now, Jack?"

"About six years."

"Six years. Where was you all that time?"

"The last three years I was in Austria."

"Australia?"

"No, Austria - you know, in Europe."

"Can't say as I do. What you been doing there?"

"Oh, I sort of worked in the occupation."

"Then you was in the Army?"

"No, I worked there as a civilian."

"Ain't it wonderful the way our young people are getting over the world today? What does Herbie write from Korea, Kitty? I don't suppose you got over there, Jack?"

"No, not that far."

Florence Gibble saw me and came over. She lived across the street from Grandma Hershey. We chatted for awhile, and I asked her about the library for which she had been an active sponsor. "Oh," Mrs. Gibble replied, "the library is going downhill, but what can you expect when the librarian drinks?"

"Drinks?" I answered, surprised.

"Why, of course, that Mrs. Shorey drinks. Everybody knows that last week they had to drive her home. They found a bottle in her desk drawer."

"But I thought she was an older woman."

"That's just what makes it so disgraceful. No one will support the library as long as they keep that woman in there. That's what comes from bringing people in from out of town. She comes from somewhere in Ohio, and they say she had to get out of there."

By then the cars had arrived, and everyone went home to their chicken dinner. Sunday dinner in the Hershey household was soon ready because most of the work had been done the day before, in order to follow the Bible's injunction against work on the Sabbath. A casserole - it was almost always chicken - had been in the oven during church service. When she was younger, Grandma used to kill them herself; now they came fresh from Trimmer's store, to wind up on the table as pot pie cooked in the Pennsylvania Dutch manner.

Delicious, but crying out for a nice chilled bottle of white wine - any kind, I didn't care, because the water in Lititz was dreadful. It was heavily chlorinated to the point of being almost undrinkable, and formed a hard crust in the pipes and a big ring around the bathtub. In that house, of course, wine was out of the question, mostly for religious reasons, but also because a great uncle had lost his farm - drank it away, they said, at the bar of the Warwick Tavern. Although wine was out, I managed to sneak in half a dozen bottles of beer. I told Grandma it was ginger ale. Her eyes weren't good enough to tell the difference, but they were good enough to spot a bottle of whiskey; those I had to hide in the grandfather clock.

Just as the big city crowds and noise of Boston had almost knocked me off my feet, the stillness of summer and the slow pace of village life made me itchy and restless, bored and in need of action. After a few weeks, I had had enough and began to rethink that original decision to put off the job hunt until after Labor Day. Although I dreaded the prospect, just sitting idly day after day in Lititz seemed less and less a good idea.

The following week found me registered in the Pickwick Arms Hotel on the East Side of Manhattan, in a tiny, unairconditioned room. There was a single bed, a closet, a bath barely big enough for the essentials, a desk and a chair. The window opened onto 51st Street, shimmering in the haze of an August heat wave. On the desk sat a telephone and a massive, three-inch directory. All I needed was the will to start dialing.

Dialing for what? The answer to that question had been eluding me, but was now becoming a little clearer, though I was too confused to give it much organized thought. I sorely needed someone to talk things over with in order to come up with a realistic plan of action. Essentially, my work for the past two years had been public relations for the US government, directing a fairly sophisticated, multi-faceted operation. In 1953 I had barely heard the term PR, and had no idea what it meant. Moving into the public relations field would have been a natural transition, but at the time I didn't know enough to even consider it.

Instead, I focused on my last job in Vienna, administering the film library for Austria - admittedly boring and uncreative. But, I told myself, it didn't have to be, not if one could become involved in the creative side of documentaries such as those being made for the *March of Time*, or even educational films for classroom use. At any rate, film seemed to be a field worth exploring.

So I opened the Yellow Pages section of the telephone directory and under "Film" started with the letter "A," intending to work through all the companies listed alphabetically. Almost immediately I came to a listing for Association Films. The girl who answered put me onto a Mr. Bingham. He seemed very friendly, much more so than I had expected, with my preconception of business executives as hard-hearted, short-tempered tyrants. This one turned out to be anything but. After a short exchange, with a few questions, he asked me to come in the next day for a meeting with himself and his partner, a Mr. Al Frederick. We met the next morning in their offices at 347 Madison Avenue. Abercrombie & Fitch and Brooks Brothers were just across the street. This was familiar territory; I began to feel more relaxed. And even more so as we began to talk.

It quickly came out that "Association" in the company's name referred to the Young Men's Christian Association, and that Association Films was the direct descendent of the original

YMCA Film Library, which had lately been reorganized as a private company for tax purposes. Bingham and Frederick were both ex-YMCA secretaries from Brooklyn. It was like the prodigal son coming home when they learned that both I and my father had worked for the World's YMCA; they had even heard about the War Prisoners Aid Program in England.

It was not a question of whether I would be hired, that was quickly settled, but rather where in the company I would best fit in; there were several possibilities. One was a film production company called Transfilm, owned by one of their investors, which did both promotional and documentary films. Interesting.

Another was a small subsidiary, formed to explore the potential of a unique device for handling 16mm film, to which they had acquired the rights. Initial experience had led to applications in training: for step by step learning, with a high degree of user interaction. Revolutionary in 1953, the idea is totally accepted now, and most media-assisted learning incorporates it.

That subsidiary, Seminar Films Inc., was where they decided to put me - a decision to my total satisfaction. The implications for audiovisual and media-assisted learning took immediate hold in my mind as I fantasized about the unlimited uses we were about to develop. For me it combined the idealistic goal of improved learning with a practical technology-based delivery system. Once the offer was made, my acceptance was a foregone conclusion. The anticipated dread of a long drawn out job search never materialized - in fact, I never even had to make a second call. Atypical of those seeking employment, but much appreciated by me. The salary was all right too - in the five thousand dollar range - about what I had been making with the government, and without the ideological threats that menaced anyone then in government service.

One career dream had been exchanged for another: foreign service, for education and training - not a bad trade. I was able to embark on the new voyage revitalized and keen to take on the world, as I had been six years earlier. The new voyage turned out to be a rough crossing - treacherous seas, in small ships, several of which went down leaving me in one lifeboat after another. Not exactly what I had expected, but that is another story.

Notes - Chapter 36

Chapter 36, "An Alpine Mystery, was written during the early months of 2009. At the end I predicted that no one would ever know the full story behind the events that took place in Innsbruck during the summer of 1952 since I was the only living participant. That fact is probably still true, but now we know more.

Completely unanticipated details have just emerged with specific names and dates, largely confirming the hypothesis I advanced to explain the mystery. That hypothesis theorized CIA involvement and direction of an underground cell operating in the Tyrol during the early 1950's, with Wolfgang Pfaundler and Manfred Neier as active members, and with Otto von Bolschwing as somehow involved. The cell, I thought, was directed by the so called "State Department Official, Bill Espy."

On November 10, 2010 the New York Times published a story under the headline "Secret Documents Detail US Support For Former Nazis," based on a 600-page report by the Office of Special Investigations - the OSI - release of which had been resisted by the Justice Department for four years. The report describes the role of the CIA in shielding former Nazis from seizure after World War II and facilitating their entry into the US as well as blocking any subsequent attempts to have them deported - this despite full knowledge of their past history of war crimes guilt.

The report provides considerable detail of one such criminal. That is Otto von Bolschwing, who appears in my memoir as a "mysterious" character introduced to me by Pfaundler just prior to von Bolschwing's hurried departure for the US, with an entry visa in hand. "Otto's" request was simply whether I could provide any possible employment contacts for use when he got there. At the time I saw nothing unusual in this and would have gladly given him anything I had, but I had been out of the country too long to be of help. He gave me a name and phone number and asked me to get in touch if and when I returned stateside. "Otto" was the kind of person I was prepared to like: well spoken, intelligent - so much so that I called him upon my return to New York. I believe it was in the summer of 1953 that we met for a late afternoon drink in the King Cole Bar of the St. Regis hotel. He had obviously done very well for himself - which did not surprise me at all - and was now a vice president at Warner Lambert pharmaceuticals with responsibility for European operations. I don't remember what we talked about - probably a personal catch up - but plans to meet again never materialized, and we lost contact.

An incidental sidelight on the above is that Pfaundler came to the US on a visit at just about this same time. He stayed with me for a few days, but I can't recall the stated purpose of his visit. He had been a very close friend, but communication lapsed after the 1960's.

It was only long after these and other more dramatic events, recounted in Chapter 36, as I started to write this memoir, that I began to perceive a pattern in what had been only odd and unexplained happenings. This pattern as set forth seems credible, and the Times article confirms its broad outlines.

Relevant parts are the following extracts:

"In chronicling the cases of Nazis who were aided by American intelligence officials,, the report cites help that CIA officials provided to Otto von Bolschwing, an associate of Adolph Eichmann, who had helped develop the initial plans to purge Germany of the Jews' and who later worked for the CIA in the United States. In a chain of memos CIA officials debated what to do if von Bolschwing were confronted about his past - whether to deny any Nazi affiliation or 'explain it on the basis of extenuating circumstances,. The Justice Department, after learning of von Bolschwing's Nazi ties, sought to deport him in 1981. He died that year at age 72," the report said.

It is quite clear that both Pfaundler and von Bolschwing were working for the CIA .That he should be assisting a German Nazi to escape justice surprises me because of Pfaundler's service in the Wiederstand Bewegung - the anti-Nazi resistance movement - and also because of his oft expressed dislike of Germans generally. He always referred to them as "Piefke," a slang derogatory Austrian term for Germans. Specifically, what von Bolschwing had to offer US intelligence is not made clear in the article, but that such a deal was made is easy to believe given his status in the Nazi hierarchy. Others in similar positions were making similar deals. Why the arrangement lasted until 1954, and possibly thereafter, also is not made clear.

There are several other unanswered questions: Why was von Bolschwing in Innsbruck - in the Tyrol? He was obviously not from there, in fact a stranger, a German citizen. Again I must theorize. My explanation is that von Bolschwing was on the run - that it was not safe for him in either the American Zone of Germany or of Austria. I think he was being sought by US Army G-2 Intelligence as an important catch - a senior Nazi war criminal, an aide to arguably the worst of them all, Adolf Eichmann. In those long ago Cold War years the CIA and Army G-2 tended to see themselves as rivals - competitors for targets, sources and information. Von Bolschwing would have been a major trophy for Army G-2, but at the same time he was an active source for the CIA, in whose interest it was to protect him - to keep him and his secrets out of the hands of Army G-2.

Which brings us back to the question, why was he in Innsbruck? The answer is that Innsbruck was in the French Zone of Occupation; Army G-2 could not operate there. French occupation authorities were extremely sensitive to any perceived encroachment by the US into their Zone - the more so if it were clandestine. (In this respect, a good question is, how did the CIA manage to do it? It's hard to imagine that there could have been some kind of understanding, but equally hard to believe that the French were unaware of a CIA presence.)

In Innsbruck von Bolschwing was at least temporarily beyond the reach of Army G-2, but time was precious for a second reason. It is more than likely that he was also being pursued by Israeli agents, just as his chief, Eichmann, was kidnapped in Argentina and secretly transported back to Israel for trial and execution. Israeli agents would not be concerned with borders or the right to operate anywhere they chose. Either way, from both of these threats, von Bolschwing had to get out, and quickly.

This leaves unresolved the question of that late night call and my emergency transport of Mr. "X" out of town. The Times article establishes the connection between the CIA and von Bolschwing. My own experience establishes the link between these two and Pfaundler, and between him and the other characters involved in that late night call, particularly "Bill Espy." It is beyond reasonable doubt that all these incidents were part of CIA operations in postwar Austria, in the Tyrol.

But without additional revelations, or more detail, we still do not know exactly what happened that night since no one involved would speak. That it was a CIA get-together of some sort seems obvious. I am inclined to stay with my original version - that it was just a reunion of wartime resistance alumni. It is possible that operational matters were discussed. But that it was a serious planning session for an immediate objective is doubtful. A professional organization does not mix important detailed discussions with a night of wining and dining. No, a reunion party that simply got out of hand is the best explanation

Further clarification will have to await the release of additional documents on this murky corner of US foreign policy, and my small involvement in it.

Notes - Chapter 37

Ilse left Austria for Africa in the winter of 1952 where she married a mysterious man named Aristide Hubrich, more familiarly known as "Bud." He was well known in Innsbruck but had left for South Africa just prior to my arrival. He was about thirty years old, but had a past that didn't bear close scrutiny. Apparently he had been a dedicated Nazi party supporter, liked to wear uniforms, and had gone to the US, after the war but was deported - possibly because of his political history. Ilse joined him in Zambia where they were married and lived for about three years until he returned home one day and announced that the government had given him twenty-four hours to leave the country. With that, he packed his things and caught the next flight to London, leaving Ilse to settle their affairs and join him as soon as she could. As with other parts of his past, he never explained the reason for this abrupt expulsion, not even to Ilse. My own theory is that he was involved in weapons smuggling to the factions then fighting in the Congo. At any rate they lived in London where two daughters were born before Ilse decided she had had enough of the marriage and left him. She obtained certification as an Official Tour Guide and thereby managed to support herself and the girls, leading tours around England and Scotland, especially for German speaking groups Years passed with this satisfying independent lifestyle. The eldest daughter, Karen, emigrated to the US, to New York, at the age of eighteen where she continued the food service career she had started in London. She, of course, had heard about me and the long ago relationship with her mother, so that when my name came up in another connection, Karen decided to promote a reunion. The opportunity arose during a forthcoming visit by Ilse to New York. I was living in Westport, Connecticut, at the time, so it was easy to arrange a get-together dinner in the city. We were both coming off failed marriages, but without either desire or plans for a second attempt. However, with me, it was as though the intervening years had never existed. I had long regretted my casual treatment of Ilse; now fate was giving me a second chance. On her side, she loved living in London, the theater, the museums, her small apartment and the constant travel. This was not easy to give up. I suppose my suit made up in intensity what it had lacked earlier because we were married in Westport on December 8, 1980.

www.ingramcontent.com/pod-product-compliance
Lightning Source LLC
Chambersburg PA
CBHW071235160426
43196CB00009B/1065